D1590406

Library of
Davidson College

The Untempered Wind

Forty Years in Palestine

by Christina Jones

Longman

LONGMAN GROUP LTD
London

Associated companies, branches and representatives
throughout the world

© Longman Group Ltd 1975

All rights reserved. No part of this publication
may be reproduced, stored in a retrieval system,
or transmitted in any form or by any means,
electronic, mechanical, photocopying, recording
or otherwise, without the prior permission of
the Copyright owner.

First published 1975

ISBN 0 582 78052 7

956.94
J76u

77-6147

Dedication

To Willard, and our son Richard.

Acknowledgements

We are indebted to the following for permission to reproduce copyright material:

Guardian Newspapers Ltd. for an extract from an article in *Manchester Guardian* 9 November 1967; Harper's Magazine Inc. for an extract from "Israel's Policy of Reprisal" on the title page of *Harper's Magazine* March 1955; The Controller of Her Majesty's Stationery Office for extracts from *The Balfour Memorandum* of 11.8.1919 (PRO FO 371/4185), *Report on Land Settlements, Immigration and Development* 1930 (Cmd. 3686), *The Royal Commission of Inquiry into the Disturbances of 1936* (Cmd. 5479), *Commission to see how the Partition Plan of the Royal Commission could be Implemented* (Cmd. 5854) and *British White Paper 1939* (Cmd. 6019); The World Council of Churches for an extract from *The Report of a Conference on Arab Refugee Problems*, Beirut 1951.

PHOTOGRAPHS

We are indebted to Rex Features Ltd., for permission to reproduce the two photographs of Refugee Camps.

Contents

List of Illustrations

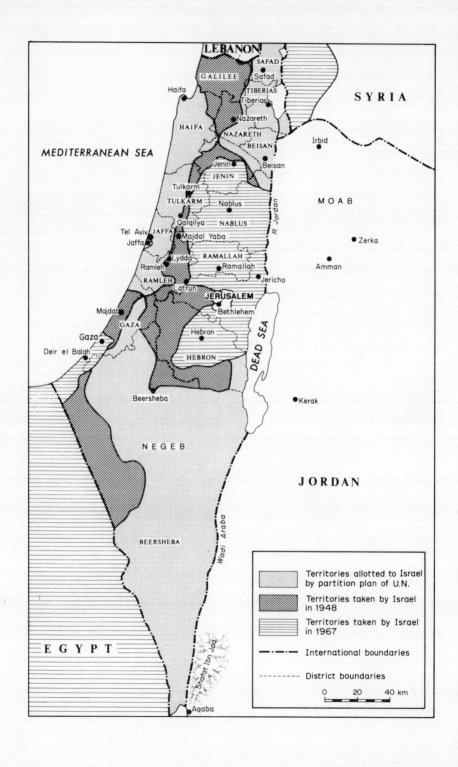

LEBANON
SAFAD
GALILEE
Safad
TIBERIAS
Haifa
Tiberias
SYRIA
Nazareth
HAIFA
NAZARETH
BEISAN
Irbid
MEDITERRANEAN SEA
Jenin
Beisan
JENIN
MOAB
Tulkarm
TULKARM
Nablus
R. Jordan
Qalqilya
NABLUS
Zerka
Tel Aviv
JAFFA
Majdal Yaba
Jaffa
Lydda
RAMALLAH
Amman
Ramleh
Ramallah
RAMLEH
Jericho
Latrun
JERUSALEM
Majdal
Bethlehem
GAZA
Hebron
Gaza
DEAD SEA
Deir el Balah
HEBRON
Beersheba
Kerak
NEGEB
JORDAN
BEERSHEBA
Wadi Araba
EGYPT
Sharat Ibn Jad
Aqaba

Territories allotted to Israel
by partition plan of U.N.

Territories taken by Israel
in 1948

Territories taken by Israel
in 1967

International boundaries

District boundaries

0   20   40 km

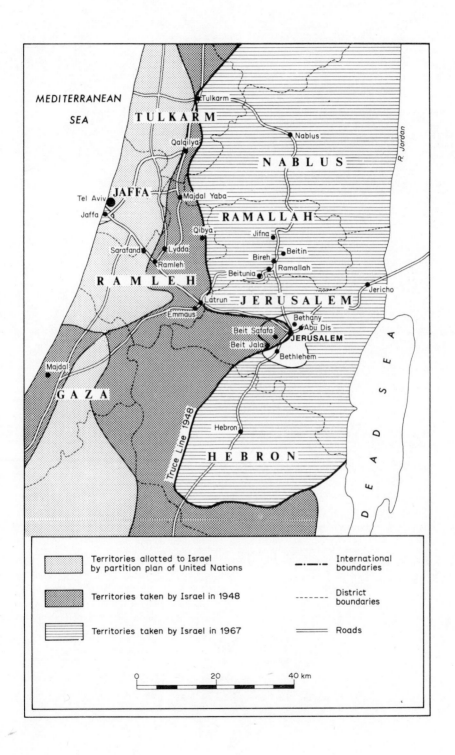

MEDITERRANEAN
SEA

TULKARM
•Tulkarm
Qalqilya•
•Nablus

N A B L U S

Tel Aviv•   **JAFFA**
•Majdal Yaba
Jaffa•

R A M A L L A H

Qibya•
•Jifna
Sarafand•   •Lydda
Ramleh•   Bireh•   •Beitin
R A M L E H   Beitunia•   •Ramallah
•Jericho

Latrun•   **J E R U S A L E M**
Emmaus•
Bethany•
Beit Safafa•   •Abu Dis
Beit Jala•   **JERUSALEM**
Majdal•   Bethlehem•

G A Z A

Hebron•

H E B R O N

R. Jordan

D E A D   S E A

Truce Line 1948

Territories allotted to Israel
by partition plan of United Nations

Territories taken by Israel in 1948

Territories taken by Israel in 1967

— · — · —   International
boundaries

- - - - - - -   District
boundaries

═══════   Roads

0   20   40 km

". . . a good land, a land of brooks of water,
of fountains and springs
flowing forth in valleys and hills;
A land of wheat and barley,
of vines and fig trees and pomegranates;
a land of olive trees and honey; . . ."

(*Deuteronomy*, Chapter 8,
verses vii–viii)

Newcomers to Palestine

The *Braga*, coal-burning cargo ship of the French Fabre Line with a small complement of passengers, arrived in Palestine on the last Saturday in September 1922, twenty-eight days out of New York. Some of the passengers were from that starry-eyed generation which was to help build a Brave New World now that the "war to end war" was over, my husband and I among them. When the peace treaty was signed at Versailles in 1919, a League of Nations was set up to prevent aggression on the part of any member and to institute a forum where international problems could be discussed in an atmosphere of peace and reason. We were entering an era of world brotherhood and our generation was to help bring it about. It was a great challenge to the young people of the post-war era.

We had a good voyage on our small ship. The sea had been calm and stopovers for the discharge of cargo made possible delightful excursions ashore at the Azores, Lisbon, and the Piraeus. Companions were congenial and we all easily adapted ourselves to the restrictions and inconveniences of a Fabre liner of that period.

It was not until we neared the eastern end of the Mediterranean that we had our first indication that perhaps the high hopes of the Versailles Conference were not going to be realized all at once. When we were close to Asia Minor, our captain was told to stand by for possible emergency. Turkey was driving the Greeks out of Smyrna, and his ship might be needed to help with evacuation of civilians. It was a jarring note in our peaceful existence, and had we known more we might have noted it as an omen of things to come. Apparently, the many problems created by the defeat of Turkey in the war and the distribution of the dismembered Ottoman Empire were not to be solved easily. Fortunately, the *Braga* was not needed, as British and American warships in the Mediterranean hastened to the relief of Smyrna and were more than adequate for the emergency. After this short delay, we proceeded to the Near East, and if doubts had arisen about the era of peace, we did not know enough to be unduly alarmed. After all, there was this wonderful League of Nations to hold the nations steady.

On this beautiful September day, we were to step on the soil of Palestine for the first time, the land of Bethlehem, Nazareth, and Jerusalem, and of the One we had learned about whose life had made it a holy land for millions of Christians throughout the world. We knew it was also a land of memory for the Jews. We were to learn later that it was a sacred place for Muslims, too. We would enter Palestine as people through the ages had entered it, at the exciting port of Jaffa. As we sailed near it, we tried to recall Bible stories and even Greek mythology which had given Jaffa more colour than that of just a port city.

We remembered that Jonah had sailed from Jaffa when he was trying to escape a difficult assignment in Nineveh, only to run into more trouble. At a later date, Peter, the impetuous disciple of Jesus, had a dream when he was sleeping in the home of Simon the Tanner, a dream that was to take him out of his narrow Jewish nationalism and broaden his concept of God and race so that he could go to the home of Cornelius, the Roman centurion, commune with him and eat at his table, and later go to Rome and martyrdom. Here also was the home of Dorcas, famous for her good works, whom Peter restored to health. Her name and example have been perpetuated in countless church sewing-circles throughout Christendom.

We find the story of Andromeda of great beauty, daughter of Cepheus and Cassiopea in Greek mythology. One tradition is that she was chained to one of the big rocks still seen as you enter Jaffa harbour. Perseus of the winged feet hastened to Jaffa, slew the monster in a bloody fight, rescued Andromeda, married her and presumably lived happily ever after.

It was late in the afternoon when our ship dropped anchor a short distance from the shore. The afternoon wind had whipped the waves into what seemed to me alarming heights and the small boats which came out to take passengers and cargo to the shore looked fragile as the crews breasted the waves, but they rowed vigorously and efficiently, avoiding rocks and swells, intoning strange songs assuringly.

A rope-ladder was swung over the side of the ship, down which we were to descend to the bobbing boats. The slender, shaky ladder and the high waves were not comforting as I stood at the top rung of the ladder. My husband went down with alacrity, then called instructions to me to come down slowly and wait at the lowest rung until the boat was on the upsweep, and then jump. Alas, I waited too long and jumped too late. Strong arms caught me and settled me on a wooden spar and I was safe, and had quite literally fallen into the arms of the Near East. Oarsmen steered us safely through the rocks that lay on our way to shore and it was good to feel our feet on solid ground.

Edward Kelsey, Secretary of the Friends' Mission, and Marion his wife were there to greet us and help us through all the intricacies of Customs. They had spent hours in the heat of the day and were thankful when we could set out in the early evening for Ramallah, 2,850 feet above Jaffa on one of the hills around Jerusalem. As we drove out from the city, we were aware of dusty roads, palm trees, the delicate fragrance of orange blossoms, and a feeling that the sky had dropped and was closer to us here than anywhere else on earth.

The stars, too, were clearly visible in the evening light, and in the coming days I was to think often of the sky and the stars as we saw them for the first time in Palestine, and I could understand how it had come about that stars had played such an important part in the lives of the peoples of the Near East, how it was in this area that astrology was born, and why so many stars had Arabic names.

We soon forgot the heat of Jaffa as we left the coastal plain and began the climb to the hills in the cooler night air. In less than two hours we were in Ramallah and at our new home, Friends' Boys' School, standing stark and strong and treeless on a high point in the village. During the war, the Turkish armies had cut down trees all over the country to get fuel for their trains, and such trees as there were on the school grounds had gone, too. In the dim light, we could see the German and Russian towers on the Mount of Olives ten miles to the south, and we could look towards the west and see the lights of Jaffa by the sea. We had arrived, and could only hope that we would be of use.

We were appointed to the Friends' School in Ramallah by the American Friends' Board of Missions with headquarters in Richmond, Indiana. Willard was to be principal of the Boys' School and, as a wife, I was to supplement and complement his work as best I could. I had hoped we would have a home of our own but the situation required that we live in the school building, and this we accepted if it was for the better interests of the school.

Our knowledge of Palestine was mostly of the biblical country of our Sunday-school days, and we knew almost nothing of the modern Palestine, of its history since Old Testament times, of its language, of the people who were presently living in it. In fact our ignorance far, far exceeded our knowledge. The Board had told us as we left that the need for teachers was critical, and we thought we might be able to help in that field and learn as we taught.

We were close enough to world events to remember reading of the dramatic entry of General Allenby into Jerusalem on 11 December 1917, and the thrill it gave a war-weary world needing some "noble" incident to get its mind off the dreadful carnage of three years of war. Pictures of General Allenby had been flashed around the world showing how he entered the Old City, that part of Jerusalem within the walls built by Suleiman the Magnificent in the early years of the sixteenth century, not as a conqueror riding a horse with a sword in his hand but unarmed, his head uncovered, and walking humbly into this revered city. He wanted it that way, as he felt that he could not ride where his Lord had walked. The First World War, for a brief period, had taken on the aspect of a crusade or Holy War. Allenby took the city without fighting and made his formal entry two days after the Turkish garrison had surrendered. A British military government followed until a mandate was given to Great Britain in July 1922. As far as we knew, this episode in the war was to be a great blessing for the people of Palestine, for they were now freed from four centuries of Turkish rule. More than fifty years later we still have much to learn about the colourful, sometimes tragic, but always exciting history of the years from AD 33 to 1917.

The first and most important thing we had to learn was that we were living in the Arab World, that Palestine was not the land of the Hebrews; that the Arab population was approximately 600,000, the Jewish population around 60,000, many of whom were fairly recent immigrants. In time we had also to learn that the term Arab did not necessarily stand for race as much as for what scholars call Arabization, applied to those people whose language is Arabic, whose culture is Arabic, and who, through process of assimilation, have some Arab racial heritage. There are Christian Arabs as well as Muslim Arabs, although the latter are predominant.

Yes, there was much to learn, but our immediate task was to get acquainted with the Mission and the school, for our teaching was to begin within three days of our arrival. Teaching was possible because the language of instruction in most of the secondary classes was English. It seemed strange to us that the pupils were learning the language of the teachers. But in this instance there was little alternative. In the first place, there were no modern text books in Arabic easily available for years after the war. In the second place, the newly established Mandate government had three official languages, English, Arabic, and, at the insistence of the newly formed Jewish Agency, Hebrew. Hence, it was important for our boys to know English well as it would open up posts for them in government, especially for those boys who would not go on to colleges and universities. And lastly, many of our boys would go to colleges where English was the language of instruction, and a good foundation in English would make college work easier for them.

The government set up the Palestine Matriculation, a particularly difficult examination, and students passing it could enter the sophomore year of the American University of Beirut. Later, our students sat for the London University Matriculation Examination, which was also recognized as a pass into the sophomore class at the university. The examinations allowed a good deal of latitude in history and the sciences, but in English we were sent a list each year of the books, poems, and drama we must study. Included were plays of Shakespeare, novels by authors such as Hardy and Eliot, and selections from the great British poets. Emphasis was placed on composition, grammar and précis. Foreign students sat for the same examination that was set for British students. Although English was the language of instruction, Friends' Boys' School took pride in its emphasis on Arabic literature, grammar, and syntax, and programmes and plays in Arabic were important events of the school year.

Much of what I have written was to be learned slowly, sometimes painfully, but our first task was to take a look at the school. We found that we had fifty boarding students and twenty-five day-boys. It was the policy of the Mission then to stress the boarding-school aspect of the work and keep the day-boys to a minimum. In the course of time, we had twice as many boarders, but day-boys far outnumbered them. The exclusiveness of a boarding-school had to give way to pressures for education and the door had to be opened wider to the community of Ramallah and surrounding villages.

We had arrived late Saturday evening and were introduced to our school duties after an early breakfast on Monday morning. Because of our arrival so close to the beginning of school, it was wisely decided that Willard should spend the first two or three months getting to know the boys and the school routine before taking over, but he would be needed in the classroom full-time. I can see that blackboard now as I write fifty years later. Fifty-two hours of teaching were scheduled for us. In addition, Willard was to take his turn at dormitory duty and, since I could not share in that, I was to keep the boys' accounts, as they were not allowed to keep money in their cupboards or in their pockets. I had not yet seen any Palestine money but all that day I was school banker, and, for the next three years, I would record every copy-book, eraser, pencil, pen-point, stamp and sundry other items for every boarder in school. Classes began each morning at eight o'clock and we were on our way to a life that was strenuous but never dull. The fact that I was a bride was a handicap, for a bride should be young and, if young, how could she know enough to teach secondary classes? One other chore assigned to me was to prepare six boys each week to recite English poems on Friday afternoon when the whole school met to hear them, and to hear six boys recite in Arabic. The latter poems went off with éclat, but the English ones were less spectacular and rendered with less enthusiasm, I'm afraid.

Willard took over full responsibility after Christmas vacation and carried on his full-time teaching schedule. We were young in 1922, with energy unlimited, and were happy in our work. The magic of Palestine was a constant inspiration and the desire for education was a driving force that was stimulating indeed.

Our boys came from Christian and Muslim homes and a few were Armenians. We had not realized how widely the Arab World had opened its doors to Armenians during the war until we went to Palestine. Turkey, considering the Armenian community subversive, being Christian and friendly to the West, had driven them out ruthlessly. In addition to a large community in Palestine, there were many Armenians in Lebanon, Syria, Iraq, and Iran free to enter the business and professional life of these countries and also free to live their own lives. Jerusalem was attractive to them because the famous cathedral of St James, with what have been described as "fabulous" treasures, had been long in Jerusalem, and the beautifully maintained Armenian Quarter was a haven for them until they could take care of themselves. It was to serve them again in 1948. Our boys came to us from all over Palestine and in later years from Transjordan also, and this helped us to get better acquainted with Palestine as a whole, as parents visited the school and as we visited the boys in their homes during the summer vacation. In time the language did not seem so strange, as our ears became attuned to it and we learned to form words and use the lovely expressions that came into the everyday speech of the people. The humblest peasants greeted you with them and knew how to be the perfect hosts.

Arabic is a beautiful, gracious language, perhaps the richest of the Semitic languages, not to be easily learned. I used to tell our friends that their language was a conspiracy designed to keep us from finding life too easy among them. Although an ancient language, it had adapted to changing times, and did so without losing its beauty and character. It was most frustrating to me as I tried to build up the Arabic section of the school library not to be able to read all the books. I learned to read the hymns in Meeting, but was not always sure what I was singing; but if the tune was familiar, I trusted that the words in Arabic meant the same thing as the English. It was comforting when the boys confessed that they could not always understand speeches in the classical language, which was the Arabic of the learned and must be used on formal occasions. Their speech is coloured with figurative language and proverbs abound!

The following are some of the homely everyday expressions which I still love. When a service is performed by the hands, a simple thank you is inadequate and the proper thank you is, "Peace to your hands." When kind words are spoken, one says, "Peace to your lips." The morning greeting is: "May your day be full of happiness," and we reply, "May yours be full of light." When one is a guest the host says, "You honour us with your presence. My house is your house," and he must put the best he has at the disposal of his guest even if it works a hardship on him and his family. On entering a home, one says: "*Salaam aleikum*—peace to you all," and the answer comes back, "And to you be peace." We admire an object of value or a piece of beautiful handwork, and before we leave the house the host presents it to us. How to accept it and let our host know it would give us pleasure to have him keep it for us was something we tried to learn, for often the gift was too valuable to accept, or to give. Even so, we have some treasures in our home that came to us in this way. One such is a silver bowl from Mecca. It was brought out for me to admire when we were guests in the home of one of our boys in Gaza. I felt it too precious for me to keep so tried to "forget" it when I left. We had not gone far when Adel caught up with us and said to me reproachfully, "My mother wants you to have it."

As in all human society, there are times when tempers run high. Anger is then expressed in picturesque language, too, and when curses are called for they are not directed so much at the object of a man's anger as at his father, grandfather, tribe or people. The most direful curse is: "May your house be destroyed." This is the time for a mediator, and nowhere in the world are the offices of a mediator or intermediary more used. Through him quarrels are settled, business transactions carried through and marriage contracts made. We often wondered what the Arabs thought of our brusque Western ways of doing things. Two boys quarrelling on the playground complain to the principal that reconciliation is impossible for "he cursed my father." It was good that school-boys could usually make peace quickly and the curse be soon forgotten. We were constantly learning that it would take time before we would understand this ancient culture, but it was worth studying.

As we tried to adjust to our new life, we were increasingly conscious of the fact that we were exceedingly lucky in having come into a work that was already well-established and respected in the country. Friends—Quakers—had been in Ramallah for a long time. All the pioneer work had been done, and from the beginning in happy relations with the people of Palestine. The first Quakers had visited Ramallah as early as 1869, when a party of two American and two British Quakers spent several days in the village. They were Eli and Sibyl Jones of Maine, Lloyd Fox of England and Ellen Claire Miller of Edinburgh. They travelled "in the love of the gospel", with no thought of establishing a permanent mission, and actually spent only a few days in Ramallah. One morning when Eli Jones was walking in the village, a young girl approached him and asked if he would not open a school for girls. When he asked who would teach in it, she said she would. Her father was a teacher and he had taught her; she had also gone to Talitha Cumi School in Jerusalem, which was a German mission school, its name taken from the words spoken by Jesus when he healed the daughter of Jairus, saying: "Maiden, arise." These Friends had with them money, given to them to distribute as they thought good, and with some of these funds the first school for girls was opened in Ramallah.

The idea of a school for girls in Palestine appealed to British Friends, and they undertook responsibility for it. American Friends had no organization then for such a project. For the next twenty years, British Friends supported it well and, in addition, added medical services.

The party travelled on to Lebanon, and while there they had occasion to meet with members of a well-established American mission which was to have a long distinguished service there. They so impressed a Dutch missionary, who had served in Ethiopia and was concerned by great need in Brummana, a village on the hills above Beirut, that he wrote to Eli and Sibyl Jones and asked them to help him start a mission to the people of Brummana. His concern appealed to New England Friends, and they accepted the challenge. British Friends were interested also, and they took on some of the responsibility for the Lebanon programme, too. With communication at best slow, it was not easy to carry on a joint programme, and by 1888 it was decided that it was better to separate the administrative work; it was agreed that New England Friends would take over the Ramallah work and (Old) England the work in the north.

New England Yearly Meeting of Friends entered into the Ramallah work with enthusiasm, and their first project was to start a boarding-school for girls in 1889. Later a Friends Meeting was set up and, save for a period when the Mission carried on small day-schools for girls in surrounding villages, the work of the Mission was concentrated in Ramallah, but certainly not limited to it as students came to the schools from all over the country. The Boys' School was opened in a house in the village in 1901 with a few boys, and it remained small until 1914.

Friends' Girls' School was well established before the First World War, when all missionaries had to return to the United States; so as soon as war ended it could begin work again quickly under the administration of Alice Whittier Jones, who had been Principal from 1906. She was much loved, and the girls welcomed her back warmly.

Friends' Boys' School did not fare so well. It did not have the long tradition of the Girls' School and it had been small. Plans were well on the way to expand it before the war, and a building was completed in the summer of 1914 on its present site, with accommodation for boarders. But events were moving in Europe that were to set up a chain reaction that continues to this day in Palestine. Its immediate effect in Palestine, as far as our mission was concerned, was to postpone the opening of the Boys' School, and the fine new building would be used first by armies, not for the peaceful arts.

The first to occupy the building were soldiers of the Turkish armies, who even stabled their horses in the big dining-room on the first floor. Friends' Boys' School is built on solid rock and the lowest floor is of stone. Marks of horses' teeth on the wooden door in the dining-room and black patches on the floor have remained as evidence of that period. When Allenby entered Palestine in 1917, the building was converted into a hospital for British soldiers and was well cared for. We were grateful to the British army for beds, sheets and other equipment they left when they pulled out in 1918. The war over, the first post-war principal was sent out from New England. He arrived in January of 1919 and the school now got off to a second start. A second principal was sent out in the summer of 1921. He remained only a year, so we were the third couple sent out in that brief period. Obviously, the first problem was to give the school stability and continuity, so necessary if a good foundation was to be laid.

On our first Sunday we went to Meeting in the morning and had our initiation into the Arabic language and a foretaste of what lay ahead if we were ever to learn it. The sermon by the Mission Secretary was in English and then translated, and the hymns, sung to familiar tunes, were in Arabic. Someone put a hymn-book into my hand in a friendly gesture, and as I looked at the strange writing and listened to the unusual sounds, I knew that I would never be able to read it or write in it. I was to have my first test in the language a few weeks later when I went with a party of British friends from Jerusalem to Taiybeh, a lovely village to the east of Ramallah overlooking the Jordan valley. The Reverend Eric Bishop was to preach in Arabic. We travelled there on donkeys, all except me: I rode the Mission Mule, a strange creature which had evidently been frightened by a camel in its younger days and could smell one a long way off. When it did so, it would make an abrupt turn and head towards home or go off the road into a vineyard. So taking trips on it was always attended with uncertainties. As we went our way, like the pilgrims to Canterbury, we passed the time with an Arabic lesson for me. Eric told me to try to recognize word-forms and sounds as he spoke, and I followed his advice; I am sure I was the most attentive person in the congregation that day. On the way home, he asked what the sermon was about and I told him *"Ya Rub* and *Walakin"*. A burst of laughter greeted this. I had told him he spoke about "The Lord and But".

We spent Sunday afternoon greeting callers, many curious no doubt to see the new workers. On Sunday evening people came to the school from the village for a "sing" in English. It was a service which they liked, for nearly all knew English and they enjoyed the informal atmosphere that was observed. I shall always remember the beautiful young woman sitting in front of me. She wore the traditional Ramallah costume, a voluminous dress of linen with broad panels of exquisite cross-stitch in intricate design. A long linen shawl, also massively embroidered, almost covered the head-dress with gold and silver coins shaped so as to form a halo-like frame for her face. Her light olive colouring, with delicate pink shining through, and her dark eyes completed a picture of great beauty. I had never seen a costume so lovely. She was a bride of only four months and was wearing her bridal dress, and the gold and silver on her head, I was to learn, was her dowry. She was fourteen years old but carried herself with the dignity of an older person. I was to see hundreds of such costumes through the years and never ceased to marvel at the ability of women who did such perfect work.

As the days passed, we tried to enter into the life of the village, attending all the main events around which the life of the village centred: engagements, weddings, Christenings, feasts for happy celebrations such as when a son or daughter returned with a college diploma or visitors came and, of course, the sad occasions when loved ones died, all of which they made meaningful in a way we of the West have too often lost in our sophistication. These events came to have meaning for us, too.

The thought that we would be living near Jerusalem was one of the wonderful aspects of our journey during the long September days on the ship, and one of my dearest hopes was that I would soon see Jerusalem. I read all I could about it and anticipated the great moment when I would enter one of the gates. But it was to be weeks before I would do so, and when I did it was to attend a meeting of the Womens' Christian Temperance Union. It seemed that with the coming in of the British there was a tremendous growth in the number of licensed grocers in Jerusalem, and obviously an increase in drinking. Muslims are forbidden to drink alcohol, but it was becoming increasingly hard for them to observe this prohibition as they met socially with British colleagues. So someone had started a WCTU in Jerusalem and, even though it was not a personal problem, it seemed urgent for me to attend. So I saw very little of Jerusalem on that first excursion, but as my hostess had an errand on David Street, she hustled me through narrow alleys with beggars lining the path to the Wailing Wall. We remained for a few minutes only, to watch some strange men wearing long cloaks, broad-brimmed hats, curls over their ears, kissing the stones and reading from their holy books. It was rather sad, as they all looked so poor and tormented. I did not understand what it was all about and there was no one there who could tell me why this ceremony was taking place. I went many times in after years but I never saw any of the educated or Western Jews at the Wall, although I understood that it had great importance to the Jewish community.

Christmas came, and during the holidays we had our real introduction to the Holy City. We visited as many shrines as possible, walked all around the inside of the walls and had magnificent views of the country from turrets and through openings; walked about the streets and discovered the *suks*, the markets, of variety and interest. Mostly, we realized that Jerusalem was a cosmopolitan city, for there were representatives of so many nations to be seen.

There are two Jerusalems, the one inside the walls and the modern one outside, the former usually called "The Old City", and it is well named, for it is ageless. If the stones could speak, they would have a great tale to tell of all that has happened within the walls, with repercussions almost to the ends of the earth through thousands of years of history.

There are eight gates to the walled city, one of them walled up and the other seven open to the nations of the world. Most of the gates have more than one name, but we of the West usually used those most familiar to the modern traveller. The names have been acquired for the most part because of their function and not in honour of anyone or of great events. Damascus Gate is so called because it is the gate that faces the north and leads to that city, although Damascus is many days' travel away. The Arabs call it *Bab el-Amud*, because at some time in the past a tall pillar dominated a colonnade of pillars leading from the entrance into the city itself. It is the finest of the gates, with massive iron doors that can be shut quickly at any sign of danger. Jaffa Gate on the east, as its name indicates, is the exit to Jaffa Road. The Arabs have a more colourful name for it, *Bab el-Khalil*. Abraham is called by the Arabs *Kahlil*, because *Khalil* means "friend" and Abraham was the Friend of God. Hebron, where he is buried, is to this day called *Khalil*, and the inhabitants, *Khalili*. Then there are Herod's Gate; New Gate, a nineteenth-century one to help solve traffic problems in and out of the Old City as increasing numbers of tourists and pilgrims came to the city; St Stephen's Gate, commemorating the first Christian martyr; Zion Gate; and the Dung Gate, called in Arabic *Mugharibah*, a much pleasanter name, because of its nearness to the Moroccan Quarter of Jerusalem. Last but of greatest interest is the Golden Gate, which has been walled up for 1,200 years. Seen from the Mount of Olives it could be mistaken at first sight for part of the wall, but two lovely arches, which the Arabs say represent Mercy and Repentance, are seen in outline and show that it was a gate. According to tradition, the Last Judgement will take place here, so the connection between repentance and mercy seems obvious.

A shopping expedition to Jerusalem was always exciting. I loved rubbing shoulders, often quite literally, with the people who filled the streets. For its size, it is possibly the most cosmopolitan city in the world. In 1930, the official report of the government listed forty languages "habitually spoken" in Jerusalem. Although the largest number of the population were Muslims, one was always more conscious of the Christians because of the diversity of religious habit of the orders one saw daily. The five ancient Churches—Greek Orthodox, Catholic or Latin, Armenian, Syrian, and Coptic—had Patriarchates and their own quarters within the walls, and their members tended to live near them. Many modern Christian denominations had also established themselves in Palestine, built churches, opened schools, had convents, monasteries, hospices for pilgrims, and scholars came from many lands for archaeological pursuits.

To add to the colour of the city, there were the peasant women from Bethlehem, Ramallah and other towns and villages in their beautifully embroidered costumes. Only the townswomen were veiled in the early days and it was not long before one rarely saw veiled women in Jerusalem. One did not need to ask village women where they came from as their costumes easily identified them.

In the nineteenth century the Arab population began to move out of the Old City, where there were already government buildings, churches, convents and schools. They built attractive homes and residential areas and had lovely gardens. Many European Jews who came to Palestine after the First World War lived in these Arab communities in happy relationship with their landlords and neighbours. During the Mandate years, a large official British community contributed much to the social and cultural life of Jerusalem and made it truly international.

We also had "colonies", not for any discriminatory reason, but simply because people of one faith or national background tended to live together. So we had a Greek Colony, a German Colony, and when an American family arrived with a dozen or so associates, the Arab people called it the American Colony. At the turn of the century there was a small English community; they were very exclusive and resented the fact that they were dependent on the Germans for services they thought their own government should provide. It was to be the American Colony and Schnellers Syrian Orphanage which would remain longest and become best known. Schnellers, a German-supported Mission, trained most of the skilled workmen and left a heritage of excellence which continues.

One interesting development in the colony was the arrival of a big party of Swedish people who, when they heard of the American Colony, sold their farms and whatever property they had, chartered a ship and came to Jerusalem to await the Second Coming. There was a time when they outnumbered the Americans and, by hard work and imagination, they made a big contribution towards the practical business of making a living. They were used to the soil and agricultural pursuits, the women were wise and clever in domestic affairs and some of the men were good in business, photography and technical skills. When Bertha married Frederick Vester, son of a German missionary who had studied woodwork in order to help young Arabs and had opened a shop for the sale of their articles of olivewood, the shop was bought jointly by the Colony and Frederick, and the American Colony Stores were started. They did a good business in the shop in the Old City for many years. The Colony became a centre for good works, too. Our mission had always maintained friendly relations with the American Colony and we were introduced to it in time and followed their continuing story through difficult times and times of success.

One other people closely associated with Jerusalem, one which acquired vast properties in the city and beyond, were the Russians. They owned property in the Old City and the New, on the Mount of Olives, and at Ain Karem, the traditional home of John the Baptist. The Church of Mary Magdalene, with its onion domes, on the slope of the Mount of Olives in the Garden of Gethsemane, and the tower on the top of the Mount are two of the most conspicuous reminders of the days before the Revolution when the Russian Church poured great wealth into Palestine.

But it was the stories of the Russian pilgrims, their piety, and their devotion that we heard about in our early days. One story told over and over again was how the bells for the tower were brought up from Jaffa. The tower is 2,680 feet above sea level and there are 224 steps from the base of the tower to the top. The story is that in April 1872 two bells arrived at Jaffa weighing twelve thousand pounds. This was in the days before there was a railway and everything had to be brought up from Jaffa to Jerusalem on a carriage road, a distance of about forty miles. To get the bells to Jerusalem presented almost insurmountable difficulties. The story goes that women solved the problem. One version is that three hundred women undertook the task. The bells were placed on a caisson and the long difficult pull began from sea level to the hills. It took three weeks for the journey, carried out as an act of devotion. The women chanted as they pulled their heavy load, their beautiful voices proof of service given with love and joy. Needless to say, some of the women became ill from exhaustion and one died.

One of our special pleasures was to go to the Russian compound in the evening to listen to the evening prayers sung by the nuns in the most glorious harmony, many of the women old and bent as they emerged from the service, but their voices, as we listened outside, sounded young and strong.

In addition to the Greeks, the Germans, the Americans, and the Russians, the Latin Church had impressive properties in Palestine, French and Italian influence being strong in the Latin groups. St George's Cathedral with its school came into the picture in the late nineteenth century, built outside the walls, and added to the congregation of the nations all seeking a place in the Holy Land. If the people of the country were sometimes suspicious of their altruistic motives, and saw in them political motives, it is not surprising, but there is no question that, regardless of government and political reasons behind government support for some of the Christian work, Palestine attracted deeply religious people, and in some marvellous way it still does and probably always will.

Though we are so conscious of the Christian witness in Palestine, the beautiful mosque, one of the world's truly magnificent buildings, dominates the scene. Incorrectly called the Mosque of Omar because of Omar's early connection with Jerusalem and the Muslim conquest of the seventh century, it serves as a reminder that Palestine has been a Muslim country for 1,300 years. The Noble Sanctuary is built on the temple area, but when the Muslims came the area was the city dump heap, and it was the Christian Patriarch who called Omar's attention to the site, for there was a tradition that it had been a holy place long before the Hebrews came. One tradition was that it was the place where Abraham was about to sacrifice Isaac, in which case it had meaning for Muslims, since Abraham is their ancestor, too. They had come to Jerusalem with knowledge of the Rock over which the Temple was built, for Mohammad had said that the Rock in Jerusalem was holy, having come from Paradise. Tradition always has associated it with Mohammad's night journey to heaven. Muslims believed that Malki-Sadek, a famous Jebusite king of one of the earliest tribes to enter Palestine from the Arabian Peninsula, worshipped God and offered sacrifices there. It was from Auraunah the Jebusite that David bought what was then a threshing-floor, when a plague threatened to destroy the Hebrews. David sacrificed on it, the plague passed, and later Solomon built his temple on it in 1004 BC. The fact that Omar himself helped clear away the accumulations of the centuries and Abdul Malek Ibn Marwan made it the heart of his beautiful sanctuary is clear evidence of the reverence the Muslims had for the Rock. Harry

Emerson Fosdick, noted American Minister, wrote the following in his book, *A Pilgrimage to Palestine*:

"Of all public places, it seems to me most worshipful. Chaste and lovely, its mosaics mellowed by time, its stained-glass glorious, its proportions filling the eye with satisfaction, its atmosphere subdued and reverential, its memories unparalleled, it is the natural place of prayer."

Perhaps it is not surprising that as time passed the legend grew that the sanctuary was not the work of human hands but that it was built by Jinn.

We have within a small area three shrines for the three religions of the Semitic World: the Church of the Holy Sepulchre for the Christians; the Dome of the Rock for the Muslims; and the Wailing Wall for the Jews. The Christian shrine has chapels for the five ancient churches: Greek Orthodox, Roman Catholic, Armenian, the Jacobite Syrian, and the Coptic. Each community guards its rights in the church jealously and many and terrible at times have been the quarrels when any rights were overstepped. In the days of the Turks, peace was maintained by making Muslims custodians, and for centuries the opening and closing ceremonies each day by a member of the Muslim family responsible have been as carefully observed as the changing of the guard at Buckingham Palace. The authenticity of the site as Calvary and the place of the Tomb of Jesus is debatable, but it has been hallowed by the prayers and vows of thousands of Christians for centuries and as such has meaning for the modern Christian.

Holy Week in Jerusalem is marked by spectacular ceremonies: it is a time for bringing out the power and the wealth of the churches and a dramatization of the last week in the life of Jesus. Two ceremonies are largely attended and attract people from the ends of the earth. The first of these is the Footwashing ceremony on Maundy Thursday, which is performed in the court of the Church. Throngs gather there in the early morning to witness it. A bright Syrian sun shines on the colourful robes of twelve bishops of the Greek Orthodox Church seated on a raised platform. The venerable Patriarch emerges from the church at a given time dressed in elaborate brocaded robes and wearing a crown heavily studded with gems of great value. He is followed by a servant carrying a basin and towel. When he reaches the platform, he is divested of his robes and in a simple tunic he mounts the platform and kneels at the feet of each bishop in turn, and simulates the act of the

Master performed in the Upper Room. One of the bishops, representing Peter, remonstrates when the Patriarch comes to him, saying he is unworthy. The words of the Master are spoken, reminding Peter and all of the beauty of service, and Peter submits, begging impulsively, "Not my feet only but my hands, and my head."

The ceremony is soon over. We leave wondering if there is any meaning in all this pomp and circumstance, and we think of the simple scene that was enacted in this same city not far from where we stand, performed with simple sincerity, lifting the humble task from servility to service.

The second big event of the week is the ceremony of the Holy Fire. There is a tradition in the Eastern Churches that on the day after the Crucifixion fire descended from heaven on the tomb of Jesus. It is believed that the miracle is repeated each year if God feels that His people have been faithful. If a person can touch the flame, he is blessed, and if he can light a candle there he can keep the blessing for his home and his church. This ceremony is at once superficial yet beautifully symbolic of the Easter services and it, like the Footwashing, takes place at the church, but inside. Crowds fill every nook and corner of the church, and amid the din of laughter and chatter, chanting, liturgy, and the heavy odour of burning incense, the people wait for the miracle. Many there are frankly cynical, but there are always a large number of devout pilgrims who believe in it, holding their candles reverently. Expectancy mounts as the moments pass, but finally the Patriarch who has led in the liturgies enters the chapel built over the tomb, and now even the wise ones grow tense. At last the fires burst forth from openings in the wall of the rotunda. Those nearest rush to light their candles. Some hurry away with bundles of lighted tapers for the crowd outside or to put in lanterns to be carried to their home churches. The majority hold their lighted candles high so that those near can light their candles from them. Soon the whole church is filled with the light of a thousand candles. Whatever the effect on us of this ceremony, we are reminded that light always has been used as a Christian symbol, and Jesus is spoken of as the Light of the World.

We have here only a hint of the wealth of history, story, and legends of Jerusalem. There is so much that is of interest within and outside the walls that there is no end. Before leaving Jerusalem for the present, it may be well to climb the Mount of Olives to catch the view from Jerusalem as it will help us to understand why its geographical position has played such an important role in its history and once seen can never be forgotten.

Unlike most capitals of the world, Jerusalem has no river. When one stands on the eastern slope of Olivet and gazes down into the valley below, one realizes what it has meant to Jerusalem to have the desert almost at its very door. The scene inspires awe, for from a height of 2,500 feet above sea level we look down on the lowest depression on the surface of the earth. The Dead Sea lies in it, 1,280 feet below sea level, and stretches forty-eight miles to the south. No organic life can exist in this sea but it is rich in chemicals; it is estimated that it contains about 2,000 million tons of potash and 900 million tons of magnesium bromide. In the heart of this scene of desolation lies the oasis called Jericho, which, because of its orange groves, date-palms, banana groves, vegetable and flower gardens, the Arabs call *Eriha*, Place of Fragrance. A clear, overflowing fountain, fed from springs in the Judean Hills, makes this a fruitful, happy sight. From the same spot on Olivet, however, a very different picture may be seen. Simply by facing the west, one can look to the lower hills of the Shephelah and the Maritime Plain to a scene infinitely fair. There, in the early spring, the fields are ripening to the harvest; trees bearing figs, olives, almonds, apricots are coming to fruition, and in the late months orange groves are pure gold; and the blue Mediterranean gives a sense of vast horizons. The contrast from the desert view is all the more striking because the distance is so short. In ancient days Jerusalem was the centre of a country which was, as told to the Hebrews weary of desert life, "a land of hills and valleys, and drinketh of the rain of heaven . . . of great and goodly cities, houses full of good things, wells and vineyards and olive trees. . ."

Before Abraham came to Palestine, Jerusalem was a centre of worship where Melchizedek was called "The Priest of the Most High God". Interestingly enough, Jesus is described in the Book of Hebrews as "a priest of the order of Melchizedek". The city of Jerusalem is for ever linked with the story of mankind from the days of the Hittites and the Scythians to Allenby. There have been times when the streets ran with blood, when its shrines were scenes of battle rather than places of prayer for followers of the Prince of Peace. It has known the armies of Sennacherib and Cyrus, Thotmes and Ptolemy, Alexander and Titus, Pompey and Anthony, and Vespasian, Mohammad, Richard, Saladin, Mohammad Ali, Napoleon and Allenby, names which reflect more than three thousand years of the history of Palestine and the races of men who have had a foothold in that country for a longer or a shorter time. Palestine has never been left to shape her own destiny, either in the ancient world or in the modern one. Because of her unique geographical situation, she has been called a Bridge, a Highway, the Belgium of Antiquity, the Heartland of the World. No single metaphor seems adequate to describe this country or the city most closely identified with it. I think that in all the years I was to go about the ordinary business of the day, buying carrots or going to the dressmakers near the Via Dolorosa, I was never to take the city for granted. For some years, I kept the funds for the refugee schools in Ramallah in a bank with the following address: Ottoman Bank, Prison of Christ, Via Dolorosa, Jerusalem. What a story there is in these names!

We didn't dream, however, when we landed in Jaffa in September 1922, that we were to live in that ancient land through many years in one of its most critical eras. Nor did we know that there was already set in motion the movement that was to mount in such complexity as to threaten the peace of the world. As we review the years since, we realize that the First World War, the war that was to end war, had only set the stage for future wars.

I am glad and grateful that for most of our years in Palestine it was not a partitioned country. Those were years when we moved about freely, each religious community free to worship after its own manner, and with its own religious courts to care for many matters that belong only to civil courts in our Western lands. We shopped together, attended movies together; Muslim, Christian, and Jew worked in government offices, Jewish people from Tel Aviv spent their summers in Ramallah living in Arab homes and hotels, and there seemed to be happiness and progress for all. In our early days, there was tremendous enthusiasm for education, and people looked to the West for leadership in government and trade, and in fact, for the co-operation that would bring Palestine into the great new era that was opening up in the West through science, technology, and all avenues of learning.

The Arab people were not unmindful that there was a time when it was they who took to Europe the culture of Greece, of Mesopotamia and of Egypt, and so filled the vacuum between the fall of Rome and the Renaissance, that period which we have called the Dark Ages. In those years, European scholars were learning Arabic in order to learn of the civilization of the Greeks and the Romans on which Europe was to develop and have her re-birth. That was also the period, according to modern historians, of the finest flowering of Jewish scholarship, as the Jews worked in co-operation with the Arabs.

The Arabs now realized that the West was opening up a new epoch in the life of mankind and they were eager and ready to enter into it.

Preparing the boys for their external examinations so that they could enter good universities, trying to create a home-life for the boarding-pupils, picnics to the valleys in the winter season when the wild flowers were in profusion, plays and school programmes, sports, intramural and with our brother-schools in Jerusalem, and social occasions with the Girls' School, all filled our days with pleasures and problems and challenges. It was a good time to be in Palestine, and it gave us a chance to get to know the country and its people in a period of relative quiet. I use the word "relative" advisedly, as there was an undercurrent of unease, since promises made to the Arab people during the war had been compromised by promises made to an alien people. But the Arabs had faith in the integrity of the British, who had been appointed to care for them for the next thirty years, and felt that their rights would be fully protected.

So the early years passed. There were compensations for the busy days. There were afternoon and early evening walks toward the village when the sun was sinking into the sea, especially lovely as the rainy season approached and the sunsets took on an added brilliance, changing the blue Mediterranean to deepest rose. At these times one felt close to an earlier people who worshipped the sun, the physical manifestation of the Creator, the Giver of life. The sun having set, we would retrace our steps and thrill to the afterglow which enfolded the village of Bireh to the east and the hills around with an evening benediction.

Not the least of our blessings, before tourists darted in and out of the country, were the days when eminent scholars took time to visit places of historical or biblical interest, or to remain to carry out archaeological research, and our boys had the experience of hearing some of the best speakers both England and America could provide. In fact, we had so many Ph.Ds come our way that one of my students asked me if all Americans were doctors!

But events were moving which would break into the comparatively even tenor of our days and which were to affect them more deeply than we would have dared to think then. How these events affected the lives of the people of Palestine, their fortunes, even their identity, is a tragic story. Much has been written about the Palestine Problem, scholarly works beyond my ability. My purpose is to tell the story as we lived it with the dispossessed, tell how they met disaster, and how lack of understanding by those who should have taken time to learn before making far-reaching decisions has created suffering and sorrow beyond description. Two wrongs cannot make a right: it would seem we have yet to learn that simple truth.

Background to Unrest

One of the ironies of history is that peace treaties too often have in them the seeds of future wars. During the First World War, the slogan "The war to end war" was made to seem like a justification for all the carnage and suffering endured by civilians and the sacrifice of the best of our young men. Instead, it merely started a chain reaction that has not yet run its course more than fifty years later. During the Second World War, I used to wish that someone would be brave enough to revive the "war to end war" slogan even if it was not realistic.

When America sent its first soldiers to Europe in 1917, no one could have foreseen that America was to be involved in foreign wars for a large part of the century. The First World War took American soldiers to Europe; the second to two areas of the world, Europe and the Pacific; two undeclared wars since then have involved America in the Far East, and there is the ever-present danger of being drawn into a conflict in the Middle East. Nations apparently do not learn from history, or from one another. The United States has not been helped by the experience of France in Vietnam or by the failure of the British in Palestine, even though ample documents and the experience of trained diplomats are readily available.

My husband and I were in Palestine when the Second World War ended. On the day the news came of the surrender of Japan, I made the following rather brief observation in my diary:

[1945: 15 August] With the surrender of Japan, the war is over. The longer stretch of winning the peace lies ahead. The use of the atomic bomb in the last dreadful days should have a sobering effect. Scientists seem more fearful than elated over this use of their latest invention; and well they may be!

If the remark about the "longer stretch of winning the peace" was pessimistic, it was realistic. I was remembering our hopes in 1918 and was only too conscious of the situation in Palestine. Peace might have come to the rest of the world but it was all too obvious that we were not to have its blessings in our little country right away; the signs were all too plain. Palestine was not a theatre of war between 1939 and 1945, but we were very conscious of war in the Mediterranean as hundreds of soldiers on leave were a familiar sight. Refugees from Poland and other European areas were concentrated in camps and towns in Palestine; Africans, fighting on the British side, were in Palestine in great numbers and were a common sight in Jerusalem as they enjoyed the Old City, the shops, and the climate of Palestine. We had all the problems of high prices and rationing and of being unable to replace equipment; but wages rose, and we managed. There were those older ones who remembered the tragic days of the First World War and they were thankful that this time the war was not being fought on their soil. But there had been no real peace in Palestine since 1918, and all hoped that with the end of the Second World War the problems which had kept the country unsettled would be solved.

Thirty years have passed since that memorable day in 1945, and the problem of Palestine has not been resolved. To understand why it has taken so long one must go back to a period even before the First World War, to see what was happening that could have brought about a situation which has cost so much in men, money, human relations and peace. It is not my purpose to go into the problem at length; many excellent books are available, written by scholars and historians, and we are bombarded with reports, dialogue, and propaganda, some subtle, some blatant, through the daily news media. A brief outline of some of the basic facts, however, may be helpful at this point in order that we may be able to interpret the news thoughtfully and, if at all possible, unemotionally.

We may begin by trying to answer some of the questions most commonly asked of those of us who have lived in Palestine or any part of the Middle East. We all wish we had the answers, especially when we are asked for a solution! We are asked why there is conflict, why the Arabs hate the Jews, why the Arabs are not willing to sell their land to the Jews, why the refugees won't accept compensation for their lands and be happy to go to another part of the Middle East, and the inevitable: don't the Arabs need the Jews, for aren't the Jews making the desert bloom like the rose? The questions too often do not indicate a desire for information; there is in them implied criticism of the Arabs. Since the first question will take longer to answer than the others, we will leave it to the last.

In the first place, the Arabs do not hate the Jews. They hate political Zionism, but not the Jews as people. Jews have lived in Arab lands for centuries and have never been exposed to racial and religious persecution such as they have suffered in our Western

countries. When the Arabs came from Arabia in the seventh century, Jews living in the Levant welcomed them and assisted them.
In Spain, Jewish and Muslim scholars worked in the closest relationship and helped establish some of the great universities which took
Europe out of that period we call the Dark Ages. It was the
Christians who drove the Jews out of Spain, after the Arab Empire
came to an end about 1492, and many of the Jews were welcomed
in Arab countries. Those of us who read *Ivanhoe* when we were in
school will remember that after the trial of Rebecca, she and her
father decided to go to Spain, where they would be safe; that was
in the time of Richard the Lion-Heart in the twelfth century, when
the Arabs ruled Spain. If the Jews in Beirut, Damascus, Cairo and
Baghdad have had trouble recently, it is due to the advent of
political Zionism in their midst. The chief rabbis of Cairo and
Baghdad have openly denounced political Zionism, which they
regard as contrary to the teachings of their prophets.

"Why don't you sell your land to the Jews, or accept compensation for the land they occupy?" That question was asked in
Jerusalem in 1958 by an American minister during a panel discussion with prominent Arabs at which I was present. The answer
given with quiet restraint by our friend Musa Bey Nasir, a highly-
regarded government official, a Christian Arab, was: "Would you
be willing to sell your country?" Regardless of where the refugees
are, or in whatever circumstances they live, whether in camps or
in the affluent society of Kuwait or Saudi Arabia, Palestine is still
their home and is not for sale. Their roots are deep in the soil of
the land of their ancestral homes, their shrines, and their history.
Some of the inhabitants of Palestine are descended from people
who were there before Abraham came in, and their customs were
adopted by the Jews, as the Hebrews, a desert people, learned to
live in a land of "great and goodly cities which thou buildest not,
and houses full of good things which thou filledst not, and wells
digged which thou diggedst not, vineyards and olive trees which
thou plantedst not." (*Deuteronomy* 6:10–11.) Other peoples came
in with the Arab conquest in the seventh century, settled, inter-
married and merged into the life of the population. Greeks, Romans,
and Crusaders played their part on the stage, and many remained to
mingle with the people. Regardless of their racial inheritance,
Palestinians considered themselves Arabs, a word that no longer
means one of the original Arabs but one who by language, tradition,
culture and social influence is "Arabized", and he may be a citizen
of any one of the countries stretching from the Atlantic in the west
to the Persian border in the east: from Morocco to Egypt; Syria,

which includes Lebanon and Palestine; Iraq, and the Arabian Peninsula. The people of Palestine feel a strong bond with all this area.

"Don't the Arabs need the Jews?" With all due respect and
admiration for the scientific and technological knowledge which
the Jews of the Western World have brought to Palestine, one
must know that Palestine was a progressing little country when they
began to come in 1918, that there was a government that was
Western and administratively excellent, though handicapped by
policies made in London. One must also remember that vast sums
of money and equipment have been given to the Jews to work with.
Perhaps no comparable number of people in history have ever been
given so much in so short a time or, because of influence throughout the world, been able to impose their ambitions on another people
as the present inhabitants of Israel have done. Miracles of development have been taking place in the rest of the Arab World, but
these are not so well publicized. Intellectual capacity and manual
skills are not limited to one small section of the human family, as
progress in the Arab World and other areas proves. Yes, the Arabs
need the Jews just as we all need each other, and our usefulness to
each other calls for co-operation, not domination. If the Zionists
mean to develop a normal state in the Arab World, they will need
the Arabs more than the Arabs need them. The people of the Middle
East have survived for a long, long time and created great civilizations, as all who read must know.

Since so much has been written about the Jews making the
desert bloom, a word about the Arab farmer should be noted here.
Palestine was not a desert at the beginning of this century, or ever
in history. It is the southwestern tip or horn of the Fertile Crescent,
that region, fed from northern mountain streams, which includes
Syria, Lebanon, and Mesopotamia. In Palestine, the rain from
heaven, which averages twenty-seven inches per annum, falls in
the months between November and April. The land has also in the
summer months the benefit of heavy dews from the Mediterranean
which are as important as the rains of winter. There are only two
seasons in Palestine. During the rainy season, sub-tropical Jericho
is balmy, Jaffa and the sea-coast towns are temperate, and in the
hill-country the cold winds blow piercingly from the Mediterranean,
and from the north and the north-west, occasionally bringing snow.
When summer comes, Ramallah and the hill-country around
Jerusalem are pleasantly temperate, the coast is hot, and Jericho
almost unbearable after seven o'clock in the morning. This variety
of climate determines the agricultural features of Palestine and
guarantees a succession of fresh fruits and vegetables throughout

the year. Our really difficult days in school usually came in May and September, when the sirocco blew in on us from the east, hot and dust-laden. The vegetation suffered, falling before it as before a blast. We read in *Ezekiel*, 17:10, "Shall it not utterly wither when the east wind toucheth? It shall wither in the furrows where it grew;" and again in *Ezekiel*, 19:12, "The east wind drieth up her fruit." Our boys might have nose-bleeds, become tired and irritable when the east wind hit us. Needless to say, we never thought it bothered their teachers! On the whole, however, for all-year-round living, the climate in and around Jerusalem was as fine as one could wish for.

To read one's Bible is to realize how close to nature the people of Palestine have always lived and how well they knew how to use the land in all its variety. The Bible is full of references to the sun and the moon and the stars, the mountains and the valleys, the trees and the flowers, the vines, the olive, the almond, the fig and the pomegranate. No passage in the Bible confirms this picture of Palestine before the Hebrews entered it better than that found in *Numbers*, 13:16–23. There it tells how Moses sent scouts into Palestine to spy out the land, and they came back bearing a branch cut from a vine bearing a single cluster of grapes, some pome-granates and figs. These were the fruits of the land, they reported, and truly it was a land flowing with milk and honey, the natives were strong, and the cities fortified and powerful. Three thousand years later, we have eaten the grapes of Hebron from whence the spies cut theirs and we can testify to the fact that they have lost none of their excellence.

And not only in Hebron were there grapes. A favourite walk from Ramallah in the late summer for us was to go to Beitin, ancient Bethel, in the late afternoon to enjoy the setting of that village and to visit the homes of our students. We would usually be invited to the vineyard to enjoy the grapes still on the vine. On the hills, the vines are not put on trellises but grow close to the ground. The rainy season over, the summer dews will ripen them. As soon as the clusters of grapes appear in the spring, the farmer lifts them from the ground and supports them with smooth stones. When he prunes the vines, he covers the plants lightly with the leaves and twigs. Nightly mists that sweep up from the west soak the covering, which forms a blanket protecting the fruit from the hot sun of noonday and retaining the moisture necessary for growth. Thus it was that we would be allowed to fold back the blanket of leaves and twigs and find a beautiful cluster of white grapes, firm and unblemished and a miracle of succulence.

As Jesus went about Palestine teaching in his time, he drew his illustrations from the life about him, and these illustrations let us know about the country, too. Humble people could get his meaning, for they knew foolish men who built their houses on sand, the sowers who let their seeds fall on stony ground, the merchants who, too eager to save, put their new wine in old goat-skin bottles; they could appreciate the care of the shepherd for his sheep and his concern for the lost one, what happened when a ploughman did not keep his eye on the plough as he cut through the stony ground, or burdened his oxen with an uneven yoke. And I am sure a burst of laughter greeted his illustration of the foolish person who would sew a new patch on old cloth, for there were probably many such in the listening crowd. He had only to lift his eyes to the hills to remind them that a city set on a hill could not be hid, for so many Palestinian towns and villages are to this day set on hills. When he said, "I am the vine, my Father is the husbandman," he was reminding them that without God the soul would not live. That, too, they could quickly understand, for they knew how to care for grapes. And a tired mother would remember as she kneaded her bread each day that the Kingdom of Heaven was like the yeast she was using.

Lest we may seem to be too eulogistic about the Palestinian farmer, let us read the observations of a successful Iowa farmer, Robert Meredith, which he made in 1891, in his book *Around the World on Sixty Dollars*: "Nothing can exceed the beauty of the orange groves and gardens around Joppa, which is surrounded by fertile plains which produce crops of wheat, barley, and grapes, all without irrigation. Tall date-palms bearing five or six bunches of fruit as large as a flour barrel hung below the leaves add beauty to the scene." He was fascinated by "this old city flourishing before Abraham ever came to the Promised Land," by the clever way fishermen cast their nets, by the camels laden with wheat, grapes, fruits and vegetables of every kind, by the donkeys laden with burdens of men and produce, and the busy streets lined with shops full of exotic objects. When he reached Esdraelon in the north, a marvellous scene met his eye. The plain was filled with several hundred teams ploughing the earth and sowing seeds widely. He thought this was the finest piece of land he had ever seen, surpassing in fertility, if not in beauty, the great San Joaquin Valley in California.

We will now note what experts with the John Hope Simpson Commission of Inquiry into Disturbances, after riots in 1929, had to say about the Arab farmer:

"He is a competent and able agriculturist and there is little doubt that were he given the chance of learning better methods, and the capital which is a necessary preliminary to their employment, he would readily improve his position. A good deal of ridicule has been poured upon his nail plough which he uses. In the stony country on the hills, no other plough would be able to do the work at all . . . ; it performs very slowly, it is true, but thoroughly all the functions for which a combination of modern machines is required, a plough, a roller, and a harrow. The ploughing of a *felaheen* (farmer) is above reproach. His field prepared for sowing is never inferior to that prepared by the most perfect implements, and sometimes it even surpasses all others. Its defect is only in its slowness."

We come now to the most important question of all: why is there a conflict in Palestine? It would not be difficult to explain if there were not the difficult task of untangling a web of deceit that has become more of a maze with the passing years. A problem that started in Palestine has now spread throughout the Arab World and into the governments of most of Europe and the United States of America, to the point of threatening a confrontation between the Great Powers. In its simplest terms, it is a situation in which the inalienable rights of the people of Palestine, derived from centuries of continuous living in and possession of the land, are being denied them to satisfy the ephemeral rights of a people whose ancestors lived there for a relatively brief span in the history of that land and who were expelled from it nearly two thousand years ago. If such a claim can be seriously recognized and other countries followed suit, our world would be a topsy-turvy one indeed. The Palestinians are being told that they cannot set the clock back thirty years or so, but the Zionists get support for turning the clock back 2,000 years. If the immigration of some sections of the Jewish people were all that were involved, the problem would be relatively simple, as Jewish people have gone there in the past and been accepted. But Zionist claims go beyond that, and to understand the significance of their claims and Arab resistance to them, we must follow what was happening in Europe in Jewish communities and what was going on in the Arab World at the turn of the century.

In his great book, *The Arab Awakening* (1938), George Antonius, a Jerusalem Arab, begins with the following sentence: "The story of the Arab National Movement opens in Syria in 1847, with the foundation of a modest literary society under American patronage."

It was at a meeting of the society that Ibrahim Yazefi, in a stirring poem, called on the Arabs to rise against their Ottoman rulers. Arab national aspirations had to be advanced secretly, but enough strength had come to the movement by 1913 for the nationalists to hold an Arab Congress in Paris. Secret societies were formed in such widely separated centres as Paris, Constantinople, Damascus and Beirut, but not without danger. Many Arabs suffered martyrdom and exile during the years. It is not surprising, then, that when war broke out in Europe in 1914, with Britain and her allies pitted against Germany and Turkey, Arab sympathies and hopes were with the Western Allies.

With a strong Germany allied with Turkey, Britain's interests in the Near East were threatened. The Suez Canal was her life-line to India and the Far East colonies. A second danger was that Turkey might use the Caliphate to arouse the Muslim World to a Holy War. In order to protect the Canal, large forces of empire troops were dispatched to Egypt and a move made to win the Arabs to the side of the West. Britain had able administrators in Egypt. Sir Henry McMahon was the highly respected High Commissioner in Egypt and the Sudan. Mr Ronald Storrs, later Sir Ronald, described by T. E. Lawrence as the most brilliant scholar in the Near East, was the Oriental Secretary of the British Residency in Cairo. He knew Arabic well and had wide knowledge of the country. We were to know him in our early years in Palestine as the Governor of Jerusalem and as a lecturer on many subjects, especially on Dante. Lieutenant-Colonel G. F. Clayton, an able soldier, was Chief of Civil and Military Intelligence; he also later served in Palestine. Dr D. G. Hogarth, an eminent scholar, archaeologist and Arabist, spent the war years in Cairo on the staff of the Arab Bureau. In these men Britain had exceedingly able negotiators and advisers, and if she was to win the Arabs over, the Sharif of Mecca was their man.

Sharif Hussein of Mecca was descended from the family of the Prophet, the House of Hashem, a family revered in the Muslim World. He and his wife and three sons spent sixteen years in Constantinople, not exactly as hostages but according to the Turkish Government's method of keeping its empire under control. He was made Grand Sharif of Mecca in 1908 and returned as guardian of the Holy Places also. During his exile, he had learned a great deal about Turkey and also about European diplomats, and while he may have been disillusioned with some, he preferred the British and trusted them. So it was fortunate for Britain that they had someone of his prestige in the Arab World with whom to negotiate for Arab support. Sharif Hussein was open to British proposals as he had no loyalty to his Turkish overlords. Sir Henry McMahon had sufficient confidence in Sharif Hussein to start in July 1915 a correspondence with him to win his support, Mr Storrs and others having laid the ground-work. The correspondence, with its promises and evasions, kept secret for many years, is known in history as the Hussein-McMahon correspondence. The substance of the letters was that in return for Arab support in the war effort, Great Britain would assure the independence of the Arab people. Sharif Hussein was careful to be clear about boundaries, which were indicated in detail, and emphasis was placed again and again on the complete independence of the Arabs. He was reasonably understanding of the problems of Britain in relation to her allies, France and Russia, and was willing to waive certain details until after the war, but it was to be understood that "any concession designed to give France or any other power possession of a single square foot of territory in those parts is out of the question." The reply was that Britain did not intend to conclude any peace whatsoever of which the freedom of the Arab people and their liberation from German or Turkish domination did not form an essential condition. The courtship over, for better or worse, the union of the Arabs and Great Britain was consummated, and on 5 June 1916 Sharif Hussein sent two of his three sons, Ali and Feisal, to the tomb of Hamza in the Arabian Desert to declare the independence of the Arabs from their Turkish overlords. It was a dramatic moment and a turning-point in the long, colourful history of the Arab people; and it could not have come at a better time for the Western Allies, who were suffering heavy losses on land and on sea.

For Britain and her allies, the Hussein-McMahon letters had reached a happy conclusion, but for the Arabs it would produce a bitter harvest. For unknown to the Arabs, and we must believe also to the British negotiators in Egypt, for they were all "honourable men" serving their country as best they could, diplomatic exchanges were going on in another theatre of the war quite contrary to those in the Arab World.

Almost as soon as the support of the Arabs was secured, Britain, France, and Russia entered into negotiations which started as a series of notes but were to have serious impact in the Arab World. These notes contained plans for the division of the spoils of war when the Ottoman Empire would be dismembered, so that each country would get what it wanted most. Russia was to get warm ports at last and control of the Dardanelles; Syria would fall to France, and Britain would get Palestine, Transjordan and Iraq. Britain would now have complete control of the Suez Canal. Details of the area each country was to have were outlined, save for the question of Jerusalem, where all three countries had special interests, and it was even suggested that it might become an international city.

The Russian Revolution interrupted the smooth functioning of these plans, for when the Bolshevik Government discovered the secret documents in December 1917, they published them. It was the first inkling that the Arabs had of the Sykes-Picot correspondence and of the men most involved. Sir Mark Sykes was a British student of Eastern Affairs, writer and scholar, and Monsieur F. Georges-Picot served as French Consul-General in Syria with the consulate in Beirut. To complicate matters further, the timing of these disclosures was a blow to the Arabs, for only a month earlier, on 2 November 1917, Britain had issued the Balfour Declaration, another secret agreement which we will deal with later. It should be further noted that the Balfour Declaration was issued only five weeks before General Allenby entered Palestine, and that with his defeat of the Turkish army the war was over in the Near East and it was the end of the Ottoman Empire. If the Arabs felt that they had been victims of duplicity, it is understandable, for both revelations came as a complete surprise to them and to Sharif Hussein especially.

For the Western Allies, the Arab Revolt had been a success. They could now concentrate all their resources on the war in Europe. The United States had come into the picture, too, and the tide had turned. Dr Hogarth made this assessment after the war: "Had the Arab Revolt never done anything else than frustrate the combined march of the Turks and Germans to Southern Arabia in 1916, we should owe it more than we have paid to this day." General Allenby also paid high tribute to Arab support and wrote feelingly of the way his troops were welcomed by the Palestinians. They were greeted as liberators, and Arabs who had been serving in the Turkish armies joined them and gave valuable information about Turkish plans.

One of those Palestinians who took part in enlisting soldiers for the British army was the young Amin el-Husseini, a member of a prominent Jerusalem family. He was later to be disillusioned, to challenge British policies and be exiled, but his first response to the British was one of enthusiasm and loyalty.

So far the story has been of the hopes and aspirations of the Arabs. They had been assured of their independence and they were now to have a rebirth of their great past and to join with the West in the new age that was opening up for mankind in science, technology, education and peace. Their hopes ran high. They were willing to accept for a limited period an alien government, however, if it seemed inevitable.

When we went to Palestine, so soon after the war, schools were filled with eager pupils, business was picking up and there was a general air of hopefulness. The Mandate Government, which had guaranteed that "nothing shall be done to prejudice the rights of the Palestinians," was trying to perform its duties as well and as fairly as possible under a dual responsibility. It is possible that the Hussein-McMahon and Sykes-Picot negotiations, devious as they were, could have been resolved and dismissed as wartime expediency, if a new movement had not been injected into the scene which was to negate the fine promises of the war, to keep Palestine in a state of unrest, to carry the whole Middle East into a war situation, and ultimately to threaten the peace of the world.

The announcement of the Balfour Declaration on 2 November 1917 was possibly the least expected development in the First World War, and may prove to have been its greatest mistake. The timing alone should be kept in mind if one is to understand the mood of the Arabs today. They had joined the Allies in good faith, had fought with them as allies for eighteen months in a war for independence, during which one-eighth of the people of Syria, Lebanon and Palestine died; 300,000 of them from hunger, disease and malnutrition. Now at the moment of victory, the future of the people of Palestine was threatened. The story of the price the people of Lebanon and Syria paid is a tragic one indeed. When General Allenby entered Palestine, he found "a population shrunken to half its size by hunger, exile and deportation."

We must turn now to the historical document to follow the steps which led up to it, see what was in it and why it has created such a crisis in the world today. It was actually a letter written by Mr A. J. Balfour, British Foreign Secretary, to Lord Rothschild, a Jewish financier, and read as follows:

"His Majesty's government view with favour the establishment in Palestine of a national home for the Jewish people and will use their best endeavours to facilitate the achievement of this object, it being clearly understood that nothing will be done which may prejudice the civil and religious rights of existing non-Jewish communities in Palestine or the rights and political status enjoyed by Jews in any other country."

There were 60,000 Jews at the most in Palestine when this document was released, and 600,000 Arabs. Yet the Palestinians were referred to as "the existing non-Jewish community", as though they were an insignificant minority. It should also be remembered that Palestine was not Britain's to dispose of. Sharif Hussein immediately protested against the Declaration, as did all Arabs, and asked for an explanation. Commander Hogarth was sent at once to Jedda with the explicit assurance from the British Government to Sharif Hussein that "Jewish settlement would be consistent with the political and economic freedom of the Arab population." While the Balfour Declaration had included only civil and religious rights, the Hogarth message added political and economic freedom, a hopeful addition.

The Balfour Declaration undertook three obligations: one, to favour the establishment of a homeland for the Jews; two, to protect the civil and religious rights of the indigenous population; three, to do nothing to prejudice the rights and political status enjoyed by Jews in any other country. How they intended to carry out the latter obligation in countries not under their jurisdiction, it is hard to know, but the phrase was put in to appease those British Jews who opposed the Declaration and who feared that it would prejudice rights Jews had won in the countries of their birth. When Lord Montagu, the only Jew in the British cabinet at that time, learned of the letter Mr Balfour had sent to Rothschild, he wrote a remarkably prophetic protest to the British Government, made public in 1966, part of which follows:

> "Zionism has always seemed to me to be a mischievous political creed, untenable by any patriotic citizen of the UK . . . It is inconceivable that Zionism should be officially recognized by the British Government and that Mr Balfour should be authorized to say that Palestine should be reconstructed (reconstituted) as a national home for the Jewish people . . . I assert that there is not a Jewish nation . . . When the Jews are told that Palestine is their national home, every country will immediately desire to get rid of its Jewish citizens and you will find a population in Palestine driving out the present inhabitants, taking all the best in the country, drawn from all quarters of the globe, speaking every language on the face of the earth, and incapable of communicating with one another except by means of an interpreter . . . I have always understood from the Jews before Zionism that to bring the Jews back to form a nation in the country from which they were dispersed would require divine leadership . . . I have never heard it suggested even by their most fervent admirers, that either Mr Balfour or Lord Rothschild

would prove to be the Messiah . . . I would say to Lord Rothschild that the government will be prepared to do everything in
their power to obtain for Jews in Palestine complete liberty of
settlement and life on an equality with the inhabitants of that
country who profess other religious beliefs. I would ask that
the Government go no further." 23 August 1917.

Without going into the history of the Jews in Europe, we must
note, however, that the Zionist Movement which culminated in the
Balfour Declaration had its beginning there. Their lot had not been
easy for centuries, but by 1874 most western European countries
had granted Jews full rights of citizenship and there was a good
deal of assimilation in those countries as a result. Eastern European
Jews had not yet attained full citizen status but, while they might
want it, they feared assimilation and looked upon it with apprehension. They cherished their traditions and way of life and wanted
to preserve them. The Dreyfus case in France and pogroms in
Russia towards the end of the century pointed to an increase of
anti-Semitism, and this group felt that to maintain their identity
they must find a place where they would not be an unwanted
minority. Their spokesman, an Austrian journalist and playwright,
Theodor Herzl, who had attended the Dreyfus trial in France,
began to feel that the time had come when the Jewish people
must have a place of their own. He claimed that while Jews in
some countries were living in security and comfort, eastern European Jews did not feel free from persecution.

Herzl gave impetus to their desires by publishing a pamphlet
called *The Jewish State* in 1896, which laid before the Jews a plan
to secure from the Sultan in Turkey permission for the Jews to
settle in Palestine because of their ancient association with that
country. He thought that if the Jews could pay high tribute for
the Sultan's protection, the plan would appeal to him, as his large
debts were well known. The most important factor in any agreement, however, was that Palestine was to be a Jewish state. The
Jews, in turn, would promise to safeguard Muslim and Christian
interests, but they themselves must be the dominant people. That
this pamphlet met with a fervent response among some Jews is
evidenced by the fact that within a year, in 1897, a great conference was held in Basle, Switzerland. As a result, Zionism was
launched as a factor to be reckoned with in the modern world.

When Sultan Abdul-Hamid was approached on the subject of
Palestine, he rejected the plea and the offer of financial aid. One
report is that he told the Zionists that they might get the country

without paying for it some day, but that Palestine was already inhabited, and in no circumstances would the population be displaced to make a Jewish state possible.

Britain then came forward with an offer of land in Uganda in British East Africa for the creation of a Jewish colony with full power of local autonomy. This offer was vehemently rejected, although according to some writers Herzl and a few other Zionists felt that, desirable as Palestine would be, the Jewish state could be created elsewhere. The general view, however, was that Palestine would offer a better rallying cry than Uganda or any other place if the movement was to grow and get the financial support it would need from Jews everywhere. The fact that Palestine had a population of 600,000 Arabs did not seem unsurmountable, as they thought the Arabs would be willing to sell their land and go to some other part of the Arab World. They did not know what was going on in the Arab World or the character of the people of Palestine, but they soon learned that they would have to use some means other than money to get the country.

Turkey had refused to consider their offer, but as war loomed and Turkey and Germany were giving evidence of an alliance, the Zionists appealed to Germany on the grounds of similar cultural background suggesting that a Zionist state would be an advantage to such an alliance. Germany was not impressed, and it was not until Great Britain was approached during the First World War and showed signs of being able to win in the Middle East that Germany realized her mistake. The Arab Revolt was unexpected, and it was to change the situation completely at the eastern end of the Mediterranean and force Germany to send some of her army there to bolster the Turkish army.

Early in 1917, Great Britain and her Allies were hard-pressed. The Allied cause in Europe was in a serious situation. The Russian army was demoralized, Rumania was defeated, the Italians had suffered a great defeat at Caporetto, France was not strong enough to start a major offensive. The United States had declared war on 6 April 1917, but there were not yet any American divisions in Europe, and millions of tons of British shipping had been sunk by German submarines. The time was propitious for the Zionists to approach Britain with an offer of help. They chose Dr Chaim Weizmann, a distinguished Jewish chemist living in England, for the task of consulting members of the British war cabinet. Mr Arthur Balfour was the man to approach. Dr Weizmann was able to assure Great Britain of the support of Jews throughout the world in return for the advancement of Zionist aims. There are many explanations given for Britain's support of the Zionist wishes, including the oft-told one that it was a reward for the contribution Dr Weizmann made in the field of chemistry. Dr Weizmann made an official approach to the Foreign Office in these words: "We must respectfully point out that in submitting our resolution, we entrusted our national and Zionist destiny to the Foreign Office and the Imperial War Cabinet in the hope that the problem would be considered in the light of imperial interests and the precepts for which the Entente stands." Lloyd George, then Prime Minister of England, admitted frankly that "the Zionists' leaders gave us a definite promise that, if the Allies committed themselves to giving them facilities for the establishment of a national home for the Jews in Palestine, they would do their best to rally Jewish support throughout the world to the Allied cause. They kept their word." He was later to confess, as reported in the Royal Commission Report in 1937, that the launching of the Balfour Declaration in 1917 was for "propaganda reasons".

The imperial interests to which Dr Weizmann addressed himself were crucial at the moment. Great Britain wished to win over the strong Zionist elements in Germany and Austria who were at that time negotiating with the Central Powers, Turkey and Germany, for a Turkish declaration similar to the Balfour one, by providing them with a positive interest in an Allied victory, and at the same time to give the Jews who had been active in overthrowing the Czarist regime in Russia an incentive for remaining in the war. They were also eager to win over Jews in allied countries who were hostile to Russia. But Britain's chief interest was in securing Palestine for herself in order to have complete control of the Suez Canal because of her possessions in India and the Far East.

One wishes that the Jewish people could know more of the reaction of Sharif Hussein to the Balfour Declaration. Naturally, he was dismayed and unbelieving, and demanded at once an explanation from the British Government. As has been stated, Commander Hogarth was sent to Jedda with a message which went beyond the terms of the Balfour Declaration, which mentioned only civil and religious rights for the "existing non-Jewish population", to include political and economic freedom. Hussein's reply was that if the aim of the Declaration was for purely humanitarian reasons to provide a haven for persecuted Jews, he would do all he could to help, sanctuaries of all creeds would be respected and safeguarded . . . but "under no circumstances would Arab claim to sovereignty be surrendered." As proof of his humanitarian pledge, Sharif Hussein sent messages to all his people urging them to maintain their faith in Britain and especially urged his sons to quiet the fears of their soldiers. He even published a call to the people of Palestine to remind them of the commands of their sacred books on the duties of hospitality and tolerance and asked them to welcome the persecuted Jews as brothers and co-operate with them for the common good. When our reporters and writers and the President of the United States speak of the "age-old enmities" between Arabs and Jews, they show an ignorance of history which is most unfortunate.

If Sharif Hussein failed, it was because he did not sense the ambiguities in the correspondence with McMahon. He took time to inquire into all aspects of Allied intentions, but he was not told of the Sykes-Picot agreements or of negotiations with the Zionists. It was a matter of trusting too much and having too much faith in the integrity of the British. It was also his first direct personal experience of Western diplomacy, and he may not have fully realized how desperate the Allies were. When we heard Sir Ronald Storrs speak on the Palestine Problem at Bryn Mawr College many years ago, my husband asked him if he would be willing to explain the apparent conflict of promises, as Sir Ronald was one of the most active of the Egypt staff in the negotiations. He could only answer that it was a case of the right hand not knowing what the left hand was doing. The staff in Egypt, according to him, was not told of the Sykes-Picot Treaty and had acted in good faith. The blame must therefore rest on the Foreign Office.

Britain was granted the Mandate for Palestine by the League of Nations in 1922, and the first High Commissioner sent to Palestine was Sir Herbert Samuel, a dedicated Zionist. He drove to his residence in Jerusalem in an armoured car through silent streets and in an atmosphere of sullen hostility, according to the story we were told soon after. Sir Herbert served for five years, and it is a tribute to his wisdom and fairness that his accomplishments were so great and that he won the friendship of many Arabs. But the opposition to the Balfour Declaration lived on, and Britain never again sent a member of the Jewish faith to that position. Sir Herbert's son, Edwin Samuel, remained as a government official in Palestine until the end of the Mandate.

During the years that followed, from 1922 until the British left Palestine on 15 May 1948, there was no peace in the Holy Land, and frequent eruptions of violence kept the country in a constant state of tension. Eighteen commissions came out during the years to study the causes of unrest, riots and rebellion; inevitably, they all agreed that the terms of the Balfour Declaration could not be implemented, since Zionist demands went far beyond what Britain maintained were her intentions when it was issued. Two of these commissions, one American and one British, must be studied if one is to understand the present crisis. A third commission sent out by the United Nations was a disappointment to the Palestinians, for the members seemed to have come out more to confirm decisions already made than to go into the basic causes and arrive at a solution after careful study. Its report to the United Nations was based largely on the reports of the Royal and Peel Commissions, which the British Government had rejected. These reports we will discuss later, and I shall take up first the King-Crane Commission.

America was swept into the First World War on a wave of idealism. President Wilson had been re-elected on a peace ticket, yet at a most critical time for the Allies in 1917 he could no longer resist pressures for American involvement in a war so vast that the name "World War" was coined. How American participation affected the course of the war is a well-known story of a young nation going to the help of the older ones from which the new nation was built, and how together they were to create a new world order. President Wilson took with him to the Peace Conference high hopes. Intellectually and professionally he was well prepared. His achievements had been formidable as lawyer, professor of Juris-prudence, Political Economy and Politics, President of Princeton University, and Governor of the State of New Jersey; he was then serving his second term as President of the United States. How-ever, it is probable that he was not fully informed of many aspects of the war, and he was faced with factors which disturbed him as he met the statesmen in Paris to make the Peace Treaty. Before going to the Peace Conference, he had agreed to the Balfour Declara-tion on the advice of Mr Justice Brandeis, but when he discovered the terms and conditions surrounding it he was disillusioned, for it con-flicted with one of his most cherished theories of government, which was the self-determination of small nations. So, although he had given his assent to the Balfour Declaration, he was now convinced that the wishes of the Arab people should be considered.

Others who had studied the situation were concerned also, among them British officials who were well informed of the situation in the Arab World, especially Sir Mark Sykes, but in a memorandum to the British Government on 11 August 1919, Mr Balfour stated: "In Palestine, we do not propose even to go through the form of consulting the wishes of the present population of the country . . . the Four Powers are committed to Zionism . . . and Zionism, be it right or wrong, good or bad, is rested in age-old traditions, in present needs, in future hopes, of profounder import than the desires and prejudices of 700,000 Arabs who now inhabit that ancient land." Hardly a responsible statement from one who held high office in his government. This was his response to a request from President Wilson that a commission should be sent to the Arab countries which had participated in the war and to whom promises had been made and accepted in good faith, to find out what they wanted in the form of government and the future of their territories. It is to President Wilson's credit that he persisted and finally sent out an American Commission in June 1919. He chose Dr King, President of Oberlin College, and Mr Charles R. Crane, a businessman, to head this Commission.

The King-Crane Commission was welcomed in the Arab World, and faith in America was strong. After weeks of travel and conferences with leaders in every area they produced a report which, for clear-thinking, perception and vision, has not been surpassed, and which, if it had been implemented, might have prevented the present crisis in the Middle East. As we look at it in retrospect, it takes on added significance and reality. It was treated at first as confidential, but before President Wilson was able to give it his full attention, he went on a speaking tour in an effort to get the United States into the League of Nations, which was also one of his cherished hopes, but illness followed and the crucial report was shelved. It was not until 1947 that it was officially published. A scholarly study of the report was published in 1963. The author of this study is Harry N. Howard, the title *The King-Crane Report, An American Inquiry in the Middle East*, and it reveals the breadth and width and depth of the amazing work done by the commission in a relatively short period of time. These extracts are from the Report itself:

". . . We recommend serious modifications of the extreme Zionist programme for Palestine of unlimited immigration of Jews, looking finally to making Palestine distinctly a Jewish state. . . . For a national home for the Jewish people is not equivalent to making Palestine into a Jewish State; nor can the erection of such a Jewish State be accomplished without the gravest trespass upon the civil and religious rights of the existing non-Jewish communities in Palestine. The fact came out repeatedly in the Commission's conferences with Jewish representatives that the Zionists looked forward to a practically complete dispossession of the present non-Jewish inhabitants of Palestine, by various forms of purchase.

Library of
Davidson College

"In his address of 4 July 1918, President Wilson laid down the following principle as one of the four great ends for which the associated peoples of the world were fighting . . . 'The settlement of every question, whether of territory, of sovereignty, of economic arrangement, or of political relationship upon the basis of the free acceptance of that settlement by the people immediately concerned, and not upon the basis of the material interest or advantage of any other nation or people which may desire a different settlement for the sake of its own exterior influence or mastery . . .' If that principle is to rule, and if the wishes of Palestine's population are to be decisive as to what is to be done with Palestine, then it is to be remembered that THE NON-JEWISH POPULATION OF PALESTINE—NEARLY NINE-TENTHS OF THE WHOLE—ARE EMPHATICALLY AGAINST THE ENTIRE ZIONIST PRO-GRAMME. The tables show that there was no one thing upon which the population were more agreed than this. To sub-ject a people so minded to unlimited Jewish immigration, and to steady financial and social pressure to surrender the land, would be a gross violation of the principles just quoted, and of the people's rights, though it kept within the forms of the law . . . No British officer consulted by the Commissioners believed that the Zionist programme could be carried out except by force of arms . . . Decisions requiring armies to carry out are sometimes necessary, but they are surely not gratuitously to be taken in the interests of serious injustice. For the initial claim, often submitted by Zionist representatives, that they have a *right* to Palestine, based on an occupation of nearly 2,000 years ago, can hardly be seriously considered."

A third historical decision which has created the existing ten-sions and violence in the Near East was made in the United Nations on 29 November 1947. That will come into this story later, but perhaps the reader will now begin to see how true is the following item from the *Manchester Guardian*, an important British news-paper. It was written after the Israeli blitz of June 1967.

[1967: 9 November] "As far as Britain and its reputation is concerned, the Balfour Declaration is the seemingly innocuous tip
   of an iceberg of deception. That is something which every English-
   man ought to remember when he considers the present situation
   in the Middle East . . ."

The tangled web of deceit has brought us to a very dangerous moment in world history. Anyone who would understand it more fully than this brief sketch allows can find many books written by able scholars who trace the threads of the story with skill and perception. He would be hard of heart indeed who does not sympathize with the sufferings of the Jewish people, especially in the days of Hitler, but to ask an innocent predominantly Muslim people to experience exile and suffering to atone for the sins of the Christian West is hardly the way to justice.

The Tangled Web

The years between the two World Wars were not an era of peace for Palestine. Britain was entrusted by the League of Nations with a mandate for a thirty-year period during which she was to give advice and assistance to the people of Palestine until they were able to stand alone. It was really a trusteeship with responsibilities and limitations. The Arabs, having joined the Western Allies under assurances of independence, accepted the Mandate, trusting that their civil, religious, political and economic rights would be respected, and they were encouraged by the promise that nothing would be done in regard to immigration and land purchase without their consent.

For the Zionists, the terms of the Balfour Declaration were less than they had hoped for, but it at least gave them entry into Palestine and was a step toward their ambition to become a majority through immigration and eventually to have a state. To that end, they brought forward certain definite demands, outlined even before Britain had been officially granted the Mandate, which were noted by the King-Crane Commission. The demands indicated clearly that they wanted to be a separate people, and to that end they insisted on the following:

  1. Recognition of "historical rights"; 2. that the Balfour Declaration be fully carried out; 3. that a Jewish Agency be set up for the purpose of "advising and co-operating with the government in all matters relating to the Jewish population in Palestine;" 4. that rights of immigration and close settlement on the land be recognized; 5. that they would set up their own schools; and lastly, that Hebrew be made an official language.

In these days when America is agonizing over school bussing to achieve racial integration, the insistence of the Jews on having their own schools gives one cause for thought. Another interesting aspect of the programme was the demand that Hebrew be made an official language. One wonders how they expected to enter into the economic and social life of a great area of the world where Arabic was spoken, if in the "ingathering" the newcomers were to learn a language as limited as ancient Hebrew. In their stipulation that "the terms of the Balfour Declaration be fully carried out" they apparently forgot that it included the proviso that "nothing would be done to prejudice the civil and religious rights of the existing non-Jewish population." They had already read into the Declaration more than was intended.

Those were the Zionists' terms and the Mandate accepted them. In time the Jewish Agency was practically a government within a government. A fact not lost on the Arab population was that in all their communications the Zionists referred to the Palestinians as the "existing non-Jewish population" or "the other section of the country". We were not surprised when, on a television programme in recent months, Golda Meir simply repudiated any knowledge of the Palestinians; they did not exist, she declared, therefore there was no group with whom she could communicate. We arrived in Palestine a year later than she did, and were in the midst of a people officially called Palestinians.

So the post-war era, anticipated so hopefully by the Arabs who had suffered so much during the war, started out under the worst possible auspices. The King-Crane Report, with its perceptive observations and warnings, was to remain in the archives of the United States, and the light it could have shed on the problem, which could have shown the way to a sane consideration of the impossible task set for the Mandate Government of Palestine, was blacked out.

The obvious happened. There were frequent protests against administrative policies and growing fear among the Arabs that their future was threatened by the Jewish immigration the government was pledged to facilitate. When in 1929 there was a Zionist Congress in Zurich and headlines coming from it reiterated the slogan which was becoming familiar to the Arabs, "Palestine is to become as Hebrew as England is English and America is American," serious riots broke out. The month was August, when many of the British officials were on holiday. The High Commissioner, Lord Plummer, who had boasted that he could maintain order with a small force of British soldiers, was not in the country at the time, and his small force was not able to control the situation adequately. The outbreak was spontaneous and without leadership, and was soon spent, but not before Jews in certain areas, particularly Hebron and Safed, suffered a great deal. I was in Jerusalem the following Friday, shopping for school supplies, and was at Jaffa Gate when people were coming from the mosque, and from their mood and the shouting that accompanied it, I feared that a new

outbreak was imminent. I had been shopping in a Jewish store and
the owner, one who had lived in Palestine before the war, in great
agitation exclaimed: "We were happy in Palestine before these
European Jews came here, now we have nothing but trouble." I
must confess that I was glad to get back to Ramallah that day.
This incident should have been a warning to the government in
London, as it showed how close to the surface antagonism lay; and
urgent steps should then have been taken to clarify with actions,
not words, how the Mandate Government was to fulfil its responsibilities to the Arabs as well as the Jews.

The crisis over, immigration continued, but during the first years
of the Mandate it did not seem to constitute too great a threat, for
the Jews did not flock to Palestine as the Zionists had hoped. The
Palestinians could even joke about it. When asked to define a
Zionist, they would answer: "He is a Jew who gives money to
another Jew to send still another Jew to Palestine." In the *Hand-
book of Palestine* published in 1930, we find that in 1928, 2,178
Jews settled in Palestine and 2,168 left. Nor was it easy to buy land.
What they did buy was mostly from absentee landowners who had
been given the land in Turkish days and lived in Beirut. Palestinians
farmed the land and lived on it, paying an annual share of the
crops to the owners. Unfortunately, when Jews bought the land,
the Arabs who had lived on it for generations were forced to leave,
as a Zionist rule was that the new immigrants were to till the soil.
This policy created a serious problem in the Twenties for it dispossessed a large number of farmer folk who knew only farming
and for whom there was now no work. The Mandate allowed
Jewish immigrants to use state lands, again without considering
their first responsibility to the indigenous population. Yet it is
interesting to note that until the State of Israel was established
following the Partition of Palestine in 1948, they acquired by purchase less than seven per cent of the land they now control. Arabs
did not easily part with their property, and some who might have
been tempted to accept the high price the Zionists were prepared to
pay did not dare risk the contempt, or worse, of their neighbours
and kinsmen. Ramallah became a summer resort after the First
World War, and people from Jaffa and other coastal parts came up
on the hills to get away from the heat. Many Jewish people came,
too. We know of some Ramallah people who were offered good
money by Jews for some of their land, but not a single Ramallah
person sold a foot of land to the Zionist organization.

The next serious outbreak of Arab hostility started in 1936, when
there was a sudden rise in immigration due to Hitler's persecution

of the Jews. This gave credence to Zionist claims that they must have a country of their own, and pressures were brought on Jews in Germany to believe that Palestine was their only hope. Many German Jews went to other European countries where they could live securely with full rights of citizenship, many went to England, many more would have gone to the United States if American immigration laws had been more flexible. The conscience of the world was stirred by the sufferings of the Jews in Germany, and to many the idea of their return to Palestine seemed to be an ideal solution. Interestingly enough, as they had opened their doors to the Armenians, Palestinians might have offered a place where Jews too would have found shelter, had it not been for Zionist political policies.

The crisis in the Jewish world which suddenly brought in great numbers, legally and illegally, alarmed the Palestinians, and they met the threat with a revolt against British policies in 1936. Jewish immigration had leaped from less than 5,000 in 1930 to 61,000 in 1935. The government put down the revolt with great severity, Jewish terrorist gangs were formed to protect their colonies, and the Haganah, the semi-official army of the Jewish Agency, was also well armed.

The situation called for another commission, and the one that came out bore the imposing title of "The Royal Commission of Inquiry into the Disturbances of 1936." This Commission had the advantage of access to valuable historical material, documents which had heretofore never been made public, all showing the incompatibility of the promises given in the Balfour Declaration. The Commission admitted at one point that "we think it sufficient to state that the British Government has never accepted the Arab case." Beginning with that assumption, they did not consider that it was necessary for them to go into the historical background of the problem in regard to the Arabs but rather to consider what the Balfour Declaration really meant. So, apparently not having studied both sides historically, they acted on the principle that claims were equal, and on that basis they could only recommend dividing the country into two, to create two separate states. It reminds one of a solution made by Solomon when two women claimed the same baby. The Commission claimed that their solution was based on practicality, obligations, and justice to both Jews and Arabs. Noble sentiments, but completely lacking in understanding, for the solution failed on all three counts. In 1936, while the Jews were still a minority, they were to be given an area of Palestine much larger than the land they owned, which included 300,000 Arabs. Since a

Jewish State was the ultimate goal of the Zionist Organization, and had been from the beginning of the movement, it would also mean the displacement of the Arab population in some areas. But that did not seem too much to ask of them. The Commission even appealed to the Arabs to be willing to sacrifice their lands to make room for a Jewish State. Yet at one point in the report we read:

"Can it be the duty of the Mandatory or indeed in the interests of the National Home itself to allow immigrants to come into the country in large numbers without regard to an increasing hostility which from time to time finds expression in violent disorder? The issue is quite plain and should be squarely faced by everyone concerned. Do the Jewish people wish that Palestine should offer a refuge to the maximum number of Jews?"

It also admitted that the promises to the Jews and to the Arabs were irreconcilable, and that the Mandate in its existing form was unworkable.

After this report, which was published in 1937, the Arab rebellion continuing against the Mandate Government, another commission was sent out in 1938 to see how the Partition Plan of the Royal Commission Report could be implemented. Its function, stated clearly by the new commission, was purely technical and not to be a study of the principles involved. This Commission valiantly went to work within this restricted sphere, but it had to conclude that since they were only a fact-finding body they could not advise what should be done. Hopefully they suggested: "But there is still a possibility that both sides may be willing to accept a compromise. We cannot be confident that this will happen, but we put forward our proposal in the hope that it may form the basis of a settlement negotiation." They could not advise, but they evidently felt it their duty to point out the following:

"As far as Jerusalem is concerned, Muslim and Christian sentiment should be taken into account. Muslims would resent most deeply the setting up of a Jewish State in close proximity to the Old City . . . But it is not only Muslim opinion which is to be considered in this matter. Jerusalem is sacred to the Christian faith, and not only the Old City within which stands the Church of the Holy Sepulchre itself and the Way of the Cross, but also places within the surrounding area, such as the Garden of Gethsemane, Bethlehem and the Church of the Nativity, the village of Bethany, and the road to Emmaus; all are hallowed to the Christians by the most precious association . . . So with all sympathy for the Jewish claims to Jerusalem for its historic, cultural, and religious meaning for them, and its exclusion from the Jewish State would deprive that state of a considerable population and substantial revenue . . . apart from the practical difficulties of implementing partition, the religious and political objections to the Jewish claims must be held to be decisive."

This report was published in November 1938. Soon after, early in 1939, Britain issued a White Paper in which the government rejected entirely the Partition Scheme proposed by this latest commission:

"His Majesty's Government, after careful study of the Partition Commission Report, have reached the conclusion that this further examination has shown that the political, administrative, and financial difficulties involved in the proposal to create independent Arab and Jewish States inside Palestine are so great that this solution of the problem is impracticable . . . it is clear that the surest foundation of peace and progress in Palestine would be an understanding. His Majesty's Government therefore now declares unequivocally that it is not part of their policy that Palestine should become a Jewish State. They would regard it as contrary to their obligations to the Arab people under the Mandate as well as assurances which have been given to the Arab people in the past, that the Arab population should remain subjects of a Jewish State against their will."

This was a strong, clear statement, and the Zionist response to it was one of rage, for although the Royal Commission Report had not given them all they had hoped for, they had been willing to take what they could get at the moment. The Arabs, on the other hand, felt that at last their case was being understood.

The Mandate Government now worked on a plan for the limitation of immigration, and there was a ray of hope for the Palestinians. Great Britain may have seen the war clouds forming in 1939 and certainly could not afford to lose the friendship of the Arabs of the Middle East, so that her latest pledge may have again been expediency. If not, it was prescient, for when the war came at the end of that year North Africa and the Mediterranean became great theatres of war and Britain again needed the Arab World, and especially a peaceful Palestine. The Arabs agreed not to prejudice the Mandate Government during the war, in the belief that when it was over their problem would be settled. Eight thousand Arabs assisted in the war effort in various capacities and still trusted Great Britain.

The Zionists, on their part, also aided the British Government, as they were willing to fight against the Nazis. Many of them were in the Haganah, the military arm of the Jewish Agency, many had been trained as soldiers in Europe, and when there was a threat of a German parachute invasion of Palestine during the war, Britain trained many of the Jews in commando tactics. This training was to stand the Jews in good stead after the war, and they possibly anticipated that it would be so, as they were beginning to fear the end of their hopes for a state and decided that they must find a way to speed up its realization; and force was the answer.

The Zionists, having lost hope in Britain, turned to the next country that could help: the United States of America. They now realized that the British were not prepared to go as far as necessary in furthering their plans, and America, with its influential Jewish community, should be cultivated. To that end, a conference was held in the Biltmore Hotel in New York in May 1942. Six hundred delegates attended and adopted a belligerent programme, declaring that:

> "The new world order that will follow victory cannot be established on foundations of peace, justice, and equality, unless the problem of the Jewish homelessness is finally solved. The conference urges that the gates of Palestine be opened, that the Jewish Agency be vested with the necessary control of immigration into Palestine and with the necessary authority for upbuilding the country, including the development of uncultivated lands; and that Palestine be established as a Jewish Commonwealth integrated in the structure of the new democratic world. Then and only then will the age-old wrong to the Jewish people be righted."

As in Britain in 1917, when the Balfour Declaration was announced and most of the Jewish community there opposed it, there was strong opposition in some Jewish circles in the United States to the Biltmore Declaration and its demands, not all for the same reasons. There were those who opposed it because they awaited a Messiah, and their return to Palestine was based on religion, not politics. Another group, Revisionists, thought it did not go far enough: they wanted Transjordan to be included in the Jewish State. Still another group, Marxists, opposed it on Communist grounds.

There were, however, amidst all the emotion and irrationality propounded at this conference, non-Zionist Jews who saw in the movement grave danger in a drive for Jewish nationhood. They favoured a bi-national state in Palestine, where Arab and Jew co-operated, for they saw that as the only hope of peace in the Arab World and a realization of the prophetic traditions of Judaism. Among them were Dr Judah Magnes, under whose leadership a great university had already arisen on Mount Scopus in Jerusalem, a monument to the finest in cultural and spiritual Zionism. He often visited us in Ramallah and we followed his work with interest. We still remember how after the riots in 1929, when he tried to open the new college year with an address that was conciliatory, he was booed through most of it. His address was titled *Not as Other Nations*, and he wanted to tell his students that a military political state was not necessarily the genius of the Jewish people, and that they had other contributions to make. Those of us who admired Dr Magnes and were glad for his leadership were deeply moved by his vision and courage at that time. He continued to give this type of leadership to the university. Mrs Magnes said to Willard one day, when Dr Magnes was under attack for his stand on an issue and Willard wondered if it was hard for him: "When he says what he thinks he must, he lets nothing worry him." Others were Martin Buber, a philosopher of renown, and Henrietta Szold, well known for distinguished social work and founder of Hadassah. Through their efforts and the work of others, an American Council for Judaism was formed which included reform rabbis and leading Americans of the Jewish faith in many walks of life. They were greatly disturbed by the militancy exhibited at the Biltmore Con-ference, and maintained that the Jews were a religious community. Like Lord Montagu thirty years earlier, they feared that a political emphasis would jeopardize the welfare and status of Jews living in other parts of the world, including America. They advocated a democratic and political solution for Palestine in which all would be treated equally. Dr Elmer Berger, a New York rabbi, gave the Council brave and wise leadership for more than twenty years and, although no longer with the Council, he continues to work for peace in Palestine and understanding in America.

Not the least of the factors which the Zionists seized on to get help from the general public was the belief of many Christians in prophecy, Christians who saw in the return of the Jews to Pales-tine the battle of Armageddon which would usher in a thousand years of peace. I remember when I was in New York, during the Second World War, waiting for a place in a convoy, a charming Christian woman when she learned that I was on my way to Pales-tine gushed: "You lucky woman, you will be there for Armaged-don." People like her had great joy in the thought that they were

actually seeing the fulfilment of prophecy, and they failed to remember the conditions under which such a return would come
about, or even to read their Bibles carefully to see if the prophecies
might not have been fulfilled in an ancient day. A study of political
Zionism would have been revealing and helpful; a study of the
teachings of Jesus even more important. Surely, among Christians
there was great sympathy for the Jewish people but complete
ignorance of the Palestinians whom they were willing to sacrifice.

For the Zionists, the end of the war was the occasion to increase
their efforts to get rid of the British Mandate and to turn to the
United States. With the British out, the Zionists felt that they could
handle the Arab population, for the Arabs were militarily weak and
they were strong. And so the next three years, 1945 to 1948, were
to be the most difficult and tragic ones for both government and
people since 1918.

With this explanation, perhaps too simplified, we may at least
have a broader perspective on the present crisis. We will now return to the diaries, because it is with the everyday life of the
people at this critical time that we are most concerned. Life became
a series of crises.

At Friends' Boys' School our first crisis actually took place in
February 1945.

[12 February] Mr Stabler, of the American Consulate, came out today and gave an excellent talk on Lincoln which the boys seemed
to enjoy. Following the talk, he presented us with a new edition
of *Compton's Encyclopaedia*. We were delighted to have such a
good reference work for the library and accepted it with pleasure.
Little did we know that before bedtime it would precipitate a
crisis. While Willard was working in his office in the evening,
a delegation of older boys entered. They were excited and angry,
for the book contained an insult. What was the trouble? One of
the boys placed a volume of the encyclopaedia on Willard's
desk and pointed to the page of the flags of the world. When he
was looking through the volume just for pleasure, he had found
as the flag of Palestine the Jewish flag with the Star of David on
it. It was rather a shock to Willard, too, and was not only evidence of American ignorance of the situation, but of the Zionists'
attempts to create the idea that Palestine was already a Jewish
State. Willard promised the boys that it could be corrected and
that he would take the matter up with the American Consulate.

Meanwhile, he would like to have the volume remain with him and assured the boys that he knew the American government would not intentionally insult them.

Willard took the matter to the Consulate and the following day the Consul-General came out to the school. He explained to the boys that he had not known of the flag, and hoped they would believe him when he told them that our government did not know, either, and had only wanted to make a gift to the school and thought the encyclopaedia would be useful. Then, taking a pen from his pocket, and in the face of the assembly, he inked over the flag and peace was restored. I have learned since that the same flag was put into the British *Encyclopaedia Britannica* as the flag of Palestine in the early days of the Mandate. The Arabs protested then and were told by the editors that the insertion of the Zionist flag was "somewhat premature". This crisis within the confines of a modest boarding-school was an indication of the temper of the Arab people.

One other cause of friction and unease with the Palestinians was the singing of the Jewish National Anthem at all their concerts. The Mandate Government officials stood for it as they did for *God Save the King*. When challenged, they explained that for them it was only a courtesy gesture; but this was not convincing to the Arabs. Our students enjoyed symphony concerts and several had season tickets, but in time ugly incidents arose because they refused to stand for the *Hai Tikvah*, so we had to stop going.

[31 December] The year has been an exciting and momentous one for the world. The great war is over and we pray that there will never be another. But it does not look like peace for Palestine. The Zionists have hardly waited for the war to be over to begin their war against the Mandate Government, and it is going to be a hard one. The timing suits them well, for the home government is war-weary and faces the big task of reconstruction, and the Mandate Government here faces more difficulties with America coming into the picture on the Zionist side. Britain cannot afford to break with the USA and the American press ties the hands of the Mandate Government. Last Thursday, the 27th, terrorists bombed the Central Intelligence Department building in Jerusalem. Much damage was done and valuable records were lost. They have been blowing up railway lines between Haifa and Cairo. We will hope for a happier year in 1946 . . . but the prospect is not particularly bright.

[1946: 1 February] The rainy season starts out well; we have had both rain and snow, for which we have been grateful. Our big problem has been the lack of electricity from time to time, as the Zionist terrorists have been cutting us off from our Jerusalem supply. The boys have been wonderful and accept the oil lamps with good nature and are most helpful in caring for the Lux ones.

[17 February] Rain and snow today added to the general wetness all around us. The younger boys will get out in the snow as long as there is any. We have been drying small boys' shoes all day. Thirty-two pairs were brought into our sitting-room tonight before the boys went to bed, and thirty-two pairs of stockings. We have built a big fire in the fireplace and must stay up until late now to get them dry. I don't know why little boys' socks smell so, but they do! We are in the midst of semester exams and I feel sorry for the boys who have to sit for three-hour examinations in the unheated auditorium. It is hard for me and I can walk about and keep warm gloves on while I am invigilating.

The big news at the beginning of the year was that another commission was coming out to Palestine and that it would be an Anglo-American Commission. Following the war, ended only months earlier, America's prestige throughout the world was high, except in the Arab World. By having the conference in the Biltmore Hotel, the Zionists had cleverly brought America into the problem of Palestine, as the conference had great publicity and influential Jews were caught into the Zionist programme. We have noted the decisions made there. As a result of propaganda, the American press carried criticism of Britain's policies almost daily, and soon Congress was speaking out too. Britain, which had suffered so much during the six years of war that it was no longer able to cope with all the conflicting problems and the constant criticism, finally asked America to join in a study of the situation in Palestine on the spot. President Truman was demanding that Britain allow 100,000 Jewish immigrants into Palestine at once. It was easy for him to make such a demand, but it would be Britain that would have to implement it and make it acceptable to the Arab population, to say nothing about finding room for them. Truman had everything to gain politically at home by making such a humane gesture. Britain probably thought that a committee of an equal number of British and Americans would give a report that would take some of the burden off the government and mitigate American criticism. The only flaw in the proposal was that the American government would not be responsible for carrying out any proposals the Commission might make. Nevertheless, the Anglo-American Commission was duly appointed and came to Palestine in March 1946. The reaction of the Palestinians was: "Another Commission! This one will involve American politics and will get us nowhere."

[14 March] The Anglo-American Commission is at work. We were invited to have lunch with Dr Aydelotte at the King David Hotel today. Dr Aydelotte is a member of the latest commission. He is a former president of Swarthmore College and is now Director of the Institute of Advanced Studies at Princeton, and a brilliant scholar. He arranged for us to attend the afternoon session of the Commission, for which we were grateful as Dr Magnes was to be one of the speakers. It was a rather impressive line-up of important men, but we wondered how much they had gone into the background of the problem. Dr Magnes was splendid and won his audience, and I expect the sympathy of the Commission, by his moderate approach and utter sincerity. He pleaded for a bi-partisan state in which all parties had equal rights, but I found it hard to agree with him or understand his insistence on the "historical rights" of the Zionists, as other countries could make similar claims to Palestine, especially Egypt. Surprisingly, he made a strong plea for the admission of the 100,000 Jews Truman is calling for; he was emotionally hardly his usual self for a bit, but he must live under great tensions and suffer over the plight of his people with so many doors shut to them. I thought he might have suggested that America had more room for them than Palestine. We admire him and can understand how troubled he is by the activities of the Zionists at the moment, which are alienating both the British and moderate Arabs. It is sad, as he came out to Palestine with such high hopes and idealism. We enjoyed being with Dr Aydelotte, who had known of the Friends' work in Ramallah for many years, and he promised to try to get out to the schools. Am I being cynical? It seems that it is better not to know too much if one is to be impartial! I felt in the meeting today that members of the Commission could not make an effective report based on their limited knowledge in the brief time they would be here. Of course, I realize they are supposed to be especially able and should be expected to see what the problems are more quickly than the ordinary man!

Incidentally, all we learned from this particular commission was that they failed to offer a satisfactory solution, and later a conference of representatives of all the Arab States and of the Jews was summoned to meet in London. It had the usual result. There was no agreement save that the British should give up the Mandate and leave the Arabs and Jews to work out their own solution, which really meant war. The Arabs claimed that their chief problem was to know with whom they were dealing. Was it with the Jewish community in Palestine or a world-wide Jewry with great influence in governments and the press of many lands?

Meanwhile, we in our small corner did our best to carry on our modest work as usual.

[26 March] Several British callers at the school today. They expect serious trouble as they fear Truman's demand for those 100,000 immigrants will be implemented. It is a strange feeling to be sitting on the rim of a volcano and yet carrying on as if we were in a meadow and all were well with the world.

[27 March] Dr and Mrs Torrence from Tiberias called today; they are having a brief break from the hospital as they are very tired. Dr Torrence says he has never in all his years in Palestine seen so many discouraged missionaries or so many in hospitals. The headmaster of St Luke's School in Haifa is leaving at once to try to get teachers from England as he says he cannot go on much longer. Misery loves company! We need to meet with other workers for comfort and understanding of common problems, if for nothing else.

[18 April] Spring vacation and Easter in Jerusalem. We have not taken part in the usual services for a long time as we usually give the courtesy tickets we get each year to our temporary workers, but this year there are only three of us American or British at the school and only one new person. So we decided to do everything once again and take Sylvia Clark, our able maths teacher from England, and be real tourists. With all the British wives and children out of the country and few VIP's from anywhere else, thanks to our tickets we were able to get the best seats and the VIP treatment. It was rather nice to be in the crowd and to see how meaningful the ceremony was for pilgrims from other countries. We hurried from the Footwashing ceremony to the mosque area hoping to see the Muslim *Nebi Musa* procession . . . but today there was none. The *Nebi Musa* celebration is based on a supposition that the tomb of Moses is on the West Bank of the Jordan near Jericho. The Turkish Government, fearing that Christians attending the Easter celebrations in Jerusalem in great numbers might try to take possession of the city, instituted an annual pilgrimage of Muslims to this shrine, which culminates in a procession to Jerusalem on the day of the Footwashing, where they remain until after Friday prayers. It is a long walk from the shrine near Jericho and a steep climb, and it is most moving to see the last stages as the procession reaches the mosque. To-day there was no procession but the Muslims were gathered in the mosque area in great numbers. However, we went into the old Rawdat al-Ma'arif School, now a police billet, from where we could have an excellent view of the celebrations. We lost Willard somewhere and, to our astonishment, finally saw him in the mosque area seemingly unaware that in the troubled times he might be mistaken for a European Jew and that would start trouble. Fortunately, one of our Old Boys saw him and stayed with him until he got out. To complete the morning, we went the short distance to the Wailing Wall to see the Jews at their prayers. It was like old times to see all three religious groups at their most ceremonious times in a small corner of the world. And how like the unpredictable and colourful East!

[20 April] We were up early this morning and off to Jerusalem to attend the ceremony of the Holy Fire. When we arrived, there were already masses of people at the Church, but we produced our tickets and were led by a private entrance to the Holy Sepulchre and to front seats. As we waited through the long morning, we were in the midst of a happy, expectant crowd. The time was enlivened by demonstrations by delegations from many sections of the country who marched around the rotunda of the Holy Sepulchre, shouting slogans, and at times it was more like a political rally than a religious ceremony. They carried colourful banners as they marched. Police were there to keep order, first-aid services were set up, and most necessary fire-extinguishers were easily available, for the danger of fire was great with so many candles ready to be lighted in the great rush at the last tense moment when the fire would issue from the openings in the chapel wall. Although the crowd was gay, even the sophisticates could not but respect older women in drab clothing reverently praying as they waited for the miracle, and it was comforting to know that they would not be disappointed. When the dark building was finally lighted, it gathered us all into the spirit of sharing in the candle-lighting ceremony.

[25 May] An historic day in Transjordania. The Emir Abdullah, son of the Sharif of Mecca and a leader in the Arab Revolt in 1916, was crowned King of the Hashemite Kingdom of Jordan under the aegis of the British Government, which has administered a mandate there since the end of the First World War. The British are astute to include the Hashemite name, for Hashem was the name of the Prophet Mohammad's grandfather and this will be a daily reminder to the Muslim world of Abdullah's descent from that famous family. We have several Transjordanian boys in school. They asked permission to attend the ceremonies and invited Willard to go with them. They came home rather late, as the bus they had chartered was a poor one which gave them no end of trouble, including not getting them to the ceremony in time; but they were in good spirits and thought they had had a wonderful day. It is a small country King Abdullah will reign over, mostly 300,000 Bedouin, but the move is a belated recognition by the British of its debt to the sons of the Sharif Hussein.

[10 June] Jewish terrorists burned three trains at three points simultaneously, doing great damage. The Arabs have called a meeting at Bludan, Lebanon, to discuss the Palestine Problem, as it is evident that the situation is worsening. The terrorists are getting bolder and the Mandate Government weaker in administration.

[13 June] Jerusalem celebrated King George's birthday today. I managed to get to Jerusalem in time to get my reserved seat in front of the YMCA to watch the King's birthday parade. One wonders how many more times a parade for a British king will be possible in Jerusalem. It was an impressive parade, with all branches of the army represented, even the women's. I especially enjoyed the camel corps from Transjordan; it was beautiful, colourful and exotic after the grim display of so much war material.

[17 June] Reports of serious damage to bridges across the Jordan River and to Egypt, four in all. That may isolate us for a bit. We are being warned that we may have even more serious incidents any day now. If the USA could only keep its hands off, it would be easier for Britain. There is a growing feeling that knowledge of American support, not necessarily official, makes the terrorists bolder.

[18 June] A reception at the American Consulate tonight—met many interesting people and quite a variety, from a Greek Princess to an American Petroleum Company head. I settled for a coca-cola and thus kept what little balance I had left from a bout with a fever. More outrages in Jerusalem and Tel Aviv. All cars were inspected on the way out from Jerusalem. They report trouble in Haifa, too.

[29 June] A truly momentous day in Palestine. Woke up to learn that the government was getting down to the business of doing something about terrorism. The Jewish Agency was searched and important Jewish officials have been arrested. There is a curfew over most of the country, and a firm statement has been made by the High Commissioner that a new period has begun. It was a sudden and unexpected move, which has left us stunned. We do not know how long this operation will last. With Commencement near, we have to think of getting our boys home safely.

It was to be years before we would learn what was behind this drastic move of the government, but we all agreed then that the Mandate Government must have been on strong ground in order to carry out this operation. Zionists' demands had been increasing and, fearful that they would not obtain all they had hoped for and also that time was running out, they had stepped up their terrorist acts. The situation which brought about the latest move by the government was that telegrams had been intercepted which proved that the Jewish Agency leaders, including Ben Gurion, were in touch with the Irgun Svai Leumi and the Stern Gang, and of course the Haganah, and were presently planning "an isolated act of violence" to warn the Mandate Government that worse things might happen if the demands of the Zionists were not met. Our only English newspaper was the *Jerusalem Post*, and we always noted that following an account of terrorist activity, the editor deplored it, disavowed any official connection, then proceeded to justify it because of the sufferings of the Jews through the centuries.

[30 June] Searches are going on all over Palestine for caches of arms. The terrorists say the government will have to dig up the whole country. How tense everything and everyone is! The Government must have had positive evidence of some kind to occupy the Jewish Agency. Quantities of arms have been found in an underground armoury near Haifa.

[22 July] Another tragic day. I was at my desk after lunch getting a letter ready to mail to our son, when Willard came in with the news of the bombing of the Secretariat in the King David Hotel. The entire wing in which the Secretariat was housed was destroyed. The accounts that have come in since then are ghastly, as rescuers cannot get at the bodies. From all accounts the death toll is high. This is the most dastardly act yet by the terrorists, as the whole staff was at work at one o'clock, an hour before closing hours. Charlie Mogannam, who graduated last year, is reported killed; the Khouri brothers of the previous year are injured or dead; Ramallah is mourning tonight as all Palestine must be.

[23 July] Palestine is in mourning and we are all shocked at the immensity of the tragedy. The death toll seems to be mounting to over one hundred, and the injured to fifty. Willard attended the funeral of Charlie Mogannam this morning. This attack on such an important target seems to be retaliation for the action of the government against the Jewish Agency. One wonders how long the British can stand this continual harassment and ruthless killing.

[1 August] A big debate is going on in London on what to do next about Palestine. Someone has come up with the suggestion of cantons as in Switzerland. America may some day regret ever getting involved with the question of Palestine and wish herself out.

Terrorist acts continued throughout the summer and until the end of the year. We were plagued by constant curfews, periods without electricity, reports of refugee ships trying to make port at Haifa and Jaffa, of arms being smuggled in for the Zionists, of British soldiers and police being shot, of still more bombings, of the beautiful, modern post-office in Jerusalem under constant threat, and each night a list of stolen cars announced on the air.

In spite of it all, we opened school as usual at the beginning of October and tried to maintain as normal a situation as possible. We had many visitors and we tried to share them with the boys for they were usually interesting and gifted. Reported acts of terrorism became our daily fare and we even began to accept them as part of life and prayed that some day some light would be shed on our problem in other parts of the world so that a solution might come.

Mounting Tensions, 1947

The first days of the New Year were a foretaste of things to come, but, fortunately, we did not have to see it all at once. Sufficient unto the day! Terrorism in various parts of the country was a warning to the government that the Zionists were stepping up their war and that they were strong enough to carry on with it. They felt now that they had the backing of the USA and that gave them confidence.

Our immediate problem at the school, and for the whole country for that matter, was water. The rains were late and our cisterns low. They had been cleaned and checked for leaks, for nothing could be more disastrous than a leaky cistern in Palestine. All was in readiness, but the rains had not come in the late fall and we were anxious. The bright sunshine was lovely, but only rain, and rain in abundance, would be beautiful weather now. All over the country people were gathering in the churches and mosques to pray for rain.

I remember so well our first rainy season, in 1922, when the rains were late and I had yet to learn how serious that was. One evening, late in November as I was working on papers, the rain began and came down in torrents. To my surprise I heard children singing in the streets and clapping their hands as they sang. I ran out to the front gate to see what was happening and watched a procession of happy children thanking Allah for his goodness and mercy and for the special blessing of rain. In those days, when the rains were late and the prayers of the priests and the congregations had not been answered, the oldest woman in the village, seated on a donkey, would lead a procession to the church, praying as they went. It was hoped that Allah would hear the prayers of one who had lived a long and good life and was now interceding for her children and grandchildren. If that failed, then the children would lead the prayers, for Allah would have pity on them and send the rain. Eventually the rains would come. Allah was great and merciful and, while he might have to teach them a lesson, he did not always chide. As the years passed, I too was to learn the wonder of rain and, like the children, wanted to get out in it and let it soak into my very being. And I understood as I had never done before how dire was the threat announced by the prophets: "There shall be no dew or rain these years but according to my word." The winter rains assured the people of grain for their daily bread, and the heavy dews that rolled up in great clouds from the western sea on summer nights brought on the grapes, figs and the wonderful vegetables we enjoyed all summer, and filled the olives for the harvest in the fall; life itself.

The first really big rain came on the thirteenth of January. A party of us went into Jerusalem to visit the Dome of the Rock that morning. The sun was shining when we took the bus in Ramallah and as always we enjoyed the trip over the road of so much history and memory. Arriving at Damascus Gate, we walked into the Old City through the narrow cobbled streets, being greeted by the merchants as we passed their shops with the usual *salaams*. At the mosque, we were struck by an unusual sight. A heavy, black cloud that one could almost touch had formed a backdrop for the Dome, almost enfolding it, deepening the blues of the ancient tiles as if by magic, as though a jinn had touched them. We put off our shoes and covered our feet with the sandals provided for visitors, wisely, for the dust of the street should not defile that sacred place, or spoil the beautiful rugs, and at leisure we enjoyed the overwhelming magnificence of the interior: the mosaics in exquisite design and colour, the glow of the "storied windows richly dight, casting a dim religious light", put there by skilled hands more than a thousand years before, the rugs made lovingly to adorn the shrine, the Rock with its traditions that go back so far into antiquity, and not least, the friendly sheikh who took pride in telling us its story.

But, alas, we had to return to the present world, drab after so much colour and beauty, so thanking our friendly sheikh, we set out. The heavens had opened. That awesome black cloud had burst and we were in a deluge. We were totally unprepared for rain and, since there seemed no sign of clearing, we went out into it running as quickly as we could to the covered and partly-covered *suks* to get to Damascus Gate and our bus for home. It was wonderful to be in Jerusalem on such a day. Everyone we met was smiling and all greeted us with "*Allah Akbar*—God is Great." It rained steadily for twenty-six hours. The earth literally soaked it up, the springs were full again, and to our joy, we had twenty-four inches of water in our biggest cistern. We would need more rain for the summer months but we no longer needed to worry; Allah was not forgetting us. A happy omen, we hoped, for the coming year; but the coming months were to bring the sad event of Partition and the end of a name we had come to love: Palestine. We will follow from my diary some of the events of these months as they affected the country and the future of the people whose lot we shared.

[1947: 18 January] Terrorist activities are becoming so alarming that talks are about to begin in London on the matter and, I suppose, on what steps are to be taken to stop them. The Mandate Government cannot seem to cope with the situation and is handicapped by the world press, particularly that of the United States. They will probably follow their usual custom, send out another commission to study the causes of the troubles, as though they did not know. The commission will learn very little that is new and not achieve any more than the others. One thing seems clear, the Zionists want Britain out and Britain wants to stay.

[26 January] The big news tonight is disturbing. A civilian, a former Major in the British Army, was kidnapped this afternoon. A terrorist is to be hanged tomorrow and the Stern Gang has threatened to hang a British soldier in retaliation if he is not reprieved. The fear is that Major Collins is the marked man.

[27 January] Judge Wyndham was kidnapped today while holding court in Tel Aviv. The High Commissioner has warned the Jewish Agency that if the two men are not returned unharmed at once, military rule will be placed over specific areas of Palestine. Meantime, curfews have been placed over a good deal of the country.

[28 January] Judge Wyndham was released at eight-thirty tonight. Major Collins, not yet. No details were given on the news beyond that.

[30 January] Major Collins has been released unharmed. He thinks he was held in a cave but he does not know where, and that is all that has been made public. We wonder what the government's next move will be.

[31 January] The government's next move has caused a sensation. It has announced that all British women and children are to be evacuated from Palestine so that the army and the police may be free to carry on their duties without anxiety for their families. We wonder if bigger and more serious issues are involved. Sylvia Clark, who teaches with us, is British and was in Jerusalem when they were taking British women and children to barracks pending evacuation, but she did not realize she would be involved. She wants to stay if possible and we surely want her.

[1 February] Willard wrote to the District Officer this morning and got permission for Sylvia to stay, but she is to remain on the school grounds. We think she should be safe in Ramallah. But the British families are stunned by the order. They were separated so much during the war and now were so happily reunited and enjoying life in Palestine that they are crushed. Some are making strong protests. Such drastic action must indicate a drastic situation. The wife of the Chief Secretary was sent out immediately without warning, to her dismay and bewilderment. The general feeling is that something will be imposed on Palestine, but no one knows what it will be. Meantime, barbed-wire, the ugliest and cruellest feature of our "advanced" civilization, is being unrolled and put up all over Jerusalem, and we cannot move about freely. Jerusalem is already zoned and is almost partitioned now.

[3 February] Today was the Prophet's birthday. There was a feeling on the part of some that we should close school for the day, but most of the teachers felt that it was not a good time to have so many students roaming about the streets. Luckily, we were able to get Sheikh Fahoum from Nazareth, who is visiting his son in Ramallah, to speak to the boys in chapel. He did so most acceptably in a gentle, fatherly way and the boys liked it. We provided a special dinner and the Muslim boys gave sweets to all the boarders; a kind and thoughtful gesture. A soccer game between the Staff and the First Team ended to everyone's satisfaction in a victory for the boys, 3–2. A movie of the wonderful story of Madame Curie ended the day. I think a good time was had by all. I do feel sorry for the British families who were all so happy here and wish I could help some of them.

[12 February] The radio tonight reports that the London talks have ended in failure. It would seem that Britain may impose a solution but may also want the Palestine Problem placed before the United Nations. Some are predicting that if it goes to the UN, Russia will back the Arabs and the United States the Zionists in the Security Council. It may become the occasion of that war with Russia we hear so much about.

[13 February] Two lonely Englishmen came in tonight and had supper with us. When the nine-thirty news broadcast the fact that Palestine was to come before the UN in September, they began to count on their fingers and gave up. They see no hope of having their wives back before the end of the year. This decision will keep the country in a continued state of tension all year unless something explodes soon. Just why so much diplomacy, so many commissions, so much violence has grown out of a flimsy promise made in the heat of war, and one practically every commission has agreed was impossible of a just fulfilment, is past belief. No one now is willing to face the essential facts; we need statesmen at the moment with courage to face them and to do something before it is too late.

[18 February] Bevin was on the air tonight speaking on British policy. He confirmed the fact that the Palestine Problem will go to the UN in September. His government's plan is to have Britain remain in Palestine for five years under a trusteeship plan; to increase the immigration quota to 4,000 a month for the next two years, to allow local authorities control over land transfers, and to create an independent bi-national, unitary state by the end of the five years. I am afraid this will be rejected by both Arabs and Jews. The Arabs will feel that it will bring in too many immigrants, the Zionists will reject it because it will kill their hope of a Jewish State, which has been their aim from the beginning. More terrorist activity at nine o'clock tonight; it could be their answer to Bevin.

[1 March] Our boys played football against St George's today. We all went in, for it is one of the most important games of the season. While the game was going on and I was sitting on the balcony of the headmaster's house overlooking the field, enjoying a cup of tea, we were startled by a loud explosion which sounded too near for comfort. I remarked to Mr Sibson that it couldn't be terrorists this time as it was still the Sabbath and they did not usually break it. Some of our friends thought they planned their strategy during the Sabbath and as soon as the sun went down set out to carry out their plots. In moments the sirens went and we learned that it was in truth the terrorists at work; and this time it was the British Officers' Club. We tried to get our boys home right away but had difficulty, as all the roads going out from Jerusalem were closed for an hour or two. The radio reports thirty officers killed and many wounded. There were fourteen "incidents" in all reported on the nine-thirty news and the prospect of martial law in many Jewish areas.

The next few months were indeed critical. Attacks against British soldiers and police escalated as the decision to take the matter to the UN meant delay. There was also the possibility of rejection of the British plan, unwelcome as it was. We tried to carry on school as normally as possible but it was not easy for the older boys, who felt that they should be out helping the Palestinians who were trying to organize themselves into some kind of irregular force to protest against the latest decisions. But we did carry on fairly well and the boys worked hard.

Great Britain did take the Palestine Problem to the UN in May, and as we expected, a commission was sent out at the end of May to study the situation and prepare a report for the sessions of the UN beginning in September. This committee was known familiarly as UNSCOP: United Nations Special Committee on Palestine. They spent two months in the country and made a report at the end of August; actually two reports, one a majority report and the other a minority one.

Almost coincidental with UNSCOP's inquiry, there was the *Exodus* affair, which made the government's situation more difficult and which was to get tremendous sympathy in the United States for the Zionists. The *Exodus* was an old Chesapeake excursion boat, which sailed from France with over four thousand illegal immigrants on board. It was hardly seaworthy. It was not the first such attempt to bring into Palestine more than the legal number, but the timing was excellent for this one. It was customary when such boats came for the government to send the people to Cyprus, where they would be interned. The mounting tensions in the country and the presence of the UNSCOP may have influenced the decision to prevent a landing at Haifa and send the ship back to Sète, from which harbour she had come. France offered the immigrants asylum but they refused to accept it and the ship was ordered to Hamburg. This action was given great publicity and anti-British sentiment was aroused by well-placed propaganda. The book *Exodus*, with its well-chosen title based on this incident, became a best-seller. Written too hastily to be good literature and historically full of inaccuracies, it sold by the million and was on the reading list in high-schools and colleges all over the United States. A movie made from the book distorted the story still further, but it was accepted by the public as fact, and influenced the thinking of Americans and clouded their judgements. Americans forgot that their government turned an illegal ship away during the war when it sailed up the Hudson, and they did not bother to learn the facts in the case of *Exodus*. Another illegal ship with four thousand tried to disembark passengers at Haifa late in July, and it too was turned back. Not much was made of that because the propaganda value of *Exodus* had created the right emotional climate on behalf of the Zionists when the UN began its sessions in the fall.

Since we could not leave the country during the summer for vacation, we accepted the kind invitation of Mr and Mrs Alvin Miller of the Jerusalem YMCA to use their apartment while they were away. It was only ten miles from home but it was a wonderful change. We could keep in touch with the school summer programme and yet be away from it all. There were shots and sirens almost every night while we were in Jerusalem and sometimes during the day. If the siren sounded in the daytime, we looked at our watches, and if it was on the hour we relaxed, as there had been a regulation for some time that blasting for building or cutting rocks must be done on the hour only, so that the police would know that the explosions were for legitimate purposes. We took early morning walks in the Old City and watched the farmers set up their vegetables and fruits in the market on David Street. The Arabs shop early to get everything fresh, so these were busy places at six o'clock in the morning, and very happy places as the business of the day got under way. And when we dared go out in the evening, we walked about the Old City when quietness had descended on it and the streets were less crowded than in the morning; we enjoyed a feeling of timelessness and history as we saw on all sides evidence of the races of men who had played a part there. Always there were friendly greetings, chats with merchants who were keeping open for the late shoppers, and the offer of coffee.

One afternoon we called on the Armenian Patriarch, a venerable man of years and wisdom, and we talked of many things. He expressed sympathy for the movement of the Armenians to return to Armenia. He thought that with the turn events were taking in Palestine, Armenians felt insecure. He also felt that they were losing their identity as a people in Russia and in the United States, where they had gone in great numbers. When we spoke of the Palestine situation with its violence and emotion, he was troubled about the Christian West. He thought Christians must see the teachings of Jesus as a whole, that attempts at helpfulness often did more harm than good, for we do not always know enough about a problem to be able to pass judgements; and at times we serve best when we are silent until we do know.

When we went to his funeral some months later, my thoughts went back to that afternoon in his palace, and as the morning sun shed its light through a small window on his bier, moving slowly across it as the ceremony proceeded, it seemed like a benediction from Heaven on the life of a good man.

Late in July, two British sergeants, sunning on the beach at Nathania, were kidnapped, and for days the country was again in a state of high tension. Everyone, Americans, British, Arabs and some Jews, went about, perhaps silently, praying that they would be returned unharmed. As the days passed we began to despair. Somehow, their fate was important to all. After intensive search, garotted bodies were found one day in woods near Nathania, prepared as booby traps so that their comrades would be killed or injured when they went to take them down. I learned later from a British friend who was in the Central Intelligence Agency of the Government that there had been a mock trial. The young men were accused of being spies for an enemy government and they were thus sentenced to death. This was in retaliation for the death penalty passed on two terrorists. The death of these two sergeants deepened the gloom which was permeating the land. I met one of our older boys the next day and was touched by his remark: "How will the parents of these men feel when they learn how their sons were put to death! They were only serving their country and were not even armed when they were taken!" Many Jewish people are concerned about this, too. Rabbi Magnes, as he had done in 1929, courageously faced his students at the opening of the Hebrew University in October and in strong words deplored the "Zionist totalitarianism" which wanted to achieve its ends by violence. He did not hesitate to call the terrorists killers, brutalized men and women, and said all Jews in America should share their guilt. He called on concerned Jews to raise their voices and show concern for the "timeless values of Israel's tradition".

When the two reports of UNSCOP were presented at the UN, the majority one was favoured. It recommended partition; the minority report recommended a federal state. Maps had been carefully drawn, indicating the geographical divisions proposed. Apparently the Royal Commission report had been given some study, for while this report did not follow it exactly, it showed its influence on the committee. In order to protect the poor Arab farmers, the Mandate Government had placed restrictions on the sale of land; this report recommended lessening these restrictions. They also favoured raising the immigration quota from 1,500 to 6,250 a month, to be controlled by the Jewish Agency. Shades of the Biltmore Conference! They advised a British trusteeship for a period of two years during which their recommendations would be implemented, and finally that Jerusalem and Bethlehem would be placed under a United Nations Trusteeship. The Zionists, though not satisfied, expressed willingness to accept the majority report. It was the best they could hope for at the moment, and as they could almost count on its rejection by the Arabs, it was politically sensible for them to appear co-operative. The Arabs did reject it. They lived in Palestine and knew that no partition scheme was workable, realistic, or just. Palestine, no bigger than Vermont, to which it is most often likened, was not a flat pastoral strip which cut in two would provide comparable farming lands to both parts. At this time also, the Arabs constituted two-thirds of the population and owned most of the country. The Zionists had been able to purchase less than seven per cent of the land; the partition scheme proposed gave them forty-two per cent more. Furthermore, most of the Jewish population were comparatively recent immigrants, more than half within the previous ten-year period. Dr Magnes saw the problem clearly and warned that partition would merely create a future "irredenta and war". The present crisis in the Middle East shows how right he was and how wisely he could prophesy. And so we have had another futile mission, doing more harm than good, and a young United Nations left to struggle with more than she should have attempted in her salad days.

[17 August] We had an interesting visitor this morning. He is a German of the Jewish faith but he wanted to talk with us about Quakerism. Somewhere he had found books on the subject and had written to Philadelphia for information. A Friend there had advised him to get in touch with us. He was in a highly nervous state when he arrived as he had learned only after he got on the bus to come to Ramallah from Jerusalem that last night terrorists had entered an orange grove near Ramleh belonging to an Arab and had killed all of a three-generation family of thirteen persons. He was the only non-Arab on the bus, but no one had paid any attention to him. He said there was much excited talk, some of which he could not understand but one passenger had interpreted. He kept exclaiming, "Why wouldn't they hate us? Why wouldn't they hate us?" He is a lawyer by profession and had come to Palestine hoping to find peace of mind. As a lawyer, he rejects the Zionist claims of legal or historic rights; surely the Arabs have them if any people have, and the violence with which the "rights" of the Zionists are enforced troubles him greatly. I suggested that there were probably many like him, and he stopped pacing the floor long enough to say, "There are thousands of us, but we are trapped here. We have no right here and certainly no right to perpetrate all this violence on the people of this country. We were led to believe that it was a desert, a wilderness, and in-

stead we find it a good country—we find the people living good
lives—we like it—but it isn't ours." I invited him to go to
Meeting with me but he refused; he didn't want people in Jerusalem to know he had even come to us lest he or his son suffer
reprisals. We drank coffee together and talked about the Society
of Friends, and he left in a calmer mood. He also gave me
money to get certain Quaker books, but I was to send them to
a friend of his in Jerusalem who would pass them on to him
later.

[20 August] A big cache of arms was found in a Jewish school
today. The British have also found great quantities of uniforms
worn in all divisions of the army, also Arab clothing. It is so easy
to disguise identity in Arab clothes and get along without much
difficulty if one knows a little Arabic. One day when I was at
the American Colony, the servants pointed to a woman who
was sitting on the road nearby dressed as a Bedouin woman.
They were quite sure she was a spy. The men who blew up the
King David were dressed as Arabs, we were told.

[13 September] It is good when something happens that helps us
forget for a little time the violence, the terror, the tensions; and
today was a good one for that. For we attended a traditional,
typical Arab peace-making ceremony. It seems that ten years
ago during the Arab rebellion against the British policies, a Greek
priest and another man, both of Jifna, betrayed a Ramallah man
to the police. The Ramallah man was arrested and hanged by the
British. It was a terrible shock to Ramallah people as Jifna, like
Ramallah, is a Christian village and relations had always been
good. For ten years, however, bitter feelings had existed, and
word had come from America that there had been trouble between a Ramallah and a Jifna man in Chicago. There had been
no blood feud but the matter had not been settled, and people
in both villages thought the time had come to settle the quarrel.
An important delegation came from Jifna to Ramallah bringing
food for the feast: ten sheep, ninety pounds of rice, rich butter,
coffee and fruit. They came to the home of the Saahs, for it was
one of their men who had been betrayed.

At the proper moment, the elders took charge and made
speeches saying that bad feelings should end and all be forgiven. The Jifna family had come prepared with "blood money"
with which to recompense the family of the victim. The head
of the Saah family accepted the £333.33 from the head of the
Jifna family with much formality. Then, taking £150 from the

pile of pound notes, he returned the rest to the man from Jifna. The money he kept, he said, was to help educate the sons of the man who had been betrayed. Everyone applauded this gesture, and all seemed glad to have happy relations restored. The feast followed and, after coffee, the men of Jifna returned to their village having done their duty. The good feeling that accompanied the feast was contagious, and one felt that this was a most civilized way to settle a debt to society. The dead man could not be helped, but his children could be. In addition, an unhappy relationship with another village was ended with dignity and in peace.

September was a busy time getting ready for school and we prayed that we would be able to carry on well even if our world seemed to be tumbling down all around us. It was important to give the young the best we had at this critical time for their families, so we worked particularly hard.

[30 November] Sunday. Dr John Trever is with us. He came out from Jerusalem yesterday from the American School of Oriental Research to give the boys a talk on photography, illustrating it with his own beautiful pictures. We were glad of his coming as we were all under great tension, for we knew that the United Nations was discussing the Palestine Problem and that even while we were enjoying the fine lecture the future of our boys was being decided. He spoke again in chapel this morning, to a troubled audience, but attention was good and his sermon was helpful.

    The news of the UN recommendation to partition Palestine came on the air in the small hours of the morning. We have been expecting something like this, although all week, as the debate has been going on, we have been telling the boys that it would not, could not, happen. All the noble talk of this decision as a way to bring peace in Palestine is the most pitiful irony, to say nothing of incredible stupidity. Tragic that the young UN organization had to face such a question and that Great Britain felt she had no other recourse after the past three years of Zionist terrorism. The Arabs are being forgotten in the emotional atmosphere of the debate and their wishes apparently are of no importance, although they constitute two-thirds of the population. The great majority of the other third are not even of Palestinian birth, and the decision has been made in favour of thousands more who are not yet in Palestine. What has happened to all the fine promise of the First World War? It is not all the Zionists want, but it gives them a firm foothold and they are celebrating. Where it will end remains to be seen. Our boys are maintaining a fine spirit and, if they are not influenced from the outside, will continue to do so. We will have to try to be patient and understanding. May God give us courage for this hour.

[1 December] Classes as usual, but a three-day strike has been called for, beginning tomorrow. We will have our hands full keeping 115 boarders happy and out of trouble, some of them are so young and cannot understand. We learn that a committee has been formed to take care of Americans in case of enforced evacuation, but we hope it won't come to that. Whatever happens, the next few months will be critical.

[2 December] The day went well in the school, boys and teachers co-operating helpfully. Anger against Americans will either increase or die down, but today the atmosphere of the school has been quiet and friendly. One day-boy came with a delegation to demand that boarders be free to leave the school. There was a rumour that we had locked the gates. That was soon scotched. In the evening, the electrician came and tried to stir up trouble by urging the boys to demonstrate against the Americans. Willard managed to take him aside, quietly telling him that he had been drinking, which was true. He meekly left, confessing meantime that Christians were afraid and felt that they must show loyalty to the Arab cause because it was Christian nations that were giving their country away. What a tragic mess the Zionists have precipitated!

[3 December] The Secondaries were allowed to join a peaceful demonstration in Ramallah this morning. Some of the teachers went along. Willard went to the municipality where he was well received, drank coffee with them, but left when someone started to speak angrily about Americans and he felt that his presence embarrassed some of the Ramallah people present. Later in the day, a member of the municipality came to the school to apologize for that one rude voice. Never again did such an incident occur.

[4 December] Some of our Ramallah friends came this afternoon to ask us not to go out tomorrow during the demonstrations. We are grateful for their friendship and concern for our safety since we represent the United States in a way, but we feel that if there is any place in Palestine where Americans can be safe, it should be Ramallah. However, Ramallah is full of refugees who know our school only as an American institution and they might not appreciate our presence. If we are to live here, though, we cannot shut ourselves up in the school, and we are glad to be here to keep the school open.

[5 December] The Arab Higher Executive called off the demonstrations, much to the disappointment of the boys, who would have enjoyed the excitement, and we had classes as usual. It is always my luck to have the first class of the day with the senior boys and, when there is trouble in the country, I have to meet the protests of the boys. However, we had a delightful lesson on the poetry of Dryden and Pope! Thank goodness, the Arabs like poetry!

[6 December] What a relief, after a week of tension, to have a wedding! Jean Harb was married in the Anglican Church today, and the whole village was out. Jean wore a beautiful satin gown with long train and veil and looked lovely. The reception was held in the cinema as the guests were so many. Sweet drinks, cakes and sweets were served and favours given to all. I think it did us all good in the midst of our troubles. I thought of Hardy's poem, *The Dynasts*. Here was a ceremony as old as the ages. The evening news reports guerrilla warfare in many parts of the country.

[7 December] Many of the boarders at the Girls' School are being taken home, as parents are worried. Five went home today. Our top class is unsettled, but on the whole we keep cool. I think they will stay through. Willard, shopping for school supplies in Jerusalem today, found shopkeepers discouraged and all are sure things will get worse.

[9 December] A lovely young mother came today to tell Willard that she and her husband and the younger children were leaving the country, but she wanted her oldest son to remain at school. It was sad to see her say good-bye to him, assuring him that Mr Jones would put him on a plane and send him to them when school closed. She could not tell him where they were going, but Mr Jones would know where to send him. Obviously under great emotion, she kept remarkably calm. There is a rumour that this is one of the few Arab families living in Palestine which had sold land to the Zionists. Most of the land the Zionists have acquired, we remember, was purchased from absentee landowners who had received the land from the Ottoman government before the First World War.

We had a strange visitor this morning. He said he was from the Red Cross and had come to see if there was something he could do for us. Did we need guns to protect us from the Arabs? He could get them for us. He said he was Tommy Thomas from Cleveland, Ohio. His car had broken down and he would wait with me until it was ready. I assured him we had no guns nor needed any; we felt quite safe. He then listed first-aid supplies he could get for us and I told him they would be welcome. When he decided to leave, I urged him to wait until Willard was free, but he thought his car would be ready and he must go. It happened that a young British official was in the house reading the *New Yorker* and he continued to read while the visitor was there. As soon as "Mr Thomas" left, however, he was on the phone to headquarters. We learned later that "Mr Thomas" had taken money from Arabs by promising to get guns for them. He collected several hundred pounds and no guns were ever brought to the people who trusted him. The government caught up with him and published a warning against him. The Ramallah people are quite sure he was a spy.

[10 December] Continued reports of sniping. Mohammad Abu Aid was called for today. Three members of his family were killed and one wounded in guerrilla warfare yesterday. Mohammad is to go to Migdal to be with his mother and sisters, who have been moved there. Willard went to Rotary Club in Jerusalem today; no Arabs or Armenians attended. Roads are getting so dangerous, especially between here and Jerusalem, that the mission feels we should offer one of our buildings for an emergency hospital. The Arab Medical Association is well organized and could operate it. We will pray that it won't be needed, but I am afraid it will. Dates for the British withdrawal are now set. It is an anxious time.

[12 December] Mr and Mrs Miller of the YMCA came out from Jerusalem today. Mr Miller had heard the report of the Palestine Broadcasting Station reporter who had been at Lake Success during the partition debate. He said Zionist pressures had created delays during which they had worked on delegates from various countries and our own. The USA used its influence to grant or withhold aid to smaller countries to get them to vote for partition, which was finally achieved in an atmosphere charged with emotion and political manipulation that was, in the reporter's word, fantastic. Some delegates to the UN confessed that they cast their "yes" votes under stress, the Canadian delegate even stating publicly, "We support the plan with heavy hearts and many misgivings."

To add to our general misery, two Arab buses standing loaded at Damascus Gate today were bombed by Zionist terrorists with loss of life and many wounded. Fighting reported in Jaffa and Haifa to the north, our chief modern port between Mount Carmel and the Mediterranean. It is a beautiful city, which has had a remarkable growth since the First World War and the development of the oil industry in Saudi Arabia. I find it hard to understand what the world expects the Palestinians to do when their land has been so generously given to an alien people. Have they become so omniscient at Lake Success that they can dispose of people and countries at will? Dear Alice Jones, at the Girls' School, who grieves so over all this trouble, said today: "The sad thing is that where you should expect good judgement and honesty, you don't get it."

[18 December] The Girls' School is steadily losing its boarders as parents become increasingly anxious. Continued reports of violence, but the Arab League apparently still hopes for a change of view in the Security Council and they obviously do not want open warfare at this time. They must realize how unready the Arab countries are for war. The Palestinians do not have much hope that the UN will change its decision as long as the USA and Russia have voted for Partition.

[19 December] Dr Canaan came out to speak to the school today on "Disease and its Prevention". He was excellent, and the boys responded well. However, he is discouraged and anxious about the future. He, a Christian Arab with a Canaanite name, says the Muslim Arabs are disillusioned with Christian nations and now Christian Arabs are questioning Christianity, if this is all we have to show after nearly two thousand years. He predicts a big revolution in religion as well as in politics.

[20 December] Another attack by the terrorists on an Arab bus about three kilometres from Ramallah. Three persons killed, one of them the cousin of our maid and the school cook. He was only twenty-one and leaves a young wife and a baby son. Another was a man from Bireh. On our way to Meeting we passed several groups of angry people threatening to attack the Jewish colony of Kalendia nearby. But they have nothing to attack with and they realize they cannot do much. We are troubled by this tragedy coming so close to us, but also feel quite helpless in the midst of this constant violence. The Christmas programme was to be given in the Meeting House and, with Willard's passion for carrying on as normally as possible no matter what is happening, we had the children's programme, and it was sweet. The children see so much sorrow in the eyes of their parents that there seemed no reason to deprive them of this one hour of happiness. But I am more ready to weep than smile when I see the brave efforts of the teachers to carry on.

[23 December] Tuesday. School closed today for Christmas vacation. It is anybody's guess how many boarders will come back. We had hoped to have classes until noon, but parents were here at eight o'clock and insisted on leaving at once because of the dangers on the roads. Classes were disrupted as still another boy was called away, so we finally gave up. We have reason to believe that all the boys got home safely. Coffee-houses in Ramallah and Bireh are deserted and there is talk of closing the cinema. Ramallah is all closed down by five-thirty these days, and rumours abound.

[25 December] A strange Christmas! No one could go to Bethlehem last night because of curfews, but we tried to celebrate Christmas as usual with dinner at our place for the teachers of both schools who remain. We have had many callers, so that it was hard to get on with dinner plans. We tried to be festive, but festivity was strained. As we sat around the fire singing carols after dinner, a lovely thing happened. About nine o'clock there was a knock at the door, and when I opened it there was our Scotch-Irish friend of the British police, Mr Strachan, and a tall handsome Scot in full regalia with his bagpipes tucked under his arms. We opened the door wide and listened in a sort of dream as he played the old airs of my Scottish childhood. He remained on the balcony and the music tempered by the night air gave us comfort and, incredibly, seemed a fitting end to a day in which we had all been trying to simulate a Christmas spirit we found hard to feel. Eleanor, whose father is a Presbyterian minister on Long Island and whose grandmother in Nova Scotia spoke only Gaelic, broke the silence at the end with, "I wish my father were here." To me it was home in Scotland, six hand-knitted stockings hanging from the mantelpiece with a Jaffa orange in the toe of each. The sons and daughters of Arab orange-growers are in our schools now and will bring back baskets of oranges, if indeed they get back, for they live in an area much coveted by the Zionists. Here we are with Bethlehem only fifteen miles away and no peace. Not since the Crusades has Christianity had such a setback in the Muslim World. How good it was to hear the pipes!

[29 December] A memorable day: both happy and sad. Kamal Muhayyadin's father invited us to Deir Dewaan to spend the day. The morning was lovely as we set out, taking Floyd and Lucretia Moore from North Carolina, who are spending the year in the schools with us. Deir Dewaan seemed serenely peaceful in the warm sunshine under a blue, blue sky. Abou Kamal almost at once suggested that we take a walk through the village with Kamal for a guide. The village people greeted us in a friendly way, the children forming a procession as we moved about. We stopped to drink delicious mint tea at the coffee-house as the men smoked their *narghilis* (water-pipes), and soon we were quite ready for the big feast prepared for us. When we returned to the house, Kamal's father remarked, "Now the whole village has seen you and will know you as friends." He had lived for many years in the United States, had prospered, and loved our country. It was an exceedingly kind and thoughtful gesture at a time when the Arabs are so disappointed with America's zeal for Zionism at their expense. The *mukhtar*, head of the village, joined us for dinner, a fine man and highly regarded, who became *mukhtar* on the death of his father, when he was only fourteen. The meal was delicious, of course; roast lamb, rice, salads, fruit, sweets and coffee and, almost best of all, bread fresh from the *taboon*, the village oven. How I love the fragrant smell of the village ovens when we take a walk in the late afternoon!

As we sat around the table enjoying gracious hospitality and exchanging courtesies with our hosts, we were suddenly aware of excitement outside. Kamal turned on the radio and the noon-day news was that a terrorist act had taken place at Damascus Gate, killing thirteen people and injuring thirty-two. A car had driven down the Nablus Road with two Jewish terrorists in it. They stopped briefly at the turn where the road goes down to the gate and hurled a barrel of dynamite down the slope. It exploded there. Meantime the terrorists had escaped into the Mea Shearim Quarter of Jerusalem and were lost in the general confusion. Damascus Gate is one of the busiest in the city, with crowds going in and out because buses and taxis leave there for the villages. We were horrified at the news, and later when we learned that Thabit Su'udi of the class of 1946, our Old Boy, was one of the victims, we were sick at heart. Thabit was a tall, good-looking young man of great promise. After leaving our school and passing all his exams, he got a post with the government and was doing well. That day, when their Jewish colleagues did not turn up for work, the Arabs left their posts as they had learned that when the Jewish workers did not show up, it meant that some terrorist act would take place. Thabit had gone into the Old City and was coming out of the Gate to get the bus for home in Ramallah when the explosion occurred and he was killed instantly. It was like losing one's own son. The day ended with Willard going to the funeral to share as he could the sorrow of the family.

[30 December] Made a trip to Jerusalem today with applications for the boys who want to sit for the London Matriculation examinations in June. I found the Education Department already separated into Arab and Jewish sections. Things are chaotic, and I was sent from office to office in separate parts of the city to get all the necessary business accomplished. The big post-office is as guarded as Gibraltar and it looks almost as well fortified. I went there to get a money order for the applications and had to go to another building for it. Jerusalem streets are almost deserted and an atmosphere of fear and depression permeates the whole city. Most of the shops on Princess Mary Avenue are either closed or half-closed. The new Commercial Centre was having another fire and there were reports of attacks on Arab buses. I did manage to get home eventually, with £250, approximately $1,000.00, for the school, and the boys duly registered. This evening the radio reported a big attack on a refinery in Haifa, started by the Irgun or one of the terrorist gangs, ending in heavy loss of life. Fifty have been killed in Palestine in one day. This brings the total to date, in one month after the partition recommendation, to over five hundred dead and six or seven hundred injured. Dr Malouf, a fine Arab doctor, was killed in his car on the Bethlehem Road as he was returning from the hospital. The terrorists said "Retaliation", but he was innocent of any action against them; retaliation so often is indiscriminate.

[31 December] The year has ended on a sad note indeed for Palestine. Continued violence which threatens to mount rather than diminish, the British more evidently on the way out, and the UN with no authority, all bodes ill for the coming days. Reported theft in the post-office means a loss of most of our Christmas mail.

Each year at this time we marvel that we have pulled through so well, and wonder how far we can carry on into the next. The coming year should be a momentous one for Palestine, maybe for us, too. We wonder if it is too late for the UN to see how impossible it is going to be to impose partition, and for the United States to get a more balanced picture of the Palestine Problem and how her role in the present situation can only lead to conditions more serious than we have yet experienced. Can we say "Happy New Year" to our friends tomorrow?

The End of a Mandate

[1948: 1 January] *Kul senna wa inti salim*—"May all the year bring you peace"—was hardly fitting this morning when we were awakened at five o'clock by the sound of heavy firing from the Jerusalem area. It could have been from the village of Lifta, almost a suburb of Jerusalem, which is a prime target. Bombing in Jerusalem, too. The Arabs say we are back in the "eye for an eye" era, only this time it is ten eyes for an eye. The Mission has offered facilities if needed to the Arab Medical Association, as it is impossible for Ramallah people to get to the hospitals in Jerusalem. Arabs are already fleeing from Lifta and nearby villages and some of them need hospital care.

[2 January] Lots of trouble in the whole country today, in the Sheikh Jarrah Quarter of Jerusalem especially. Ramallah buses have stopped running as it is getting too dangerous to pass the Jewish Colony of Nebi Yacoub on the Nablus-Jerusalem Road. Homes were blown up in the Katamon Quarter by terrorists last night: it is an Arab section. More and more British police are being fired on. The Ramallah bus has bullet holes in it from being a target for snipers.

   The past week has been a difficult one for the residents in the Old City and more grim days are ahead if signs mean anything. There is a report that the Arabs have surrounded the Jewish Quarter of the Old City and are determined to fight the Partition Plan in every way possible. Official figures give 574 dead, Jews and Arabs, and one thousand injured in the first month since the UN announcement, Jews against British and Arabs, Arabs against Jews. The Zionists are still counting on Western powers to give what is not theirs to give, and to support their unrealistic claim to the country. There is a news item in the paper today that seventy-seven cases of TNT, addressed to firms in Tel Aviv and Haifa, were discovered in New Jersey. Enough to blow up most of this little country. When will America wake up?

[4 January] The rain has come at last. It started slowly but worked up to a grand climax, descending in torrents; thunder and lightning added to the celebration. We have been praying for this rain for weeks. I love to see what joy rain brings in this two-season climate. It is interesting that the word for eye and the word for springs is the same. The thought is that as the eye reveals the soul of the body, the springs reveal the soul of the land. When one is happy, the eyes shine; when the springs flow abundantly, the valleys "laugh and sing". Uncomfortable as we are during the rainy season with the rain and the wind, we do not complain. A big disaster in Jaffa today. The Arab social headquarters was destroyed by Jewish terrorists and many innocent people were killed.

[5 January] We were awakened shortly after midnight by loud explosions in Jerusalem. We learned that the Haganah had blown up the Semiramis Hotel, claiming that it was headquarters for Arab "conspirators". The Spanish Consulate is in the hotel and it has suffered greatly, too.

[6 January] I had errands in Jerusalem today. It is becoming "a deserted village" and already partitioned, with zone-passes needed to go from one part of the city to the other. Most of the Jewish shops below Zion Square seem to be closed, and Arab shops all have shutters on the windows, and the doors only partly open so that they can be closed quickly.

[7 January] Willard was in Jerusalem this morning and left only fifteen minutes before a terrible outrage occurred at Jaffa Gate, similar to the one at Damascus Gate in December. The terrorists stole an armoured car, drove it to the gate and threw a bomb into the midst of innocent people going about their business. They turned, drove back to the corner of Princess Mary Avenue, threw another bomb, then accidentally crashed into a wall. They tried to escape but three died. According to reports tonight, seventeen Arabs were killed and forty-two wounded at Jaffa Gate, many of them seriously. Jaffa and Damascus Gates are the two busiest in the city. The policy of the Zionists appears to be intimidation, to keep Arabs from coming to Jerusalem from the surrounding villages, and so to isolate Jerusalem. People from Bethlehem and Hebron use Jaffa Gate, people from Ramallah, Damascus Gate. Dr Sliman, the government doctor, has asked the use of some of our school facilities for a hospital as these outrages mount. We can turn the boys' recreation building over to the Medical Association. It is an old Arab stone house, but it will afford three wards and a dispensary and two small rooms for

critical cases. We will have to do all the cooking at the school
. . . but we pray that it won't be needed.

Arabs are already moving into Ramallah from Haifa and Jaffa,
and since the Semiramis outrage and almost nightly explosions,
Jerusalem families are moving from their lovely homes in the
Katamon and other quarters. Some have gone to Egypt and
Lebanon, others have come here. Some mail today and the
promise of telephone communication cheers us. The British
soldiers call the low bridge leading to Mount Scopus "Bloody
Bridge" as so many of their trucks and cars have been blown
up there. We have to cross it when we go in to Jerusalem, and
we just pray that civilian cars and buses are relatively safe. The
first really wonderful rain is over, the sun shines, and I run out
into it to warm my back between classes.

[12 January] Seventy-two boarders tucked away tonight. We are
delighted, as we did not know how many would get back, but we
shall miss the other forty-four. Some may come yet. I do hope
we can carry on until the spring vacation. We have accepted
some new boys into the top class who want to sit for the London
Matriculation exams, as their own schools have had to close.
Only nine boarders arrived at the Girls' School.

[13 January] What an exciting day I have had! Four boys did not
register for the London Matriculation Examinations in December,
and as this was the last date for registration and Willard could
not get away, I was elected for the doubtful pleasure of going to
Jerusalem. A lovely day and all was well until I went to the
office of the Department of Education on Ben Yehudi Street.
There I was told that the Arabic and Jewish sections were
already separated and that I would have to go to the new office
for the Arab department, on Allenby Road. As I walked down
Princess Mary Avenue, there was a stillness on that usually busy
street and on looking up at some of the buildings, I could see
snipers on the roofs. After some time at the new office, final
work was done on applications, but I could not pay the deposits
there: I was told I must go the the post-office to get money
orders. More walking from Allenby Road to the general post-
office, only to be told that the Money Order Department had
been moved to a narrow street off Allenby Road. So back I trod,
found the humble buildings that housed the special department,
then returned to the Education Building and formalities were
now completed. Both weary and hungry I sank into the Ramallah
bus at three o'clock. It was already almost filled with govern-

ment clerks and others returning home from work. I found a
seat by a window and relaxed, enjoying the local scene, when
as we started up Mount Scopus I heard a sharp crack as though
a big stone had hit the side of the bus. I paid no attention to it,
but when it happened again I was suddenly aware of the fact
that all the other passengers were bent over in their seats, crouch-
ing low. It was all so quietly done that it looked like a routine
happening, as indeed it was becoming. I followed their example
and crouched, too. The shooting followed us up the hill and
along the road almost to Shafat. The rest of the way was peaceful. This, to me, was just further confirmation of my feeling
that there is a concerted effort to shut Jerusalem off from the
villages. I'm not sure how much I would like this every day, but
the rest of the passengers accept it as a fact of life; there was no
panic or excitement of any kind, and I had to admire these
young Arabs for continuing to try to get to work in this troubled
city. For years about two hundred have gone from Ramallah to
Jerusalem each day to work in the government offices, places
of business and offices of various kinds. Not that many go now,
as the life of the city is so disrupted. We arrived home safely,
none the worse for our adventure and with only a few holes in
the bus.

[18 January] Boarders have trickled in and we are happy to have
ninety tonight: almost back to normal. There is a report that
Arabs ambushed Jews in the Hebron area and killed forty-seven.
They claim they captured ammunition and have the identity
cards of all the victims. If this is a prelude to 15 May, heaven help
us all. There were several explosions between four and five
o'clock in Jerusalem this afternoon, possibly in the Sheikh Jarrah
Quarter. Two women teachers of the Bireh Girls' School have
come to stay with us as it is too dangerous for them to go back
and forth to their homes in Jerusalem. We are glad to have them.

[1 February] Just as we had gone to bed at eleven o'clock last night,
we were startled by a loud explosion in Jerusalem. We are always
afraid that the walls may be attacked, but we learned this morning that it was the Palestine Press that had been blown up. It is
a Jewish-owned paper, the only English paper we have, and it is
a great loss to the Jews. It is not clear who is responsible, but the
Jews suspect British soldiers. It would not be surprising, as they
have many accounts to settle before they leave. The Mandate
Government continues to try to administer law, but there is a
breakdown everywhere.

[8 February] A terrific rain and a little of everything with it: thunder, hail, wind, and threat of snow. How thankful we are for it! Alice Jones came up to go over Mission books with Willard today. She is utterly discouraged. In all the years we have been here, she feels that the Mission has never faced such an uncertain and dark hour, and she cannot see what the future holds. She has written to the United Nations, and I think to her cousin, Rufus Jones, suggesting an analogy of the present crisis to the story of Jacob and Esau. Her letter: "It is a sad little land. I think the UNO has been very stupid; swayed by propaganda, emotional appeal, lobbying, selfish interests, and doubtless bribery; and ignorant of the truth, they are not fitted to decide a question of this kind. They might be useful to discuss matters of international concern. Jacob has again stolen Esau's birthright: Isaac (the UNO) is blind; Rebecca (the USA) has assisted Jacob in his scheming. I am deeply ashamed of my land and my President."

Strong words from a Quaker schoolmistress now in her late seventies. Her grief in this crisis is great as she feels so helpless. We hope she may return to the USA soon so that she may not need to be so close to the sufferings of the country and the people she first came to know in 1906.

[16 February] Never a dull moment. At quarter-past eleven this morning while classes were going on as usual, three men burst into Willard's office, ordered him to open the safe and give them all the money he had. Two carried guns and one had a hand-grenade. One detached the telephone while the others faced Willard. It was obviously well planned. Willard told them he could not give them school money but they could have what he had in his pocket. That would have been small pickings! When they continued to threaten, he walked towards them as though he was going to the safe, but quickly, and to their amazement, he disappeared through a door into a small washroom which had a door on the other side opening into a hall. He went upstairs to get help, if possible. When he didn't return and teachers and pupils were moving about in the halls, the would-be robbers left, firing three shots into the air in sheer frustration. No one was hurt, no money was taken, and school went on as usual. Two of the teachers had told Willard that a boy who had been dismissed had brought men to Ramallah to plan to rob the school and had all the details worked out. Willard had not given it much thought and certainly would not have expected an early-morning visit. The whole incident passed off so quietly that if the men hadn't fired the guns as they left, no one would have believed anything unusual had been going on.

[20 February] Mr de Bunsen, Director of Education, visited the school today. He congratulated us on being able to keep the school going so normally and thought he might try to spend a few days with us before leaving the country in May. While we were having tea, Dr Khartabil arrived from Tul Karm with an Iraqi military commander who had come to consult with the Palestinians and see how prepared they were to hold their country. It was an awkward situation for Mr de Bunsen, as he is an official of the British Mandate Government still in charge here, and the presence of officials of other Arab countries would not be officially recognized under existing circumstances. We called in Dr Khartabil's son, and we managed to talk about school; meanwhile, Mr de Bunsen hastily excused himself. Since we learn that the Israelis have had an American colonel, trained at West Point, in Palestine melding the Haganah, the Irgun and Stern gangs, and the Palmach into a well-organized army, the Mandate Government can hardly object if an Iraqi Commander has come to study the situation. Alas, he does not have an army of Palestinians to work on; only a small number of irregulars with almost no arms.

[22 February] Another big explosion in Jerusalem today: three trucks drove into Ben Yehudi Street loaded with dynamite, which exploded, rocking the centre of the whole city. Later accounts in the day reported it the worst disaster to date; casualties are many and buildings are wrecked the whole length of the street. The Arabs say special commandos were responsible, but it is not clear yet who was behind it.

[23 February] The Israelis believe that the British soldiers were behind the Ben Yehudi incident of yesterday, certainly not the government, so there are increasing attacks on British police and British soldiers, and many have been killed.

[25 February] A little comfort in the news today. Reports from Lake Success are that the Palestine Problem is again being discussed and there is less assurance that partition is the solution. The weakness, and we hope the injustice, of the Partition Plan are becoming apparent.

[28 February] Talk this week of Israeli protest meetings in Tel Aviv against the leadership of the Zionist movement. We don't know the details but the Arab press carries the story. A British officer who called today says there is something in it, but he thought the protests were more against their own terrorists who have committed so many outrages. Reports continue to come from Lake Success that the Partition Plan may be given up and a trusteeship set up, as the Security Council sees that Partition cannot be implemented without war. The Zionists have known from the beginning that it would mean war and are already preparing for it. The Arabs are willing to accept the Jewish people already in Palestine but are against unlimited immigration, which may lead to their dispossession. It is a little country to be made into two states, but Israeli plans of a nation from the Nile to the Euphrates have been well publicized.

[29 February] Three months since Partition was announced and two and a half months before the British leave. If the present crisis gains momentum, we will be in a bad way on 15 May. The Zionists are foolish to force the Arab World into an arms race. The Arabs are weak militarily now, but they may not remain this way long. The Zionists seem to be trying to take all the Partition Plan allows them before the British leave. The Mandate Government cannot fight them, and seems unable to protect the unarmed Arabs, who are the majority of the country and their responsibility.

[1 March] A train-load of British soldiers on their way out of the country was blown up today. Twenty-eight were killed and thirty-eight seriously wounded. The High Commissioner went on the air to report it and placed the blame squarely on the Jewish Community, which sits back and allows the terrorists to commit outrage after outrage. It is not enough for the Jewish Agency to claim that they have no control over terrorists. If Jewish people in the USA and other countries only understood what is being done in their name, I am sure they would take action. I *must* think they do not understand.

[2 March] Life at the school is fairly normal and happy occasions break the tensions. Our son was born in Jerusalem twenty-three years ago today. He is far away, but the teachers and household staff surprised us with a party, and made it a happy celebration. I used to like to go to Jerusalem on his birthday to sit in the garden of the government maternity hospital where he was born and recall all the happy memories of that day in 1925. There were the violets brought from the Garden of Gethsemane by

Mrs Albright, wife of the Director of the American School of Oriental Research, when the baby was only a few hours old, masses of cyclamen and anemones gathered by the girls of our Girls' School in the valleys around Ramallah, enough for everyone in the hospital; the lovely hand-made gifts from friends, and all that was done to show us our friends shared our joy. But today it was not possible to go to Jerusalem or to the garden, and we were too much concerned for our people to think of ourselves. Not until we went to dinner in the evening had we any idea that anyone knew it was an important day for us. A delicious dinner had been prepared and dear friends invited to join the staff. Cake and coffee were served in our own apartment later and we spent a pleasant evening, which was good for us all as we live amidst great tensions. Our regret was that our son could not be with us to share in our work and pleasures.

[4 March] While I was trying to teach Shakespeare to the seniors this morning, a distressing incident was taking place only a short distance from the school. Seventeen of the Haganah had come to the Ramallah-Ramleh road to attack the bus. They were surrounded by Arab irregulars and all were killed, their bodies mutilated and paraded through the town. It is the kind of brutality that goes with war, but we were badly shaken to be so near it. It is not easy to hold a school together when so much violence surrounds us. This policy of trying to cut the Arabs off from Jerusalem and from each other is taking a heavy toll of life and this time it was a bitter experience.

[6 March] The latest news is that all the British police will leave Ramallah on Tuesday morning at seven o'clock. Willard had a telegram from the American Consulate asking him to come to Jerusalem to see the Consul-General. It had to do with the police leaving. Willard found that the Consul is concerned for the safety of Americans and advised us to get our young people out, even if we feel that we cannot leave. We certainly cannot leave, but we think our young Americans should go.

[11 March] I was in the library with the senior boys this morning about nine forty-five when we were startled by the sound of a loud explosion in Jerusalem. We knew it must be serious. Soon the word came that the Jewish Agency building had been blown up. It seems to have been a clever and daring plan. A young Arab, driving an American Consulate car, stolen that morning, drove into the grounds of the Agency, delivered some boxes presumably from the American Consulate, and quickly left. In minutes there was the explosion we heard ten miles away. Eleven are reported killed and eighty-seven injured, thirty-seven in a critical condition. The Arabs are congratulating themselves on being able to do what the terrorists thought only they could do. This makes three great disasters for the Zionists close together: the Jerusalem Post building, Ben Yehudi Street, and now the Agency building. The Jews think the British police are not entirely innocent in these disasters. Violence begets violence, and we are surely seeing the horror and agony it causes, for so many innocent people are victims.

[15–16 March] Two of the stormiest days of the winter. Ramallah has been under snow and we call it the snow of the century, it is such a big one. The boys have loved it and played in it quite recklessly. Boys who have not seen snow until coming to school here cannot seem to get enough of it. We spend the evenings drying shoes and stockings, before a big fire; we sat up until two o'clock this morning drying them for the younger boys. The grounds are beautiful. Thirty-one day-old chicks got a cold reception and are spending their first days by the fire in our living-room. We are burning precious wood with abandon.

[20 March] The morning news is that America has reversed her decision on partition as she feels that she can no longer support it as Arab opposition has been too strong. The threat to world peace is one big factor in the change, according to Warren Austin, our Ambassador to the UN. The Arabs are jubilant. A trusteeship for the whole country has been recommended, but the Palestinians say they cannot accept that either. The Zionists should welcome it, but they have been working for a state for the past thirty years and are determined to rule one from the Nile to the Euphrates some day. Our electricity was cut off at half-past eleven this morning, so, no radio, no news, no lights, no refrigerator, no motor to pump water into the school, plenty of nothing. Heavy firing in the Arab sections of Jerusalem, many mortars being used. Trouble everywhere. Possibly the Zionists reply to the new developments at Lake Success.

So the days passed, each day bringing news of trouble throughout the whole country. The road to Jerusalem became increasingly dangerous as the Jews erected a small turret at the entrance to the colony of Nebi Yacoub and attacked cars passing along the road indiscriminately. Our boys had to go to Jerusalem to sit for exams,

and it was a constant worry for Willard as he feared for their
safety. They did not worry, but we were thankful when the examination days were over without any harm to them. Not all
travellers on the road were so fortunate. The government finally
stationed an armoured car opposite the turret for certain hours
each day and we tried to do our business in Jerusalem within those
hours. More and more of our American friends left the country,
and by Easter we were few. In the midst of all this, President Truman announced that he was still in favour of partition and tried to
insist that the Mandate Government allow 100,000 Jewish immigrants into Palestine at once. It was a shock, as we had hoped that
Austin's statements in the UN would bring some stability and
stop the violence. The British soldiers and police were under constant
attack.

Miss Thompson, who had served the government as a social
worker almost from the beginning of the Mandate, was killed on
the Bethlehem Road on 30 March. She was to leave Palestine in ten
days. She and a companion had driven out on the Bethlehem Road
to gather wild flowers after lunch, when the car was fired on. She
got out of the car and held up her hands to show she was an English
woman, but she was shot down. Her companion remained in the car
and was not harmed. The Zionists had often accused Miss Thompson of being pro-Arab. I think she loved the Arab people but, knowing her, I am sure she was non-partisan in her administrative
capacity. She was a remarkably able woman, and the second British
woman to be shot by Zionists.

Another disaster. The Cairo train was attacked with heavy loss
of Arab lives. There was not much sign of a truce. Since Russia
voted for partition, the Arabs were afraid they would come to the
help of the Zionists.

[1 April] The boys love April Fools' Day. Four of the youngest were
waiting for me when I started up to the main building for inspection this morning. I could see them plotting but pretended
innocence. When Said came to me and said, "A boy wants to
see you," I fell into the trap and looked about as seriously as I
could. In a few moments they said, "April fool", and went off
happily. Such a simple incident, but so comforting when our
world is going to pieces around us! We continue to hear explosions from Jerusalem and now the UN says we must have a
truce. But who is to enforce it?

[2 April] Truman's support of the Zionists makes them aggressive,
and with the Mediterranean their only outlet they accuse the

Arabs of wanting to drive them into the sea. The Palestinians say they don't want to be driven into the desert.

[9 April] We move from crisis to crisis. Yesterday, Abdul Khadir Husseini was killed at Kastel. He was a hero to the young men of Palestine and there is great sadness in the land. We did not get the news until after breakfast this morning, and word came just before chapel that there would be a day of mourning and that schools should be closed. Willard took Everett and Eleanor Reid to Haifa yesterday to get a ship for America, so was not here to help decide how to handle the situation. The day-boys were all here, so the teachers thought we should have chapel and announce there that we would not have classes. Mr Khouri was in charge of chapel today, but when he announced a hymn there was not a sound, not the rustle of books, only a vibrant silence. The teachers were all on the platform, but Mr Khouri turned to me to take over. For a moment I was quite weak. But I knew I must do something as no one else came forward. Going to the lectern, I tried to tell the boys we understood their sorrow over the death of the young leader whom they loved and who had died bravely. Then I spoke of the emergency hospital across from the auditorium filled with people sick and wounded. I talked of Lincoln's words at Gettysburg, words which many of the older boys were familiar with, that it was for us the living to see that the dead had not died in vain, and added that we must try to think also of the living who needed our compassion. I told them we had been asked to close the school for the day. Day-boys would go home and we hoped spend the day quietly, remembering the sacrifices that were being made for them.

And we did have a quiet day and a friendly one. Sadly, although the Arabs had held Kastel, the Zionists took it while they were burying their dead leader. Kastel, on the Jaffa-Jerusalem road, was important to them, another strategic site.

Willard arrived home in the early afternoon after a satisfactory trip. He got the Reids on to the ship, and on the way back his was almost the only civilian car on the road. He joined a police mail-escort at Jenin and was with it as far as Nazareth, but missed a British convoy he had been advised to join there. Much as we will miss the Reids, we are glad they are safely away.

[10 April] There was great excitement tonight when Fawzi al-Kaukji, the commander of the Arab Liberation Army, so called, passed the school, his men shooting many cartridges in the air. Kaukji is a Lebanese and has a reputation as a military man. But I wonder if he knows what he is up against in Palestine, with the Israeli forces so strong and so concentrated. He does bring with him hope and much-needed optimism; I only hope his coming adds strength to the cause here.

A beautiful young peasant woman was brought to the hospital today. She was shot when she tried to get food to her brother, who was on guard duty.

The most tragic and dastardly act of the Stern and Irgun occurred at Deir Yasin yesterday afternoon. These terrorists went into the village and massacred 250 old men, women and children and threw their bodies into the village well. Young men of the village were at work in Jerusalem and in their fields. The survivors are being cared for at Beit Safafa. It does not seem possible that it can be true, but the story is confirmed by the International Red Cross delegates and representatives of some of the consulates who have gone to the village. We wonder what the effect will be when the news reaches Lake Success. The fact that it has happened while the Mandate Government is still here indicates the attitude of the Zionists towards it and Great Britain, and sadly underlines their confidence in the support of the USA. To say that this has created panic in surrounding villages puts the situation mildly. Five men were killed near Nebi Yacoub on the Ramallah Road and others in the Sheikh Jarrah Quarter today, also.

[14 April] Two men were killed when a truck was set on fire at Nebi Yacoub tonight. We hear that the terrorists are driving through Jerusalem streets using loud-speakers to warn the people to leave or Deir Yasin will be their fate also.

More news of the horrible incident comes to us. The Arabs are surprised that Deir Yasin should be the village attacked, for the people there were thought to be too friendly to the Jews in the past. The village so near to Jerusalem is strategically located for Jewish development, but I am inclined to think it is just a part of the campaign to rid the country of Arabs in order to make more room for immigrants so that an apartheid Jewish State may be set up. I hope I am wrong. It is almost more than one can bear to be so near such a great human tragedy and such sheer brutality.

Statements made by Zionist leaders following the Deir Yasin massacre give chilling reasons for it. In his book, *The Revolt*, Begin, who commanded the Irgun Zvai Leumi, writes that the terror inspired by this massacre resulted in the "maddened uncontrolled

stampede of 635,000 Arabs . . . the political and economic signifi-
cance of this development can hardly be over-estimated." Ben
Gurion, on his part, said: "Without Deir Yasin, there would be no
Israel." And later Dr Weizmann, first president of Israel, referred to
the Arab flight as "a miraculous simplification of Israel's tasks."
(Quoted by Ambassador McDonald in *Mission to Israel*, page 176.)

As we watched events during those days, it seemed obvious that
the Zionists, fearing a reversal of the United Nations policy, were
determined to get all the territory allotted to them in the partition
scheme before the end of the Mandate Government and face the
world with a *fait accompli*. The first step was to dispossess the
Arabs. Before the British left Palestine, there were already more
than 200,000 refugees, and they did not flee from their homes with
the thought that it would be for ever. The Arabs feared that Russia
would help the Zionists, since they had voted for partition. Zionism
had opened the door for Communism and the *kibbutzim* were run
on Communist lines. As long ago as 1928 when Willard and a
friend visited Kibbutzim, they found large pictures of Lenin and
Trotsky on the walls of the common-rooms.

[17 April] Willard went to Jerusalem today. He had lunch with the
new Consul-General and Mr Stabler, who has been in the consulate for some time. They told him that all American women
are to be evacuated before the British leave, and of course any
British women who may still be about. The headmistress of our
Girls' School is British, but she says she will remain and, at the
moment, I have no intention of leaving. One project which the
British are carrying out is that of getting all German citizens out
of the country also. During the war the Germans were moved
to Sarafand, near Ramleh, where they were comfortably housed
and protected, but it has not been possible to allow them out
as Jewish hostility to them is so great. One German *probst* and
another prominent German were shot when released, and others
had difficulties, so they have remained in their German village
and their work has been cared for by an Orphan Missions Committee of which Willard is a member. They must not be in
Palestine when the British leave. Some have gone to Australia,
we hear, others have returned to Germany. There is a good deal
of valuable German property in Palestine, the Schneller Syrian
Orphanage being one institution which has served Palestine well
and has valuable equipment.

[18 April] The kind of day which could happen only in Palestine.
It started out calmly with life quite normal and the day beautiful

as it can be at this time of year. While we were having our usual Sunday tea with the teachers, Willard phoned that he was sending down some English soldiers to have tea with us. They had been attacked at Nebi Yacoub when they foolishly drove past the entrance to the colony in a captured Jewish armoured car, with the Star of David conspicuously displayed. There were six of them and they looked as though they had been in trouble. They had indeed, for they had escaped death by the Haganah and arrest by the British for trying to desert, as they did not want to return to England. We served them tea and cakes and they relaxed; but while they were enjoying this respite, an officer burst into our living-room; he was most apologetic when he saw us all so quietly drinking tea, but he quickly led our visitors away. Fighting was going on at Nebi Yacoub and we watched it from the roof of Grant Hall. Later a call came for help for the wounded, and since no ambulance was available Willard converted the station-wagon into one. By dropping the back door, we could get two stretchers into it and it served reasonably well. Willard made two trips to the Nablus hospital in the evening as it is not possible to get into Jerusalem. Some of the wounded were brought to our emergency hospital, and all of us were kept busy until late caring for them.

[19 April] We hear of the complete evacuation of Arabs from Tiberias today. Women and children are leaving Jaffa also. Ramallah is crowded with strangers trying to find rooms. They all come with stories of how they were driven out, British soldiers urging them to go as they said they could not protect them. We have a feeling that things are closing in and down on us, and Ramallah becomes increasingly vulnerable. The streets are full of weary, bewildered people. All, however, think they will be back in their homes soon and pray for the Arab armies to come to help. We continue to have school as usual; it is a little island of normality for the young and keeps them occupied constructively though surrounded by chaos. Parents express thanks and hope we can continue. There will be no holiday break as we do not know what will happen after 15 May . . . and the young people are better off in school than being in the midst of all the misery of their families.

[20 April] Several wounded were brought to our hospital from Beit Suriq, a village not far from us. They say the village is completely destroyed and that some women were burned to death in their homes. The Mandate Government appears to have given up all responsibility for the safety of the Arabs, unarmed and helpless in their simple villages. The new USA suggestion of a trusteeship is evidence of the fact that they simply do not know what is happening here. The Zionists are counting on the USA to stand by and accept a *fait accompli*, and the Arabs, having pinned their hopes on the UN, have lost faith in it.

[23 April] Fighting is going on all around us and last night many wounded were brought to Ramallah. Willard made a trip to Nablus with two men in a very critical condition. Nebi Samwil has been under heavy attack but the Arabs were able to withstand it and drove the Haganah back with many casualties. Reports of the situation in the north are distressing. The Zionists seem well on the way to having all that the Partition Plan has given them before the British leave and before the Arab armies can come in. They talk constantly of a purely Jewish State with a purely Jewish culture. Since they are such a polyglot community and reflect the cultures of the many countries they come from, one wonders just what is meant by a Jewish culture.

[26 April] We start another week without electricity. Mail is a thing of the past as the post-office is under constant threat. The Palestinians are counting on other Arab countries to come, but most of them have no armies strong enough to combat the Zionists. Lebanon and Syria, our only near neighbours, have been independent from French control for too short a time to have built up armies; Iraq is seven hundred mostly desert miles away, and Egypt is two hundred miles, with the Sinai between. No country has an air-force of any strength. The Arab Legion in Transjordan is the best equipped and best trained army, but its numbers are small compared with the Zionist army. If there must be fighting, the Legion is the best hope of the Palestinians. Jaffa is being speedily evacuated. They say twenty trucks loaded with people leave every hour. The price of petrol is sky-high. Willard paid five pounds ($20.00) for a five-gallon tin on Saturday, and they tell us that it is twenty pounds ($80.00) in some places. The International Red Cross has been called in by the British. The IRC is departing from its "prisoner-of-war only" programme and will bring in nurses to replace the British nurses. I wonder if there will be places for them, as the Zionists have surrounded the areas where all the hospitals are located.

[29 April] Graduation is usually at the beginning of July and we make quite an occasion of it, but this year we had it today. The

British will be gone in two weeks and we do not know how long we will be able to carry on with school after that. By giving up spring vacation, we have been able to get ahead of schedule, too. So today we had our annual Commencement for both schools in our auditorium. The seniors are very happy about it and we feel that we owe it to them as they have kept remarkably steady while their world seems to be toppling around them. We had the usual programme of music, speeches, and processions. The boys were very smart in their best suits and the girls lovely in white. A wonderful sense of warmth and friendliness prevailed and parents were visibly moved and happy for the occasion. Not unaware of the tragedy around us, a hospital a few yards away full of wounded people, Jaffa people in flight up into the hill country, reports of atrocities in surrounding villages, and danger of attack, we were trying to give our young people an hour that would recognize their achievements in the classroom and an hour to remember.

As the programme neared the end, one father of the graduating class, fleeing from Lydda with his family to Damascus, rushed up to the door of the auditorium and asked us to get his son at once. I happened to be the member of the staff nearest the door and I tried to tell him that the programme was almost over and it would be a pity to disturb it. It would mean going down to the front rows to get his son, perhaps creating panic. He finally submitted, but as the graduates marched out to the strains of beautiful music, he pulled his son out of the procession and took him off, leaving all his son's possessions behind. Ahmad's clothes were finally given to a refugee, who accepted them gratefully.

It has been the most moving programme we have ever had and we are glad we have done it. School will go on. We even have hopes of completing a full school year, and the graduates will spend the next few weeks preparing for external exams. How we needed such a day! Went to bed with the noise of an explosion that shook the house. Sounded like another Jerusalem incident.

[1 May] Willard tried to get to Jaffa today as he heard that flour was available, but was turned back by the British soldiers. They said fighting there was too serious. By good luck, he met an officer who told him there were rations at the camp for Europeans which he could have. So he came home terribly proud of his good luck for he had bacon, butter, tins of peaches, dry yeast and powdered milk. These will have to be used with discretion and shared wisely as we don't know when we will have such treats again.

Little as they have to fight with, the Arabs do not give up easily. What a situation! We have a government which is supposed to keep order and protect its citizens, but is helpless. It cannot attack the Jews nor can it protect the Arabs from the Zionists and stands helplessly by while village after village is destroyed and the people dispossessed. The Jewish Agency, which has been a government within the government all the years of the Mandate, is ready to form its own government in a progressing little country: not a desert, as they say, but a country that has roads, harbours, an airport, railway, rich agricultural areas, orange groves that produce wealth, and trees rich in oil, certainly not the sole property of this alien people. The Arabs of Palestine accepted the Mandate Government as its "Agency", and this is the result.

[2 May] Sunday. As we went to Meeting this morning, we were stopped again and again by anxious groups gathered for mutual council. Jaffa had fallen and the British had retired from the area. Thousands were fleeing up our way. The Katamon, the lovely Arab residential section of Jerusalem, was also in Jewish hands and most of its residents had fled. They have been under fire for weeks. Weeks ago they were telling us how weary they were as nights were a nightmare of shootings and attacks. At Meeting, we decided to open the Meeting House for the refugees, where they would at least be under cover at night, as these nights are cool. There were also benches where they could stretch out. Willard and Dr Mansur, Clerk of the Meeting, notified the mayors of Ramallah and Bireh of our decision. By six o'clock tonight families were moving in, and it looked to Willard as though they were settling in. Someone said tonight that there are probably ten thousand Jaffa people in Ramallah now.

[6 May] Nine families have partitioned the Meeting House into nine apartments. Fifty-nine people in all, and a baby due to arrive soon. The benches have been used to build up walls and blankets and gunny sacks and cloth of every kind help give the families a little privacy. I hope they will not need to stay in the Meeting House long. As for the baby, it will be welcomed and loved. Our son's baby-basket has been in the attic for years; it can be painted and decorated for the new baby and neighbours will make the layette. Everyone is helping the families. We will take turns with the Girls' School in sending up hot meals to the Meeting House as the people have little equipment for cooking.

The Zionists are boasting that partition has been accomplished; the UN seems to have had to give up the trusteeship proposal. I fear political pressures rather than good judgement and justice have won this round. We wonder if the Palestinians and other Arab states will accept a *fait accompli* and recognize a state of Israel. The only winner at the moment seems to be the Zionists. Britain has paid dearly for her part and the USA has shown up so badly through it all that she has lost the respect of much of Europe and the confidence of the Arab World; as for the UN, on which the world was building so much hope, it surely has not gained in prestige. Russia may stand to gain, but it is not clear yet what game she is playing by her support of the Partition Plan. She may realize that the USA may have a lot to learn the hard way and is glad to see us getting deeply involved.

We are down to thirty-three boarders but have enough day-boys to make a fairly good school. I could be wrong, but I think we may be the only school which is carrying on normally. We even plan an English and Arabic speaking contest for 14 May.

[10 May] Fighting at Bab-el-Wad. The Jews are trying hard to keep the road between Tel Aviv and Jerusalem open, but the Arabs have put road-blocks in the way and sit above the road and fire on the convoys. Some convoys get through at a cost, some have to turn back.

[12 May] Willard decided that he must go to Jerusalem this morning to get money from the bank lest the coming conflict last longer than we think and the time come when we would not be able to meet emergencies or our obligations. It was the money which enabled us to open school in the fall and fortunately we had not needed to touch it all summer. He found Barclays Bank getting ready to close up but they waited on him. He also brought out a good deal of money for some of our Arab friends who had not been able to go to Jerusalem for some time, so he came back with a small fortune!

His chief news for me, however, was that he had met a British officer who would be leaving with the High Commissioner and wanted to take an Oriental rug home with him. Willard offered my services as he had told the major, "My wife will help you. She loves to help people buy rugs." All too true. I did love seeing the rugs as the merchants unrolled or unfolded them for us, getting a thrill out of the whole ceremony of buying. Not having occasion to buy for ourselves very often, I usually was glad to be with others when they were buying. Although I was no authority, I knew some of the reliable merchants and that seemed to give assurance to visitors. Seeing the beauty of the rugs, feeling almost reverence for the hands that tied the knots to create the lovely designs, appreciating the fine quality of the materials used, guaranteeing endurance as well as beauty, was like a day off for me. Added to all that was the leisurely atmosphere as we sipped sweet coffee from tiny cups as bargaining went on and decisions were finally reached. Yes, buying rugs was a delightful experience.

But going to Jerusalem was no longer a game, especially today. For months Jerusalem had been a divided zoned city with snipers everywhere. Today, it would be almost impossible to find a shop open as the High Commissioner had announced only this morning that he would be leaving tomorrow night. The plan evidently is for him and his aides to go to Haifa tomorrow night, board ship next day and leave on the stroke of midnight or one minute after on the fifteenth. Jerusalem was ready for battle, even now. Five months and a half of tension and terror had caused most merchants to keep their shops only half-open. Today, most would surely be closed. So, if Willard's announcement was startling, if not reckless, I think I rather liked the idea of going to Jerusalem once more before this era ended.

The Major came for me after lunch and I must confess that I was not too optimistic about our expedition. However, it was a lovely day and adventure lay ahead. In moments we were on the Nablus Road, one of the most interesting roads in the world. On the left we soon passed the mosque at Bireh, built over the spring which tradition says was the place where Joseph and Mary discovered that the twelve-year-old Jesus was not with them and from which they had to retrace the long weary miles to find him in Jerusalem. This spring has supplied water for Bireh for centuries and continues to do so. Our drinking water came from there, too. The winter rains had been good, and the valley to the west was rich with orchards, vineyards, and fields of grain, well cultivated. Rising from the valley like a sentinel, the hill called Nebi Samuel came in view, named for the Prophet Samuel who, it is believed, is buried there. Our Arab farmers revere the peak because they say it collects the evening dews of summer nights and spreads them over the valley so that the grapes and the grain and the olives ripen and provide food for the coming months. I found myself trying to see it all so that I could treasure up this view and this trip in a special corner of my memory, for the future was so uncertain. Traces of the old Roman road could be seen plainly, calling up stories of other days. This could have been the road over which Paul walked on that fateful journey to Damascus. Now on the east is Tel el-Ful where Saul had lived; and then Shafat, where David fled from the anger of Saul and ate the shewbread. Now, in less than half an hour, we were on Mount Scopus, where we got our first awe-inspiring view of Jerusalem. Alexander in his day could have seen Jerusalem from this spot; the Romans encamped on it. Today, modern Christians of the ancient churches cross themselves when they arrive at this point and pray for a blessing on the city and for themselves. Travelling back and forth on the bus as I have done so often, watching them, I often found it difficult to keep my hand firmly by my side. Only the reminder of my stern Presbyterian childhood kept me from following their example.

One cannot look on Jerusalem from Mount Scopus without a feeling of wonder, for too much of the religious story of mankind is linked with it. From this point it almost looks like the City of Peace its name indicates. Domes and minarets, spires and crosses rise above the roof-tops, and the view beyond is of the hills south to Bethlehem and east to the hills of Moab, always impressive.

As we start down the slope of Scopus, we look to the east to the Mount of Olives. Not far from us is the British War Cemetery with its rows of crosses and a giant stone cross dominating the scene. A bronze crusader sword placed in the centre of the cross glints in the sun. Three thousand British soldiers are buried there, silent witnesses of the First World War when the deliverance of Jerusalem was hailed so joyously by the Christian World. If we had only at that time remembered that Jesus of Nazareth had lived and taught and died there, the present tragedy Palestine was facing might have been averted.

But we are on an errand today, a very human one; we are looking for a rug, and time is of the essence. Today, Jerusalem lies silent below us. We may have the city to ourselves, I thought. There were no pedestrians, no buses, no cars, no sheep or donkeys to watch out for; all that made going to Jerusalem a delight was gone. For months now Arabs trying to carry on their businesses and bringing produce to market had gone about at considerable risk. As early as January, Christians had been wearing crosses conspicuously, the men sometimes having woven straw ones on the lapels of their jackets. Most shop-keepers kept their windows and doors partly shuttered so that they could close them up quickly when the sirens warned of terrorist acts by the Zionists. We met no cars, even as we came nearer the city, and when we reached Barclays Bank at the corner of Allenby and Jaffa Road, we might have been in Petra; however, it was not temples carved from limestone, but iron shutters on windows and iron doors and brick walls that greeted us. There was no hope of getting a rug in that area.

Not willing to give up easily, we decided to drive out to the German Colony where some of the Armenian rug-merchants lived, hoping they might have taken rugs to their homes. The Arab sections of the new part of Jerusalem were deserted, as people had fled from their modern homes to safer places. Armenians, faced with the possibility of becoming refugees a second time, had tried to remain in their homes. Many had taken refuge in the Armenian Quarter of the Old City, but we hoped some were still living in the Colony and that we would find them.

We set out, but as luck would have it, our car broke down in a deserted street. We got out of the car and waited hopefully for the driver to find the trouble and repair it. Soon a big car came along, stopped, and out stepped a three-star General! To say he was upset is to put it mildly. He ordered the Major to get me out of there as quickly as possible, saw that that was easier said than done, and told me he would send his own car back. He was in a hurry to go somewhere so went on, but in a few minutes his car did return and we were back at Barclays Bank in no time.

Now what to do? Ramallah was ten miles away, our car in trouble, and not a shop open on Jaffa Road. To our relief, our car finally arrived and we were tempted to get in and give up the quest. Knowing how disappointed the Major was, however, I timidly suggested that if he would trust me I would go into the Old City to the Armenian Quarter and try to find a merchant. He quickly agreed and I started down the lonely street, but not alone for long, for the Major, handing his gun to his aide, followed me. I was truly surprised, for the Old City had been out of bounds to the Red Berets, an elite British fighting force, for some time as they had been brought in earlier to keep the Zionist terrorists under control, and they were prime targets. Major Redman was one of them, and today was wearing his Red Beret and unarmed.

It was strange walking down that street that was usually such a busy one. We did not meet a soul, and the effect of seeing only closed shops, some bricked up, others iron-shuttered, was like a dream. I did hope the major knew what he was doing but supposed he had little to lose at this late hour in Jerusalem. For myself, I did not dare tell him how hopeless our quest might be as the afternoon was passing and we had to be off the road before dark. I prayed that my good angel would direct my steps, for I hardly knew where to begin looking for a rug merchant in the maze of houses in the Armenian Quarter.

So we entered Jaffa Gate, the gate I had first entered in 1922 and a thousand times since, and it was to be the last time I would go into it from Jaffa Road for a long, long time, if ever. The Old City looked deserted, too. Few people were on the streets and every shop seemed closed. I shall never forget my relief and joy when we came to Bulos Meo's Oriental Shop on David Street near the gate to find that, although the front windows were covered and the door locked, a small door on the street going off to the left was open. I peered in and found the Meo father and brothers there and willing to show us their rugs. The tall Major had to stoop low to enter, but once inside we were soon lost in wonder at the wealth of beautiful objects on the shelves and in the cases that filled the two large rooms of the shop.

Time was slipping away; nevertheless, coffee was made and we sat on our low stools for the next hour sipping sweet fragrant nectar while our hosts brought down rug after rug from the shelves and we were as unhurried as though we had all the time in the world and all was well. After the usual bargaining, a decision was finally made, fifty good English pounds were paid for a beautiful rug, and we reluctantly set out for the lonely, awesome walk back to Barclays Bank and our car. We thanked them with the Arabic "*Khaterkum*—From our hearts we thank you," and their "*Maa Salaami*—Go in peace" seemed particularly moving as we walked that street.

How often we had heard that beautiful goodbye, "Go in peace," through the years and on how many different occasions, happy and sad! I remembered how heartbreaking it had been to me when I was quite young and new to the country, and it was the cry of a young mother weeping as her tiny baby was laid in the grave. She cried, "*Maa Salaami, ya habibti*—Go in peace, my darling."

As we hurried up Jaffa Road to the waiting car the words followed me now, for in the deserted street, in the ominous silence of a city besieged after the culmination of years of unrest, violence, political intrigue, deception and unfulfilled hopes, one almost felt the hand of death was once again on this ancient city. Certainly something we loved was gone.

But there was no time for brooding, the afternoon was far gone and Ramallah was ten miles away. Soon we passed New Gate, Damascus Gate, and were speeding along the Nablus Road, retracing our journey, and we arrived at the school just before dark.

[13 May] The High Commissioner, Sir Alan Cunningham, made his farewell speech tonight over the radio. It was a sad little speech. We listened to it on our crystal set. It was brief, simple, dignified. but must have caused him some heartbreak. He regretted that the Mandate had ended in this way, but he had faith in the verdict of history. Those of us who had seen the beginning and the end of the Mandate had only sympathy for him as he closed what history will probably say is one of the darkest moments in British colonial history. There were such high hopes back in 1922–23, such faith in the British. I think faith in the integrity of the average British official remained, but only disillusionment for its home government. Already, thousands of Palestinians are refugees and the land is ravaged by war. This government, pledged to see that nothing would be done to prejudice the rights of the Palestinians, was stealing away from Jerusalem in the dark of the night with no formalities, no flags waving, aware of failure. We went to bed tonight with the sound of British vehicles on the road to Haifa in our ears. We do not know how Sir Alan will travel. They will arrive in Haifa late tonight, board ship tomorrow, and sail on the stroke of midnight or one minute after. When we wake up on the morning of the fifteenth, there will be no Arab government to take over.

[14 May] Although a truce was to be observed in Jerusalem as the British leave, the Jews have broken it twice today and are already occupying important places. The Arab armies are supposed to come in tomorrow. We don't know what will happen, but today we had our annual speaking contest and it was a happy occasion. My husband's determination to carry on normally though the heavens fall works out well. We were so excited by the judges' decisions we had no time to sit and weep, although some of us had hearts too full for tears.

And so ends an era. But it is not an end: the seeds of the future have been sown, which may yield a bitter harvest.

The historic day had arrived, 14 May 1948. At midnight the Mandate would end and the Palestinians would be left without even a temporary government to guide and protect them. As we gathered around the dinner table that night, we were in a sombre mood. The afternoon speaking contest had eased tensions and helped divert our thoughts from the coming hour with its presage of tragedy. What would happen when the hour struck twelve, we did not know. However, we thought we had reason for optimism, as the Arab armies were to come in as soon as the British left. What we did not fully know was what help the Arab armies could give. Lebanon and Syria on our borders could not furnish more than three or four thousand men and limited supplies; Iraq, seven hundred miles away, with tremendous transport difficulties, could give only token help; and Egypt, under Farouk, had no great army trained for modern warfare. She, too, had a problem of terrain: two hundred and fifty miles, mostly desert, from her source of supply.

Transjordan, a nation of only about 300,000, had its Arab Legion. Her strength at this time was probably not more than five thousand. It was trained chiefly for desert patrol but was well disciplined under Glubb Pasha, a British general who had the confidence of King Abdullah and the devotion of his men. What could they do against the 65,000 soldiers the Zionists claimed?

The fact was that the Arab World had not been fighting battles nor building up armies during the four hundred years of the Ottoman rule. The seat of government had been Constantinople. Arab provinces and sheikdoms had furnished their quotas to the Turkish armies but had no independent armies. The Palestinians had no National Guard, such as the Jewish Haganah, in the Mandate days and in the present crisis had only a few irregulars with which to face the Zionist Haganah, the Irgun Zvai Leumi, the Stern Gang, and the Palmach. Arab strength lay in love of country and a conviction of the rightness of their inherent claims to their homes and the homes of their immediate ancestors, the soil they loved, and a determination not to yield them to an alien people.

Alas, these were claims the modern world seemed to ignore, on the age-old principle that might makes right. All told, the combined forces of the Arab armies could not, at that time, have been much more than 20,000, and it looked as though the Arab Legion would have to bear the brunt of the battle in our part of Palestine. On the other hand, the Zionists could boast of an army three times that number, compact, and under a central command. Many had fought in Europe during the Second World War and so were trained in modern warfare and in the use of modern weapons. They were also well-equipped and in the Palmach they had an elite corps of full-time regular soldiers numbering almost as many as the Arab Legion. When there was the threat of a German invasion of Palestine during the Second World War, Britain had trained them for commando action, counting on their hostility to the Germans to make them willing to undertake difficult tasks. Colonel David Marcus, West Point-trained and a reserve Officer of the USA army, had been in Palestine in the first months of 1948 and, according to no less an authority than Abba Eban, he had established training schools for officers, organized the general staff, supervised field training and written the military manual by which the Haganah became "an army of democracy". He was presently in Palestine serving as Supreme Commander of the Israeli forces. He was to be killed in Palestine during the battle at Bab-el-Wad in June, but he had created an army of considerable strength. That was the situation as we civilians saw it.

The consular corps in Jerusalem formed a truce committee during the last days of the Mandate, but it was not a success. With the British leaving Jerusalem, the truce was broken twice by the Zionists on 14 May and important places were occupied.

After dinner, Willard and I went to our apartment at Grant Hall, which was also the dormitory building for the younger boys. To-night we would be alone in the building as we had wanted to have all the boys in the main building for it was the safest place in the village, probably in the whole country. We were not sure that there would not be demonstrations against Americans at this critical hour, as America was being held largely responsible for the UN decision. We did not worry about the Girls' School, where the British head-mistress, Sylvia Clark, and Alice Whittier Jones from New England remained. Alice Jones had been principal of the Girls' School for many years but had retired in 1929. She returned to Palestine for a visit ten years later. Caught there by the Second World War, she had remained through it and stayed on as she loved the country and was loved by the people she had served. We knew that Arabs would not demonstrate against women. But they might demonstrate at a Boys' School building. After all, we Americans were the tangibles of a seemingly unfriendly government at the moment, and Ramallah was full of displaced people rebellious against the partition of their country.

The silence tonight was ominous. There had been almost no activity outside the school grounds all day. No buses ran, there were no cars on the road that passed the school, no men went to the fields, shops were closed and no business offices open. Save for occasional sounds of explosions in Jerusalem, all was quiet. After years, and particularly the last months, of violence a daily occurrence, it was a loud, menacing silence.

As the evening was chill, we built a fire and settled down to wait for midnight. We recalled how school had opened with such hope on 1 October 1947. Every bed, 115 in all, had a boy sleeping in it that night, and next morning at seven o'clock we went out to find the grounds filled with day-boys all eager to begin the new school year. Momentous discussions were even then going on at Lake Success, headquarters of the United Nations, and, if some of our older boys and their parents were pessimistic about the outcome, we tried to assure them of the American sense of justice and that she would do what was right when she understood the situation. We reminded them of the long history of friendship that had existed between America and the Near East; there was the great American University of Beirut to prove it. It had served the young people of the Near East for eighty years, and its graduates held important positions throughout the Arab world. Someone had told us that when the United Nations Organization was set up there were more graduates from the University of Beirut at San Francisco than from any other university in the world. Last, but not least, there was all that oil in the Arab World, and Palestine was between the USA and Arabia where the oil was so abundant. Were we whistling in the dark?

But as we sat alone around the fire, we had memories of many years. It was fun to recall them and it relieved the tension of the moment. We were tired almost beyond words but we were sure that we should remain awake until twelve o'clock.

By eleven o'clock, what with the stillness all around us, the dying embers of our fire, the weariness of having been up and about since six o'clock that morning and the effort to maintain a sense of normality in the school, we began to wonder if we could sit up another hour. We also began to wonder what we would do if we were awake, so it was sensible to go to bed, knowing that the next day would be even more anxious than the one just ending and we should be prepared for it. The historic moment passed, therefore, and we slept peacefully through it, having decided we should "just trust".

[15 May] Saturday morning, 15 May 1948: a day for the history books and a momentous one for the people of Palestine. We were awakened by the sound of the school bell at six o'clock as usual. Never had it sounded so beautiful, so welcome, so comforting. We had slept through the hour when the British were leaving Haifa and nothing had happened to disturb us. Willard said to the boys yesterday: "When you are old, your grand-children may ask you what you were doing the morning of 15 May 1948 when the British left Palestine. I want you to be able to say, 'I was doing my duty. I was in school.'" And bless them, every day-boy had come. Some were reviewing their lessons as they walked about waiting for classes to begin. With day-boys and our thirty boarders, we still have a fair-sized student body. There was an undercurrent of excitement, for we knew that the Arab Legion was to come and it would pass the school, as we are on the main road to Latrun and Bab-el-Wad where fighting has been going on for weeks, but for Friends' Boys' School, it was business as usual.

Bab-el-Wad (or *Wadi*) means Door or Gate of the valley. In this instance it was a narrow defile where the main road from Jaffa leaves the Coastal Plain for the climb up to Jerusalem, 2,500 feet above. The *Felaheen*, or peasants, in that area had been guarding it zealously for weeks to prevent Jewish convoys from taking relief to Jews in Jerusalem. No convoys got through easily, many had to turn back, and there were many casualties. The Arabs wanted to isolate the Jews as the terrorists had tried to isolate them during the past months. Now the Arab Legion would probably go there, for it was a most strategic spot.

About eleven o'clock, the Arab Legion forces began to come through Ramallah amidst great rejoicing. There was something impressive as they came past the school. They were quiet, dis-ciplined, and friendly as they went on to the Manara where five roads meet in Ramallah, and struck off to the Jaffa Road leading to Bab-el-Wad. If war has to be, here was a well-trained, efficient, dedicated army that was bringing comfort and re-assurance to the thousands of homeless people in our midst. Pacifist as I hope I am, I could not but be thankful for the presence of this army at this moment. We had no government, people were desperate and fearful, and the coming of the Arab Legion steadied them and brought hope. It is a terrible thing to see what war does. We have already seen maimed bodies in our small hospital and the cruelty of guns in the hands of men. Some happy celebrants shot guns into the air. "They had better save their guns for their enemies," someone murmured, but the grim words were lost in the general rejoicing.

Many explosions in Jerusalem today. We live on rumours. We

hear that Kalendia is in Arab hands and that Nebi Yacoub will be next. News comes of fighting in Tul Karm, Beisan, Beersheba, in fact everywhere.

Our hospital is full tonight. A little nine-year-old girl was brought in from Er Ram. While she was skipping a sniper's bullet hit her in the head and it is feared she is blinded. As I looked at her, with her head bandaged, all I could see was her mouth. She tried to smile when I spoke and quite irrationally my thought was: "her teeth are like pearls." Seldom had I seen such perfect ones. There was also a woman in difficult labour, but her baby died.

What a pity the Zionists have allowed a situation like this to develop in Palestine! Unless peace comes soon, it may cause the Arab World to arm as it has not done in centuries. One dreads to think of the whole Arab World in arms. If the Zionists had only been willing to place their claims before the International Court of Justice, as the Arabs have always been willing to do, all this violence and hatred might have been avoided and the two peoples could have lived together in Palestine as Arab and Jewish communities have been able to do in the rest of the Arab World. It is even more dreadful that the UNO, set up after the last war to prevent the acquisition of territory by conquest, is helpless in this first real test of its charter. For years, thoughtful Arabs and Jews, Americans and British people living in Palestine have tried to prevent this holocaust. Now, Palestine is a battlefield, and, to our sorrow, Christians in other lands see in it the hand of God.

All our boarders are quietly, and we hope securely, asleep tonight. We too must carry on as normally as possible. Parents are glad and most thankful that we are keeping on, and the boys do their part. It is not much that we can do, but we are glad that we are situated where we can keep school going. It is not easy for boys or teachers, but we pray that the worst will soon be over and peace will come to this beloved country.

Turbulent Truce

The battle for Jerusalem was to continue for a long time, ending with the Arabs retaining the Old City and the territory around it to the north, so that we in Ramallah and the northern districts were not cut off from Jerusalem. A wall was built between us and the occupied zone to the south, a wall of barbed wire and later of stone. Notes from my diary follow the events of the next six months, showing what it was like to live under the insecurity and continued fear of renewed fighting on a big scale.

[17 May] Great excitement at about half-past six tonight. We thought we were about to be attacked, the shooting seemed so near and was so loud and continuous. The first report was that Jerusalem had surrendered to the Arabs, but later reports were that it was only the Jews in the Old City who had surrendered. The report is that the Arabs had pushed into the Jewish-held sector as far as Ben Yehudi Street and that the Jews were ready to surrender, but a message from headquarters ordered the Arabs back to the walled City. The Arab Legion is sending reinforcements to Jerusalem and the battle goes on.

[19 May] Woke up to the sound of bombardment of Jerusalem which kept up until afternoon. The coming of the Legion has been good for the morale of the Palestinian irregulars who are fighting against such heavy odds. They have made some gains and hope that all Jerusalem will surrender soon. Meantime, our emergency hospital fills up with wounded civilians. Five women were brought in from Shushi today. All had severe injuries which had gone untended for seven days. The foot of one was partly gone, another had been shot through the breast and gangrene had set in; still another, a little girl of twelve, had a piece of hip-bone sticking out. They had fled to a cave, rather, dragged themselves to a cave, after they were hit. The Arab irregulars drove the Jews back, but the women, not knowing the situation and thinking that their village was still occupied, did not dare come out. On the seventh day, the Arab soldiers found them and brought them to us. Our facilities are inadequate for such emergencies, but our doctors and nurses, all volunteers, rise to the situation marvellously. Some of the serious cases will have to be taken to Nablus Hospital tomorrow.

[21 May] Our little girl died in the night. I had hoped that she might survive, but fear, hunger and exposure may have been more responsible for her death than the wound. M. Courvoisier of the International Red Cross came yesterday and arranged for us to fly the Red Cross flag over our buildings since we are caring for refugees. Willard got out on the roof of the main building and painted the four corners of the red-tiled roof white, leaving the red tiles to form a cross. We hope it will be easily seen from the air. Willard has been given a flag from Geneva to put on the station-wagon also, since it is being used as an ambulance.

[22 May] Mr Wasson, American Consul-General, was shot yesterday in Jerusalem. We do not know the details. He came only last month and was working hard to bring about peace, and probably was responsible for the Jerusalem Truce Committee that was formed before the British left. People had so hoped that Jerusalem might not become a battlefield. The peacemakers may be blessed, but their task is not an easy one. Mr Wasson's condition is reported grave and that is both sad and disturbing news.

[23 May] Mr Wasson has died, and since the consulate is in a sector under heavy fire, we cannot attend the funeral or, in fact, learn much about the circumstances. And the battle for the Holy City goes on.

[24 May] A hot sirocco is drying us all up. The flowers in our garden that have drooped all day were so lovely yesterday. The evening dew may help revive them. I wish we could recover as quickly as they will. We hear that fighting is going on, room to room, in Notre Dame, the big Latin Church and hostelry across from New Gate. We are increasingly anxious about America's attitude, as it may complicate the situation terribly. If our congressmen and senators could only keep still when they are not informed! Everything they say for the press is accepted here as official American policy; maybe it is, but we hope not.

[25 May] The battle for Jerusalem goes on apace. There is a report that Jews fleeing from Jerusalem have been caught at Bab-el-Wad and many lives lost. They must have been desperate to risk that area, but they undoubtedly feel cut off and constant siege does strange things to people. Wounded civilians were brought to the hospital from Emmaus when their home was destroyed; five of the family were killed, one of the wounded a three-year-old child.

[26 May] A plane came over Ramallah at two o'clock in the morning and dropped what seemed to be a barrel of explosives. A clear moonlight night is no longer a joy to us. The bombing may be a way of telling the Ramallah people to get out: I hope they will not go. The attack tonight may also have been an attempt to destroy the radio station, as the barrel fell just east of it in the "lake", as we call a piece of land on the Nablus Road which fills up to form a lake when the rains come. The sirocco continues to burn us up. The doctors have begun moving patients into our main building, and I am afraid many, many more will be moved in before this affair is settled.

[27 May] Another plane came over tonight at one o'clock and dropped either two or three bombs quite close to the school. We learned that one bomb made a big hole in the grounds of the Bireh Girls' School south of us. I found a piece of metal in the school dining-room and a broken window through which it had come. The metal hit the wall so hard it was covered with whitewash from the wall. This is one way to celebrate our twenty-sixth wedding anniversary.

[28 May] News today of a big battle at Bab-el-Wad. The Arabs are low on supplies and fighting in some places is slowing down. We wonder if there will not have to be a negotiated peace soon, as soldiers cannot fight without arms. King Abdullah was in Ramallah today. He received a warm welcome. Apparently he is very anxious about Jerusalem, with its association with Islam as well as with Christianity and Judaism. The beautiful Dome of the Rock looks so vulnerable; one hopes that it can be safe from attack.

[29 May] Three planes came over tonight and one report is that they dropped twenty barrels of explosives. One old man died of shock, one man was killed, and a boy injured. Otherwise, little damage was done. There are reports of similar raids on Nablus, Tul Karm, and unconfirmed ones that Irbid and Amman in Transjordan have also been bombed. We worry about the fifty-nine people in the Meeting House. We went up to see them as soon as we could this morning and found them badly frightened, as a direct hit would be tragedy indeed. I wish they were somewhere else. We have been told to have lights out at half-past nine in the evening from now on. Our small family of boarders have been wonderful through this period. Willard had called them together to talk about what they should do if we had air-raids, and to his surprise and pride the boys had already worked out strategy and had everything under control. Willard has gone to Amman with some students to see if they can sit for the London Matriculation Examinations there. The Director of Education had assured him that if Jerusalem was closed to them the papers would be sent to Amman, so they have gone off hopefully. The London Matriculation pass is a pass into the sophomore class at the American University at Beirut, so it is very important. It also means acceptance into London University. I will be alone in Grant Hall tonight. Refugees are beginning to come to the school to ask permission to sleep in dressing-rooms in the basement of the auditorium. According to the Red Cross rules, I think we may protect women and children only, so it is a problem to know what to do. The bombings may be more to create fear than for the amount of destruction they cause. Ramallah is a desired prize.

[2 June] Willard returned at four o'clock today. The examination papers had not been sent to Amman and he was advised to see if they could have been sent to Beirut. The young people were so eager to try that Willard continued to Beirut with them. At Beirut, the people responsible said that they had not received the papers and thought there had been sabotage in Jerusalem. A Jew had been in charge of registrations in Jerusalem and I think he may have decided that there would be no chance for the Arabs to get to Jerusalem after the British left, so had not bothered to send in the applications. It was a big disappointment, but Willard took the young people to interesting places in Beirut; they also saw Baalbek and came home quite happy. They were almost heroes for having had such an adventure and a dangerous journey. I was glad for news of friends, some magazines and flowers.

[5 June] We were invited to the broadcasting station tonight. While we were there an interesting thing happened. In the midst of routine broadcasting, Mr Nashashibi hurried in ready to go on the air to announce the surrender of the Hebrew University and Hadassah Hospital on Mount Scopus. Dr Judah Magnes had gone to Amman, he said, to see King Abdullah. Moments before he was to go on the air with the news, a telegram came telling him not to make the announcement. I have rarely seen a man so frustrated. Dr Magnes, an American rabbi highly regarded by the

Arabs, must have been able to persuade King Abdullah that if
the University was taken, valuable scientific research would be
destroyed. King Abdullah, himself a scholar, probably thinking
that the fighting would be over soon, could be appealed to in
this way, and would respect the wishes of Dr Magnes. This is
the second incident of the kind. The order to the Arabs to retire
to the Old Walls in Jerusalem on 17 May; now this order. The
Arabs say the war is being directed from London and from
Washington, DC.

(Incidentally, the two institutions remained on Mount Scopus,
forming an enclave in the most strategic location in the area, at
great inconvenience to the Arabs of Palestine, for the next nineteen
years. And that is another story. But I am sure Dr Magnes had not
anticipated that, if indeed he had gone to King Abdullah as
reported.)

There is talk of a truce beginning on Monday. Would that it
were peace so that our refugees could go home!

[7 June] Strange how we can get used to things. People pay little
attention to the shooting and shelling that goes on. While we
were having tea on the balcony this afternoon with guests, a
plane flew over, circled Bireh three times then went off. We
don't know if it was a Jewish or an Iraqi plane.

[11 June] School closed today and we have had a complete school
year. Wonderful! It has been strenuous as we have had no break
since Christmas, but it has been worth it and I am sure we were
wise to carry on. The truce was supposed to go into effect at
eight o'clock this morning. I wish it might mean electricity, as
we need it so much. The question is how long will it last?
According to British officers with the Arab Legion, both armies
are needing a rest and reinforcements. They are not supposed to
get reinforcements during a truce, so rest may be all they can
look forward to.

[16 June] M. Courvoisier of the International Red Cross came in
today. He told us he had been supervising the evacuation of
more than one thousand old men, women and children from the
Jewish Quarter of the Old City. Haganah prisoners and young
men of military age were taken to Amman, but the others,
civilians, will join their compatriots on the other side. M.
Courvoisier was deeply moved by the success of the operation.
He saw Arab Legion soldiers helping the older people and children
through the narrow streets of the Old City, carrying their bundles

when they got tired. One old man came along, carrying a large *Torah* wrapped in a heavy cloth. Meeting an Arab civilian whom he knew, he gave it to him to keep until he came back. The Jews who have lived in the Old City for many years are not happy about the aggressive newcomers, who they feel are not living according to their faith.

(Incidentally, Mr Albina, the Arab who was entrusted with the precious possession, did keep the *Torah* for at least fourteen years and finally turned it over to a distinguished American rabbi when he visited Jordan.)

If it is true, as Robert Graves says, that the Age of Chivalry in Europe belongs to the days of the Arab Empire, M. Courvoisier could believe it when he saw the gallantry of the Arab soldiers. We saw it so often in the coming months that we can believe the evacuation was executed humanely.

During the truce period life went on busily in Ramallah, as there were people who needed help. We made trips to the villages around us and to Jerusalem, as there were refugees to be cared for in some way and everyone was needed to help. Jifna, which in Roman days was called "Head of the fat valley" because of its olives and grain, had more than 1,000 refugees. Bir Zeit nearby, a small village, but as its name suggests, rich in oil, was crowded with refugees who were living in tents in the lovely vineyards. We moved about freely and accepted invitations to the homes of our friends with no embarrassment to them or to us. We belonged.

Count Bernadotte was in the country under United Nations auspices to work out a peace plan. He did in fact make out a plan which he hoped would make for peace, but he was not to be able to present it to the UN or ever see the UN or his own country again.

In the meantime, the Jewish buildings on Mount Scopus were to be allowed to remain temporarily in Jewish hands, but eventually to be under the UN, and neither side was to take advantage of the truce to strengthen its position. The pass at Bab-el-Wad was to remain open under International Red Cross supervision to allow the Jews on the coastal plains to send relief in the form of food and supplies to Jerusalem, enough only for the four weeks of the truce. The IRC, working in unfamiliar surroundings and knowing little of the country, was handicapped in enforcing the rules, and it was generally thought that more supplies got through than were permitted by the terms of the truce. After the final armistice was signed, Russian-born Ben Gurion thanked the Soviet Government for allowing Czechoslovakia to supply reinforcements. The Arabs had no communication with the Soviet Government, which had voted with the USA on the Partition Plan, and as there were a large number of Communists in the new state of Israel, the Arabs could not expect help from that source. Actually, they feared Russian intervention on behalf of the Zionists and remembered that Russia had competed with the USA in speedy recognition of the new state. On the other hand, Western Powers had observed the terms of the truce and, according to Glubb Pasha who commanded the Arab Legion, no aid came from them. Thus, when the truce ended on 9 July, the Arab armies may have been rested but were no stronger militarily and the Zionist forces were both rested and immeasurably stronger.

Brief excerpts from my diary tell about the next anxious days.

[9 July] The Truce ended today and fighting began at once. We have heard sounds of firing all day. The Arab radio station put on its first English broadcast tonight and we are glad it has done so. The staff of the Egyptian Red Crescent is setting up a hospital in the main building of the school but the International Red Cross will continue to use our facilities for their headquarters. The big study-hall and the big dormitory will serve as wards. One classroom is being equipped for an operating room, another will be a dispensary, one an examination room, and still another used for storage. We hope it won't be needed long. We remember that during the First World War, before the building had yet been used as a school, Turkish soldiers had been quartered in the school. Later the British used it as a hospital and the beds they left are still being used by our teachers. We realize that history does repeat itself.

[10 July] Jerusalem has been under heavy fire all day; we have heard it and seen the smoke rising from it. The Zionists are shelling the Old City. They have captured the Lydda airport and Lydda itself is in great danger.

[12 July] Big demonstration against King Abdullah in Ramallah today. There is almost panic as there is a feeling that the war is being waged half-heartedly. The Arab armies, scattered as they are and so few in number, probably cannot hold some of the territories. The Ramallah people are afraid the Zionist forces will be here soon as they well might be if the pass at Bab-el-Wad and Latrun cannot be held. The people may be expecting too much of the Arab Legion. Surely, the soldiers of the Legion stationed around us have been wonderful in their conduct during the Truce and have given a good account of themselves all along.

[13 July] A sad day for Palestinians. Lydda and Ramleh are both in Jewish hands and people are fleeing up to the hills. They had been so sure they were safe that they had made no preparations for flight and now they are reported to be leaving everything. Half of the Red Crescent Hospital equipment is still there. Khulusy Kheiri came to the house at half-past nine tonight to borrow the school station-wagon to drive towards Lydda, as he had heard that his father was in flight and he knew that his father was not well enough to walk all the way to Ramallah. Willard said he could not lend him the car but they would go together. They returned at midnight with a story of thousands of people struggling up the rough roads to the hills, of loaded cars and trucks, of people sitting by the wayside too weary to go on. Khulusy stopped often to ask about his father, who was a well-known and highly respected citizen of Ramleh, and finally someone was able to tell him that his father was seen going to a small village off the main road. It was impossible for Willard to get to the village that night so they had returned, Khulusy relieved to know that his father would be cared for.

As they were coming back they came to a spot where a terrible accident had occurred; a truck full of refugees had collided with an Arab Legion armoured car speeding down to the plains, and people had spilled out of the truck, many receiving severe injuries. They were already bringing the injured to the hospital newly set-up in our building but hardly ready to meet such an emergency. It was midnight but I had fortunately stayed up, not knowing what we might be called on to do, and Williard said: "Better go up to the school building, they will need all the help they can get." And they did, even my amateurish help. The two Egyptian doctors were called on to a tremendous night of bandaging and operating under incredibly difficult conditions. It was a dreadful night for us all as we worked into the small hours doing what we could to assist. In the midst of it all, I stood by the bedside of a young mother with a sweet baby by her side. She would not survive, but the baby would. I will never know how these young doctors got through the night, but they did a splendid job in a building which, as a hospital, could offer only space and water. Shelling went on most of the day in Jerusalem.

[14 July] Hundreds of refugees are pouring into Ramallah. Sylvia Clark reports that there must be two hundred in the Girls'

School grounds. We have read of the hardships of refugees during war; now we know what they mean. Women lose their children, babies are born on the way, everyone is exhausted, hungry, some are ill in body, all hopeless in spirit. Ramallah is in a panic, too, as we already have large numbers of refugees, more than this small village can feed or house. Meanwhile, the hospital fills up with civilians with varying degrees of injuries.

[15 July] Truck-loads of bread are coming from Amman; Arab Legion soldiers are giving their bread rations to the refugees crowded around their mess hall, which is close to our school. I saw some of them bringing out food from the table, apparently sharing their meals. A maternity ward had to be set up today, and a boy was born at seven o'clock tonight. This "maternity ward" was part of our home when we came to Ramallah in 1922! There are other babies to be cared for and a Swiss nurse has agreed to take over. The mother of one died on the way, the mother of two had a bullet in her shoulder and is waiting to have it removed. The tragic movement of people keeps up and there seems to be no end. In their panic, the people are cursing their leaders and blaming the Arab Legion for the fall of Lydda and Ramleh. I have great faith in the Legion, myself, but they have a long line to hold and they are not only far from supplies but their supplies may be getting low. It is so hard to know what is happening not only here but in England and the USA.

[17 July] Planes over Ramallah last night dropped bombs on the edge of the village. With so many refugees living in the open, it is misery compounded. Firing kept up most of the night, Bireh people seemed to be up all night as they were close to the bombing. Another truck-load of mangled bodies was brought to the hospital this morning at seven o'clock. It was ghastly and heartbreaking. Trucks continue to pass the school laden with people who may continue across the river to go on to Lebanon and Syria. Count Bernadotte continues on his peace mission. Able as he is, he cannot possibly know the minds of the Arabs and their inability to understand why they should be the victims of a Western problem. Count Bernadotte expresses optimism; I hope he has good reason for it.

[18 July] Sunday. Panic in Ramallah today. They say the Zionists are only a few miles from Ramallah. Many refugees and some Ramallah people have gone to Transjordan and Lebanon; others sit in their homes and weep. I have tried to comfort our friends by telling them that the Legion will hold Ramallah no matter what. So help me, what do I know about such things? But someone has to think that. The walk to Meeting at the Girls' School was difficult. The road was lined with hundreds of refugees holding on to the few possessions they have left, and such pathetic possessions. There will be a terrible reckoning some day if this continues.

[19 July] Ran up to see Mrs Cadora this morning as we knew her garden was filled with refugees. I literally had to step over people to get into the house. The refugees were making breakfast on their little fires; they have used up the Cadora wood, almost emptied their cistern, and would seem to have settled down. Naameh said that the smells keep her family from rest day and night, but they cannot turn the refugees away. She thinks our Women's Club should set up a milk centre so that the babies can have something nourishing. She has asked me to take it up with the International Red Cross Delegates. Many refugees are leaving Ramallah, but they are reluctant to go to Jericho as they think it is unhealthy and, since they expect to go home soon, it is not worthwhile going so far. The hills around Jerusalem form a barrier that frightens them. Generally, there is disappointment with the Arab League on which they had built their hopes, and thoughtful ones suffer most. The Truce was broken in Jerusalem again.

[21 July] Today, Dr Ovid Sellers, Dean of McCormick Theological Seminary, presently in Jerusalem as Director of the American School of Oriental Research, Walter C. Klein, American Representative on the Staff of the Anglican Bishop of Jerusalem; and John D. Whiting, Secretary and Treasurer of the American Colony, Jerusalem, called to ask Willard to join them in a petition to the Federal Council of Churches in America for relief for the displaced Arabs. Willard, who had been pacing the floor thinking he ought to try to get to America to tell both Jews and Gentiles what was happening, was glad to do so. The telegram they sent read as follows:

"We regard it as our inescapable duty to place before our fellow Christians in the United States the appalling facts of the Palestine Arab Refugee Problem during the last six months; virtually half of the non-combatant Arabs of Palestine have become displaced persons, houses wrecked beyond repair and whole communities reduced to destitution. It is estimated that 200,000 Palestinian Arabs who have taken refuge in the adjacent

Arab countries are penniless. These countries have met the demands of their guests generously and resourcefully, only to find that their own slender resources are approaching exhaustion. Still more obvious is the lot of the 200,000 or more refugees who have remained within the borders of Palestine. If the Truce ends in a final peace, they will go home to bare fields, looted houses, and a shattered economy. If the Truce ends in a renewal of war, their miseries will be multiplied. Whatever happens, they now possess nothing but the clothes they stand up in and a courage that will respond eagerly to any promise of a return to normal life. This drifting multitude, close to half a million in number, is in desperate need of organized help. An International Agency, suitably equipped and liberally supported, must take charge at once. Can the Federal Council take immediate steps to spread the knowledge of this need and to promise the required aid?"

A second telegram was sent to the World Council of Churches Meeting in Geneva, as these four men were not content to ask for relief only. It was sent in August with additional signatories and was as follows:

"VISSER T'HOOFT WORLD COUNCIL MEETING
AMSTERDAM NETHERLANDS.

Following clergymen and laymen in Palestine belonging to Churches participating in World Council importune Council to examine Palestine Problem in light of principles of Christian justice with the view to recommend rectification of obvious wrongs. Total missionary enterprise imperilled by widely prevailing view that Christian World has not made impartial study of question.

JONES	FRIENDS
KLEIN	PROTESTANT EPISCOPAL CHURCH—USA
MACINNES	CHURCH OF ENGLAND
MOLL	LUTHERAN
SELLERS	PRESBYTERIAN."

Other visitors today were Mr Daoud el Issa of the Palestine Press and Dr Dajani. They are eager to get back to Jaffa and had come to see the International Red Cross about arranging for their return. Hundreds are eager to return, to get back to their places of business and farms, but the IRC cannot help them much, if at all. In the course of the day, the IRC was notified of another 10,000 women and children who are refugees. In addition to being a hospital and headquarters for the International Red Cross,

Refugee Boys' School, Ramallah, 1949

Refugee School in Ramallah, 1949: In the playground

Friends' Boys' School, Ramallah: Graduating Class, 1951

*Friends' Boys' School, Ramallah:
Prefects and the Headmaster, 1953*

Refugee Boys' School, Meeting House, Ramallah, 1949

Refugee School in Ramallah, 1949
"Please, sir . . ."

Sergeant Tel and his orphan boy, with the author: 1948

Beit Surik: a frontier village after the fighting, 1948
The Mayor and Mr Willard Jones

we have now to set up an office for the American Consul, who
will come across the lines in Jerusalem one day a week to care
for Arab Americans and students who have been accepted into
American colleges, and others. Crowds are waiting for him when
he arrives. We too are cut off from our consulate except for this
one day.

[31 July] Such a day! While I was in the midst of Saturday baking,
Willard called me to the office. There I found Sergeant Tel,
brother of Abdullah Tel who is commanding the Arab forces in
Jerusalem, holding in his arms a pathetic bit of humanity, a boy
probably fifteen months old. He had been found by the side of
his dead mother, starving and nearly dead himself. She had fled
from her home in Ramleh or Lydda and not been able to make
it to the hills. The hospital simply could not take him and advised
trying to get a woman in the village to care for him. The truth
was that they thought he could not live and they can hardly care
for people who have a chance of survival. I called the doctor and
asked what chance there was for the child. He lifted his shoulders
and said, "*Sowa sowa*—fifty-fifty." If there is a chance, we must
do something, so I called a neighbour who is a trained nurse and
asked her if she would help me if I took the child into our home.
She was more than willing.

For the next five days and nights we worked to bring that starved
little body back to life, Willard helping with night duty, and we
were rewarded one morning when I went with his barley water.
I had taken a piece of bread with me at times to see if he would
eat, but he paid no attention to it; he craved liquids. This morning,
however, he sat up and with a firm hand pointed to the bread.
That was when he began to take an interest in life, also. His cot
faced a large mirror over a dressing-table and I found him again
and again playing with the little boy in the mirror with great
delight. He must have been fundamentally sturdy, for he came back
to health quickly once he had recovered from a severe dysentery
caused by hunger. The day came when Sergeant Tel arrived to take
him to his home, as he had promised, and together we rode into
Jerusalem where a nurse was waiting to take the boy across the
River Jordan to his home in Irbid. I asked Mohammad Tel if his
wife knew he was taking a boy to her and he smiled and said, "No,
but she will be happy." Mohammad felt that Allah had led him to
the child and he was responsible. We finally had three babies
brought to us under similar conditions, in each case an Arab Legion
soldier carrying the child a long way and later taking the child to

his home. One of the soldiers who had no children was sure Allah had given him this child, and I have rarely seen a happier man than he was when he came to take the bright-eyed, six-month-old baby to his wife, who had longed for a child through several years of marriage. As long as we lived at the school, Muklis, for that was the name our friend had given the boy, was brought to us at Christmas, and we always had a gift for him under the tree. He was a beautiful child and apparently a great joy to his new parents.

[9 August] Took one of our babies to the American Colony Baby Home today and hope he will be happy there. It was not easy to give him up, but it may be some time before his foster father can take him, and the hospital is well-staffed to care for children. We have several requests from people, both Arab and Western, who want to adopt children, but there are surprisingly few available for adoption as Arab families consider any child born into the big family a family responsibility, so that even if a parent or parents die, the child is not without family. I went on into the Old City after leaving the baby and, as usual these days, saw a man being taken on a stretcher to the Austrian Hospice, which has been turned into a hospital. There may be a truce, but it is a "shooting" one. (Commander Hutchison, writing a book years later, called his book *Violent Truce*.)

[16 August] Woke to the sound of heavy bombardment in Jeru-salem. It began at half-past three this morning but we do not know who started it. Boys and parents are coming to ask about school in the fall. The hospital is still in our main building and the Board at home say they cannot help us financially so we hardly know what to do. The Board have even suggested that we take a furlough and just not open for the present. I feel sure that if they really knew what is happening they would not urge such a drastic step. Parents are wanting their sons and daughters in school and they will pay all they can towards school fees. Unfortunately, for most of them, their money is frozen in banks on the other side of the Truce line. If we could freeze the boys until bank accounts are unfrozen, it would be a solution, but since we cannot we have decided to open and hope for the best. We have a precious fund, a small one, in the safe, and we will start with that. As the Arabs say, it is on our heads now.

[26 August] John and Grace Whiting, from the American Colony, have been with us for some days. John suffers from acute asthma and needed to get away from the constant firing going on around the Colony. We took them back to Jerusalem in the afternoon. As we stepped out of the car, mortars began to fall around us followed by firing. How casual we are getting about this sort of thing! One man was being treated at the American Colony First-Aid station. He had been wounded on six different occasions and cheerfully talked about it, and is ready to go back as soon as he is well. "A man must defend his home," he said.

[28 August] We have announced on the air that schools will open as usual at the end of September. General approval all around; and we are glad the decision has been made public. Willard feels that we must try to create an atmosphere of hope and normalcy as much as possible, and it gives parents hope to have something done for their children. The power-plant in Jerusalem was blown up today. We don't know by whom, but it dashes any hope of electricity in the near future. A more personal catastrophe: Tiger, the dog, ate our Sunday roast while I was upstairs this afternoon, an expensive lesson for me!

[2 September] A committee of responsible former government officials, working voluntarily, decided that a census was needed if a relief programme must be set-up. They achieved it by ordering a curfew between twelve noon and six o'clock in the evening, a most efficient method and a wise thing to do. Relief is coming to us and we welcome this action. We are told that the street sweepers in the Old City continue to do their work although they do not know who will pay them. The Old City is kept clean and sanitary.

[9 September] Had my first flight in a plane today, through the kind offices of Colonel Goldie of the Arab Legion, and I was thrilled that it could be over the Jordan Valley to Amman. It took less than half-an-hour. One cannot realize how twisting and winding the River Jordan is until one sees it from the air. It is just as though someone had let loose a spool of ribbon and let it fall where it would. Flying in a small plane was like sitting on the back of a bird, having a bird's-eye view of the world.

[17 September] The country is in a state of shock at the newest outrage by the Stern Gang. Count Bernadotte was assassinated this afternoon in front of the YMCA building in the occupied zone in Jerusalem. He had arrived at the Kalendia airport this morning and been out to Ramallah to see the Second-in-Command of the Arab Legion, Colonel Lash, Lash Bey, as we call him, and

the cars passed the school as they were on their way to Jerusalem for dinner. As his entourage was leaving the YMCA, a jeep
blocked the road, making the three cars stop. Then, according
to report, one of four men from the jeep went to the car Count
Bernadotte was in and fired point-blank at him and at the French
Colonel Serot who sat beside him, killing him also. Two others
from the jeep fired at the wheels and radiators of the other cars
and fled. Interestingly enough, a few days ago a Swiss Red Cross
Delegate showed me a picture he had taken in Tel Aviv. It was
of a large poster which showed Count Bernadotte being kicked
out of Israel. An enormous boot filled most of the poster and
Count Bernadotte was at the toe of the boot. He is not the first
victim of Jewish terrorists and may not be the last, I am afraid.
Count Bernadotte was an official representative of the United
Nations and was here on an errand of peace. The loss of a great
and good man at this time especially is a sad blow to us all and
the country grieves. One wonders what the repercussions will be
in the United Nations.

[18 September] Since the Stern Gang are boasting of yesterday's
deed, carried out "according to plan", it is clear where responsibility lies. They even published the following statement in the
Press:

"Although in our opinion all United Nations observers are
members of foreign occupation forces, which have no right to
be on our territory, the murder of the French Colonel Serot
was due to a fatal mistake: our men thought that the officer
sitting beside Count Bernadotte was the British agent and anti-
Semite, General Lundstrom."

General Lundstrom happened to be Swedish, as his name indicates, and Count Bernadotte's Chief of Staff. We have learned
that Count Bernadotte knew of threats against his life but had
said: "We cannot allow ourselves to be frightened out of doing
our work." There is genuine sorrow everywhere, as Bernadotte
was considered one of our finest Christian statesmen and, of
course, anger that the UN should be treated with such contempt.
Apparently the report which Count Bernadotte was ready to
present to the United Nations had leaked out and was not
acceptable to the Zionists.

[20 September] A walk to Beitin (Bethel) was good for us after the
sad events of the past two days. It was a lovely trip; all the
people came out to welcome us and offer us grapes and figs and

to invite us to have coffee with them. There are seven hundred refugees in this small village and the people of the village share what they have with them. We enjoyed the hospitality of these simple people—simple in only the best sense. On the wall of one home there was the framed diploma earned by a son of the family at Oxford University in England and a picture of the young man, rather handsome in his cap and gown. I love to get into the villages, to enjoy the friendliness of the people, drink their coffee or mint tea, see them on the threshing-floor in season, and smell the ovens.

[25 September] Many, many callers today: newspaper men, UNO men, International Red Cross personnel, and parents and boys wanting to be sure we are opening school. I am afraid we will not be able to cope with boarders with the hospital still here and needed sorely. We had been too optimistic about the fighting being over by now and the refugees back in their homes. That is what we thought usually happens when there is fighting: when the fighting is over, people go back to pick up the pieces. How naive we must be, for the Zionists now have more territory than the Partition Plan gave them, and the promise of the Balfour Declaration that "nothing will be done to prejudice the civil and religious rights of the existing non-Jewish communities" (which we remember made up ninety per cent of the country in 1917) has gone with the wind. One interesting visitor was Commander Cox from North Carolina, who was in the car with Count Bernadotte when he was shot. He brought with him three UNO Truce Observers. One of the men said that his car had been shot at so many times on his way to Tel Aviv that he had turned back and was pursued by shots until he reached the monastery gates at Latrun.

[28 September] We managed to clear space enough to care for thirty-one boarders, when we thought we could take only six senior boys at the most. Two boys, with parental permission, have camp-beds on the stair landings in our building. More boarders want to come but we have reached the limit. We continue to hear explosions in Jerusalem. I hope they won't destroy the walls. It is almost an anachronism that the walls Suleiman built over still earlier foundations four centuries ago are helping the Arab armies to defend the Old City and parts of Jerusalem. We have walked on the walls in a happier day and peered through the slots made for bows and arrows. It is something more deadly that is shot from the walls today. Progress!

[1 October] Our first chapel today. And how good it is to have school going again! The boys make a good showing and we don't seem to mind if the balcony is boarded up to make room for International Red Cross supplies, and one corner of the main part of the auditorium has been made into a classroom. Recreation hour after supper will be in our living-room each evening and we will enjoy it with the boys. I have a good collection of games, jig-saw puzzles, old records, even a Caruso one, and a piano. So we will manage. Since we have no electricity, we use Lux lamps and the boys take care of them. After all, we tell them that great civilizations have grown up, great discoveries have been made in science, great books have been written and great pictures have been painted without electricity, so we can get along, too.

[6 October] We were invited to a band-concert tonight at the Arab Legion Headquarters in Beitunia. There were a number of Americans there; but some need to learn better how to handle "refreshments". We had lemon squash, thoughtfully provided for us. It is surprising and amusing at times to learn what our reputation is. Willard was quite distressed at the time of the bombing to find that the army was setting up anti-aircraft guns in a residential area. He went to headquarters and suggested that they put them down the road where there were no homes, for example. The colonel in charge looked up and smiled: "But, Mr Jones, you are a Quaker; what do you know about war?"

[12 October] Another crisis day at the school in which we were not supposed to be personally involved. The Egyptian Red Crescent Society sent up two thousand blankets to be distributed at the Feast al-Adha, the Prophet's birthday. (The Prophet's birthday corresponds to our Christmas, only it comes on a different date each year as the Muslim month is a lunar one.) Last night we had the first big rain of the season, accompanied with strong winds and cold. The two young doctors stole silently out in the night to go about the village to find the "most needy". They had prepared cards to give to them so that they could come in the morning to get blankets. They must have had a hard night. The plan was for the refugees to come to the front entrance of the building, present their cards, get the blanket and go out the back way. When I set out for class, there seemed to be thousands of refugees in the grounds. We had not been warned about the distribution and the doctors had not reckoned with the fact that there were thousands of "most needy" and that word spreads quickly. I had to struggle through the crowd, people pulling at my coat begging me to intercede, and it was with great relief that I reached my class, shaken and exhausted. It was with difficulty that I got back to Grant Hall after classes. There was no question but that all who came needed blankets, as Ramallah can be bitterly cold when the rains come. The other day in a meeting in Jerusalem, Bishop Stewart called the present fighting genocide, and today we realize how right he was. If the Palestinians were not essentially a healthy people, they could not survive. Most of the refugees could go home in no time at all, in fact they look toward their homes daily, longingly. When the lights go on in Jaffa, they look down with tear-filled eyes. One bus-driver who goes between Ramallah and Beir Zeit stops at a certain point on the road for the passengers to get out for a few moments to look down on their old homes on the plains and the sea-coast.

I shall always remember one woman as she stood under the fig tree at the door of our house with her sick baby in her arms on a warm August morning. Tall, dark-eyed, olive-skinned, dressed in the long flowing dress of her village on the plains, a light shawl covering her coined headdress and falling across her shoulders, she might have been the Madonna of the Fig Tree. But in her eyes were sorrow, bewilderment, shame at having to be seen begging and a kind of anger, not at anyone, but because of her great need. I gave her the usual bottle of milk I had prepared according to the Red Cross nurse's directions, and a small bag of lentils for the six children she had left sleeping under a tree above the village. She accepted them with the quiet dignity so natural to the village women of Palestine and a "thank you, lady, may your house be blessed." Suddenly her calm broke and she wept: "I have in my house in Ramleh plenty of lentils, and rice, olives, and oil for all my family. Now, we have nothing. What shall we do until we go back? And will there be food in the house when we go home? But never mind food; we only want to go back."

[16 October] The tide of battle shifts to the Negeb, an area greatly desired by the Zionists because it would give them a port on the Red Sea and so enable them to have access to both East and West (they have cut the Palestinians off from the Mediterranean) without using the Suez Canal. It would also cut the Asian countries off from Africa, and Palestine would no longer play her historic role as a bridge. In addition, it would not only give the Zionists a military advantage but would strengthen Israel's economy. Also a three-hour battle in Jerusalem today. People are getting almost apathetic as we are cut off from news and there is a feeling that we are not getting anywhere. Fortunately, the weather is warming up after the first rain, so that refugees will have a little respite. My supply of powdered milk is almost gone; I have enough for a few days only. I dread telling the mothers that I cannot continue.

[19 October] Reports of fighting in the Gaza Strip, and we fear that it will be the next area to go. One almost despairs of any settlement soon. But we are glad Jerusalem isn't entirely gone.

[20 October] Was surprised to have a call from Elias, the hairdresser, today. He was prepared to give me a Zotos permanent (probably thought I must be needing one) which does not require electricity. I wasn't sure I could afford such luxury, but I could not refuse as he had walked to Jerusalem from Bethlehem over the long road and he had been four hours on the way. Obviously he needs the money as he has a big family. We hear that the UN has ordered a cease-fire in the Gaza Strip. The Jews would like to control that area. Back in the Thirties, there was talk of oil and uranium to be found not far from Gaza, but explorations were unaccountably blocked at that time in London.

[21 October] Now the news is that Bethlehem is in danger, that the Egyptians are not able to hold it and that the Arab Legion is going to their help. One wonders how long the UN is going to stand by and see the country absorbed into a Jewish state. A Jewish state in world politics could be a problem, since there are Jews in so many countries with influence in government and the press. Europeans coming through think all decisions are being made in Washington. An International Red Cross delegate told me of an incident at the point where he was an observer. The Zionists had crossed the Truce lines and the Arabs had objected. Truce observers and reporters all rushed to the scene. There was a good deal of argument and finally word came that the Zionists could remain where they were but must not infringe further. An American reporter turned to a European one, amazed at the decision, and asked, "What's the story?" The gruff answer was: "Call your White House."

[23 October] There are rumours that the Arab-Jewish question is entering its last phase. All are tired and want it settled. Meanwhile, Arab Palestine has had a terrible set-back economically and in every other way. We have lost most of our professional class to the rest of the Middle East already. Palestinians do not want to leave, but there is nothing for them here and the needs of their families are great.

[25 October] A *sharkiyeh* (sirocco) has been blowing hard all day; we hope the rain that usually follows at this time of year will not come too soon. Strange to be hoping the rain will not come when we are usually praying for it; but we have not had thousands of refugees to think about before. However, the refugees will not complain, as the weather is in the hands of Allah and He knows what is best. Report tonight is that Beersheba is in Jewish hands.

Mr Irani came from Bethlehem today. He fears that Beit Jala, which adjoins Bethlehem, has suffered from shelling but thinks Bethlehem is safe. He says that a small group of Christians in Transjordan are trying to have the Old Testament removed from the Bible, and think the Quran and the New Testament are closer in religious thought. Surely the Old Testament is badly taught, and the present conflict seems to revive some of the battles recorded there. Christians are sensitive these days as they see what the Christian West has brought on them. A dreadful rumour tonight is that the USA may send in troops to end the fighting in Jerusalem! The Palestine Problem is to come before the UNO this month; we hope the events of the past year will have taught them something. If they observe the terms of the Charter, they cannot allow the Zionists to keep all they have taken by aggression beyond the Partition Plan of last year. There is increasing talk of the UN creating an international zone around Jerusalem. If that happens, Ramallah would like to be included. There is continued fear that Russian intervention is inevitable if matters are not settled soon.

[13 November] Rain began in the night and we have hundreds of refugees under the trees in this whole district who refuse to go to Jericho. The YMCA has a tremendous problem trying to carry on in a tent. Willard brought a copy of *Time* for 8 November 1948 from Amman today. In it there is an item in regard to Truman's insistence on handling Palestine as if it were above and beyond regular international matters. He seems to have taken it out of the hands of the State Department, or certainly does not listen to its advice, and one would think the people of Palestine do not need to be considered. Most of the UNO representatives here are irate, to put it mildly. One remembers Lord Balfour's reply twenty years ago when asked if the people of Palestine should not be consulted: "We have no intention of consulting the 700,000 people in Palestine *. . .*"

[14 November] This rain is cruel for people in tents and under trees. The fragile shelters they have been able to put up around them, branches of trees stuck in the ground to support gunny sacks and tar-paper, are poor shelters against the wind. Willard is getting anxious about the hundreds of children around us who have no schools or activities of any kind. He hopes some relief money can be set aside for schools even if they are temporary. Well-trained teachers are available and will work for very little or nothing at all, as they see the problem too, and they also want to be doing something. One wishes the farmers could get to their fields to sow their grain in the proper season. With the rain, they look at their fields wistfully, so near to them, knowing that ploughing should begin. In Jericho there are one thousand tents for sixteen thousand people. Warm as Jericho is, they need shelter at night and some privacy.

[21 November] My morning at the milk centre: 304 mothers came with their babies to get a cupful of warm milk. If they come through all this rain and stand about waiting in the cold to get only one small cupful, they must need a great deal more. A few sent little brothers or sisters to get the milk, which they take away in containers they have brought; battered kettles and pans, old coffee pots, whisky and beer bottles (left by the British soldiers) with the labels still on them, tin cans of all shapes and sizes, clean and otherwise. The International Red Cross gives the powdered milk and the Club has managed to get utensils and primus stoves. I wish some of the VIPs seated comfortably in New York could see what their ill-considered and uninformed decisions have brought about.

[28 November] Five hundred mothers came today to the milk centre through mud and rain. In bulk it is a good deal of milk we prepare; individually, it is too, too little. The Club members take turns each day and are most faithful. I have to go on Sundays as I have classes other mornings, but I wish I could help oftener.   •

[29 November] Another of the dates Palestinians cannot forget. It is the anniversary of the UN Partition Resolution. I hope they are having sober thoughts about it today in the UN, if they think at all. An American representing the American Red Cross was in today. He is not encouraging about the future of Palestine. He says the need for aid, as far as health and relief are concerned, is all on this side. He says the Jews do nothing for the Palestinians on their side as they regard health and relief as the responsibility of the military. Meanwhile, Willard is trying to get schools started for the refugee children and the Refugee Committee is trying to get funds.

[8 December] Went to Bethlehem today with M. Courvoisier, of the International Red Cross, through Abu Dis and over the new road. It is not an easy road as it goes up and down and around in endless fashion. Just when we think we have left Jerusalem behind us, we take a turn and there it is again. The direct road was so simple and did not burn up precious petrol as this one does, but it is closed to us now. Saw many refugees along the way living in caves, others are in tents. Christmas in Bethlehem this year is rather a mockery, with evidences of the military all about. Saw some old friends for the first time in months.

[25 December] Callers began coming at nine o'clock this morning and continued all day. They included Omar Pasha, a kindly gentleman who has been appointed over this area, and his chief magistrate, and the Vice-Mayor of Ramallah. But fighting continues in the southern part of Palestine. There are rumours that there is to be a meeting in Ramallah tomorrow of representatives of all the villages in the district to petition King Abdullah to annex this part of Palestine to Transjordan. Of course, there may be some opposition, but the majority feel that we need a stable government and union with Transjordan would provide that. We have been touched by all the expressions of friendship that have come with the Christmas season. Last year it took courage to show friendliness to Americans, although many did. This year seemed like old times.

Before ending the story of events in Palestine during 1948, we should mention the damage done to the famous mosque, the Dome of the Rock, during the long months of fighting in Jerusalem. This Noble Sanctuary, as it is called in Arabic, is the religious centre of the Muslims of the Middle East and second only to Mecca in the Muslim World. Completed in AD 691, it has been a place of prayer ever since, and is considered one of the most beautiful buildings in the world.

Professor Hayter Lewis, who wrote *The Holy Places of Jerusalem*, says of it: "There is no doubt that the mosque is one of the most beautiful buildings in the world. It may also be added that it is one of the most beautiful recorded in history." In an *Essay on the Ancient Topography of Jerusalem* by James Ferguson, we find the following appreciation:

> "The Mosque of the Rock is extraordinarily beautiful. I have visited many places and beautiful buildings of India, Europe, and other parts of the world, and as far as I can remember, I have not seen as magnificent a building as the Dome of the Rock. The symmetry and the gorgeous blending of colours I have not seen in any other building."

It is sad to say that this beautiful sanctuary did not escape serious damage. The Al-Aqsa Mosque, also a building of great beauty and reverence, is in the same area as the Dome of the Rock, and both buildings were exposed to firing from the Jewish-held area of Jerusalem. According to government records, bombs fell on no less than thirteen occasions, the largest number falling on 16 July, the day a truce was announced but before it went into effect. On that day sixty mortar-bombs fell in the area, only one of which hit the building, but it did much damage to the wooden ceiling. On 16 August, a bomb destroyed a part of the north-west wall of Al-Aqsa Mosque, killed three people, and wounded a man and a girl while they were at prayer. On the evening of the same day, twenty six-inch mortars fell and damaged the western part of the Mosque. The roof was again hit six days later. Further damage was inflicted on the Dome of the Rock on 23 September, when the area was again heavily bombed. A large number of the lovely windows were broken, thirteen of them almost beyond repair. One man was killed while at prayer. The last attack on the building was on 10 October, destroying part of the north-west side and steps leading to the high elevation on which the Mosque stands. (Attempts to repair the roof in December, in the Truce period, failed because bombs directed from the nearby Dormitio Church, held by the Jewish army, prevented men from working.) We can only hope that this building can be restored and saved for future generations, both for its sacred associations and its great beauty.

[31 December] Hard to realize on this last day of 1948 that all we have been through, and all that has happened to the people of this country, can be real. We wish we could wake up to find it has been a nightmare and that the world is normal after all.

It has been a lovely day. We have had many callers, British, American, Old Boys of the school, and the older boys of the school in for games after supper. Willard and I ended a second game of anagrams as the clock struck twelve. An anti-climax to the strains and stresses of the past twelve months! Nothing should be too difficult from now on.

Arab Exodus

The first United States Ambassador to Israel, James G. McDonald, in his book, *Mission to Israel*, tells of a conversation he had with the first President of Israel, Dr Weizmann, in the course of which Dr Weizmann referred to the flight of the Arabs as, "This miraculous simplification of Israel's tasks." If the use of violence and terrorism against an unprotected people and creating panic constitutes a miracle, then he was right. The massacre of 250 men, women and children at Deir Yasin, 9 April 1948, perpetrated while the Mandate Government was still in Palestine, was the occasion that created panic, as other villages realized that they had no government protection.

Those of us who were living in Palestine at the time are often asked why the refugees fled, for the Zionists claim that they did not need to go. We can only say that we were there and those we saw had not come away from their homes after thinking it over. The record is all too clear; most of them fled, and fled in panic to the nearest haven possible.

There was insecurity in the country before the partition decision in the UN on 29 November 1947, but in the months following partition and until the Mandate ended, there was chaos. The government lost control of the situation and public security was gone. Even before Christmas, as I said before, more than one thousand casualties were reported in clashes between Jews and Arabs.

Before the British left, the best residential Arab sections of Jerusalem were brought under Zionist control by terrorism, and more than 50,000 Arabs there had already fled to Lebanon, Syria and Egypt. Others came to Ramallah, and some to properties in the Old City which had been in their families for centuries. They were not far from their homes in any of these places and they left them furnished, fully expecting to get back in a short time. Civilians are not usually expected to remain on the firing line and they certainly were in that situation. The railway station, electric plant, post-office, government buildings and other facilities were no longer available or safe for Arabs. Jerusalem was actually a zoned city almost a year before the British left.

Jaffa, an Arab city of close to 100,000 people and the most ancient seaport of Palestine, long a link between the East and the West, was under such constant attack for months that by 2 May 1948, only about 2,000 Arabs remained. Some fled to Gaza, others came to Ramallah, many used their small fishing and rowing boats to sail up the coast to Beirut, taking almost nothing with them, and squatted on the sands to wait for the fighting to cease so that they could go back to repossess their lands and rebuild their lives.

Near the end of April the Arabs and Israelis were fighting in Haifa, one of the most important Mediterranean seaports, the Arabs battling against heavy odds. Having understood that British troops would remain in Haifa until the complete evacuation of the British within three months after 15 May, they were not prepared for this sudden departure on 15 May, nor for a heavy Israeli attack. On the afternoon of 23 April 1948, after two days of bitter fighting, the British officers in charge arranged what was supposed to be an armistice but was in reality a capitulation. Many of our Arab friends told how they left food cooking in their ovens, housewives had no time to change their dresses, men left their shops in the general panic and sought refuge over the borders in Syria and Lebanon.

To the south, around Gaza, intimidation by terrorism between January and May increased in intensity, settling into small-scale raids and guerrilla warfare during the first part of May. Atrocities and reprisals were carried out by both sides. Villages were attacked, wells and schools damaged, and in some cases completely destroyed by bombs. Roads were mined, endangering the lives of women and children fleeing from attack. Practically every Jewish colony was a military outpost, well-manned, but Arab villages were, for the most part, completely unprotected. The city of Gaza organized medical facilities for thousands pouring into it from Haifa, Jaffa, Majdal, Jerusalem and Beersheba. By 15 May 1948, there were thousands of refugees in the Gaza Strip, and by the end of July they numbered more than 200,000.

When the Mandate Government left Palestine, there were already more than 500,000 Arab refugees, and when the State of Israel was announced one minute after midnight on 15 May 1948, the Jewish Agency, which had been virtually a government within a government for years, was ready with all the necessary offices and a large well-equipped army to take over the new State.

On the other hand, the Arab population was left with no government at all, as they had been dependent entirely on the Mandate administration. That anarchy did not prevail is a great tribute to the Arab population. True, a war was going on, but among the people there remained respect for the concepts of law to which they were accustomed. Former government officials took hold in a voluntary capacity and helped in countless ways to maintain certain government functions and to get services going under incredibly difficult conditions.

Between May and the middle of July, despite one truce of nearly a month, there was much bitter fighting as the Arabs struggled to hold what was left of their country, and the Israelis to establish themselves by force in areas beyond the UN Partition lines.

By July, the truce of 11 June had broken down and Palestine was a scene of sheer tragedy. While Jerusalem was being fought over and the Old City was being defended by the Arab Legion from the walls built by Suleiman the Magnificent in the sixteenth century, the refugee population was growing. When Ramleh and Lydda fell on 12 July, 70,000 people poured into Ramallah overnight.

The Arabs finally formed a small force of irregulars poorly equipped and inadequately trained. In the last days of the Mandate, when the fate of Jerusalem as a whole was uncertain, soldiers from the Arab Legion, and some Bedouin, came to help protect the city and also to help at Bab-el-Wad. British soldiers on their way out, possibly sympathetic to the Arabs, were often willing to be "attacked" and have their guns "stolen" for a price, but that provided only a small store of weapons. Hand-grenades found their way into the markets, but they were of more danger to the civilian population than to the terrorists. As for the guns, the young irregulars hardly knew how to use them. My husband got so troubled over the number of accidents that he thought someone ought to teach the young patriots how to use them, not so much against an enemy as for their own protection.

But the real heartache was to see the breakdown of the government which had come with such hope, and which might have crowned its colonial empire with an honoured administration in a land so hallowed. Now it was defied and humiliated, forced to leave Palestine under such conditions.

By the end of the second truce in July, Ramallah, Nablus and Jericho on the West Bank of the river, and Amman, Zerka and Irbid on the East Bank had become cities of refuge, and many villages became hosts for the homeless. Refugees found shelter in caves in the hills between Jerusalem and Bethlehem and in other parts of the country.

In Amman, we found them in the old Roman amphitheatre. However, we all thought that this was temporary; there seemed no other thought than that the refugees would go home soon, so they could stand makeshift homes in the summer months. Perhaps it was just as well at that time that neither they nor we fully realized that they were never intended to go back. They were to be part of the enormous price of Israel, and already their homes were either destroyed or being made ready for aliens from other lands; their dispersion was a "miraculous simplification" for Zionist ambitions, and they were the human sacrifice of Christian atonement for what had happened in Europe.

In the early days of the Zionists, their appeal was that Palestine was a country without people and they were a people without a country. Now their call was, "We have a country, but we must also have people." There were approximately 600,000 Jews in Palestine in May 1948, and they had displaced more than that number of the indigenous population to make room for "their people". How they expected to set up an apartheid state in an area of Arab states, and carry on business and cultural relations where the language of 100,000,000 people was Arabic, one finds it hard to see. Nor was their introduction a happy one. They had forced their way into the Arab World in an atmosphere of hostility, claiming historic rights based on an ancient residence, and were now trying to force the people who had maintained the country for centuries to recognize this claim and to allow them to become dominant. As they had done in ancient days, they rejected the wise counsel of their modern prophets, men like Judah Magnes, and turned to violence rather than to the best in their traditions.

Ramallah stands high on the hills around Jerusalem and is exposed to all the winds that blow. The west wind is the prevailing one in Palestine, bringing fresh breezes and dew in summer and rain in winter. Winter winds blow hard and are cold and penetrating. The winters of 1948, 1949 and 1950 were among the most severe we ever had; they were not "tempered to the shorn lambs". As one lived in Palestine, one began to learn that there was a cyclic pattern to the weather, years of drought followed by winters of long, windy, rainy days when "the storms descended and the floods came", days that tried our souls as we taught in unheated classrooms and lived in unheated houses. The Arab farmer understood this cycle and had long since learned to adapt his plantings to it.

We were in the rainy cycle when the refugees came. Fleeing as they did from homes on the warm coastal plains in the heat of the summer, and expecting to return to their homes when the fighting stopped, they had only light clothing with them. However, even in summer Ramallah is cool at night, and sweaters and warm bedding are needed when the evening dews sweep over us. Now that winter had come, the need for clothing and bedding was desperate, especially during that first winter when we had almost nothing to give. Thousands reluctantly fled to Jericho when the rains began, but many remained in Ramallah for they thought that they would be allowed to go home any day.

[1950: 2 January] A cold rainy day. I was cold even with woollen sweater and lined shoes as I moved about from one cold room to another doing household tasks. About mid-morning I heard a knock at the door, and when I answered it there stood a refugee from Lydda whom we knew. He had his little daughter, Leila, with him. He had no coat, his tattered shoes were wet, and he was rubbing his hands to try to get some warmth into them. Lovely little bright-eyed Leila had no coat either, not even a sweater, and she shivered in her thin cotton dress and her worn-out, ill-fitting shoes. They had come from the plains, where Abu Ahmad, for that was his name, was certainly not rich but had been able to provide for his family, as he had worked for the government. I asked them to step inside, but what could I give them? I did not even have a warm fire for them to sit by. Interestingly enough, most of us, Arabs and Americans, in Ramallah had sent clothing to Germany after the war and, because of high prices, had not replaced them. Now the need had come to our very door.

"Abu Ahmad, why don't you go down to Jericho where it will be warm and sunny, where you will be able to get oranges, lemons and bananas cheaply and the hot sun will do you good?"

"I know, *Ya Sitt*," he replied, "Jericho has all this, but the papers say that we will go home in ten days and here we are near home. Jericho is far."

True, he could look down on the plains from Ramallah to the coast and the shining Mediterranean. Lydda was in the heart of the plains and everything he owned and had worked for was there, too. Fruits and vegetables grew there in abundance. Better to suffer a few days more than be so far away in Jericho when the news came to return. As I saw the eagerness in his eyes, heard it in his voice, I was silent. To the people of the coast, Jericho was not a healthy place, 4,000 feet below Ramallah, 1,100

below sea level, and it did not get the winds and the breezes from
the Great Sea which they loved.

All I could give at the moment was some of my husband's
woollen socks which I decided he could spare, and I had a part-
wool undervest. By shortening the straps of the vest, I was able
to put it on Leila. It covered her thin little body almost down to
her knees and I got some comfort from the fact that it hugged her
tummy and covered her little bottom. If they would come back
in a day or so, I might have something better. But my distress
was so great that before I knew it Abu Ahmad was comforting
me, telling me not to worry, that Allah would send help. "Maybe
we have been doing wrong, but He will forgive us and take care
of us." How often we were to hear that in the years following!

So they left with smiles and blessings on me. For a few
moments, for the second time in a few months, I was shaken as
anger and rebellion swept over me that such things could be,
that so much cruelty and suffering had come to this lovely little
country because of "man's inhumanity to man", because of
blundering and ignorance where wisdom should have been found,
in the halls of an organization established to bring in a world
where peace and justice would rule, and in the halls of governments supposed to be dedicated to freedom.

[1950: 5 February] Sunday. Snow fell all night and by five o'clock
this evening we had six and a half inches. Word came of great
hardship in the refugee camp in Jalazone, not far from Ramallah,
so Willard and M. Porchet, an International Red Cross delegate,
tried to reach it with relief. They went in the school station-
wagon but it was impossible for them to reach the camp as six
cars had stalled on the snow-covered road and were piled up
blocking the way. There were no facilities available for removing
the cars and no way around. Later, Willard went down to the
Girls' School to see how they were getting on and found Mildred
White, the principal, in bed with a severe cold. While he was
gone, a mob of men, women and children came into the school
grounds. They were from the Amary Refugee Camp, about half
a mile from the school. This camp had been set up in what had
been a flourishing vineyard but was now a sea of mud and
battered tents. They had come to the IRC, which was housed
in our school, for help, and naturally they thought the school
was responsible too. I managed to get in touch with M. Porchet,
who had been out with Willard earlier in the day although he
was recovering from a serious illness and should not have risked

the cold. I am afraid he came reluctantly as he knew there was little he could do for this large group of refugees. All he could do was to tell them to return to their tents and that he would do his best to get help tomorrow. But their tents were falling down on top of them from the weight of the snow. M. Porchet also thought that some people were trying to make trouble for the IRC, which was responsible to the UN for relief to our area. It could have been so, but these people were desperate. It was fortunate that the matter was not in my hands, for I would have been tempted to strip the school and open the doors of the auditorium and let them all in. At a critical moment, one of our Old Boys, Ali Mansur, may his tribe increase, came to the school. He had heard of the situation and said women and children could be sheltered in a new house in Bireh and the men could go to the mosque and the coffee-houses for the night. Another crisis was temporarily over.

[6 February] Monday. Fifteen inches of snow on the garden wall this morning and it is still coming down. By noon it was seventeen. Only twenty day-boys came to school, but they were in fine spirits for they were having a real adventure. They were, fortunately, warmly clad with their heads muffled in warm scarves, but the classrooms were cold so we shortened class periods and dismissed school at noon. The telephone is down, branches of trees are broken off, some not broken are weighed to the ground, roads are impassable so that we have had little communication with the outside world, save for news brought to us by three men who walked here from Jalazone Camp to see the IRC. It had taken them four hours to come a distance they could have easily done in an hour normally. We have often walked to the spring at Jalazone in a happier day for our school picnics, for in addition to the spring it was a wonderful place for wild flowers.

There was great need at the camp. The people were not able to make paths in the snow as they had no shovels, so the women could not get to the ovens to bake their bread. In many instances, they could not even open the flaps of the tents to get out at all. The three men were cold, wet, and hungry. Willard, ignoring a small-pox scare at the camp, led them to the school kitchen, the only warm place in the building. They were soon seated in a corner drinking hot tea and eating bread and cheese while their shoes were drying near the stove. I sat with them, pouring tea and replenishing the supply of food, until the IRC delegates arrived. We were able to find warm socks and scarves, and they set off through the snow to carry the good news that the IRC would get help to the camp.

As usual, I was amazed by the philosophical way in which the refugees accepted these hardships. Always they reminded us that Allah was good and that He would send help. If they could only get back to their homes they would be all right and they were sure they would get back in Allah's good time. I used to visit that camp quite often as long as we lived in Ramallah. It was quite touching in spring and summer to see onions and tomatoes planted between the tent ropes, and more often than not, a geranium! They were farm folk and loved the soil and understood it. In one of the first of the many commissions which came to Palestine to inquire into causes of trouble, the agricultural experts reported that the Arab farmer was a good farmer. Now that they had lost their lands, one could see in the efforts the refugees made to grow something that that was true.

Fortunately, these snows do not last long, but when they come, the whole country is paralysed for a few days. Here again, despite the hardship the snow brings, the farmer thanks God, for he sees in the snow precious water that will fill the springs and water the valleys, for the snow from the north-west is heavy with moisture, soaking the dry ground abundantly.

[7 February] Roads are all closed today by order of the government. Rumour is that the Arab Legion does not want to risk a tie-up on the roads at this time. There is a continuing fear that even though there has been an armistice, Israel is determined to get to the Jordan, perhaps before a formal union between the West Bank and Transjordan is signed. Walking has been difficult as the roads are icy. Trees are bent to the ground, branches are broken off, and a bitter east wind tonight makes it colder than ever. I hardly dare look out of the window as it is heartbreaking to think of the refugees living in their tents and makeshift huts within sight of us and with not enough to cover them. My bed-room is cold, but there is a metal hot-water bottle in my bed so that soon my feet and my back and the sheets will be warm, and if I carefully push the bottle to the foot of the bed and cover it with a pillow, the water will be slightly warm for my morning sponge-down. It would take a miracle indeed to share my moments of warmth with our people so very near to us. We are trying to give out everything we can, but we do not have enough of anything.

[8 February] Incredible! Snow in Jericho. I remember when "snow in Jericho" meant "your slip is showing". It is not funny here. We are told that in five centuries there is no record of snow in Jericho. Snow also in southern Palestine near Egypt. How we wish some kind fairy would give us $3,000.00 to spend on oil and heaters, it is so very cold now. One of the biggest refugee camps in the whole country is in Jericho. Thousands of refugees went there because of the warmth and lack of rain. The YMCA of Jerusalem has set up a big tent in Jericho for their programme of recreation and school-work for the boys of the camp. I wonder how they fare? Taught all morning and happily thought I was through for the day but learned that our science teacher was not able to get out for his afternoon classes, so I had to spend a double period with the seniors in the afternoon. They seemed to think I could teach them science, but I firmly told them their science was beyond me, so, at their request, we settled for grammar. When I was a young teacher in 1922, trying to be modern in my methods, the boys gravely told me that if I would teach them grammar, they would learn English more quickly. Times had not changed! School over, my friend and neighbour, Mrs Rodenko, herself a refugee, and I went up to the attic of the main building where we had a few bales of clothing and sorted out every warm garment we could find. My arms ached with the pushing and pulling of the big bales, but we got along famously and by supper-time we were ready for a distribution in the morning.

[9 February] Wonderful! The sun came out today, the roads cleared and we were able to take clothing to the little girls in our refugee school in the Meeting House. We also sent bundles of clothing to the camp at Jalazone. There is a good deal of troop movement of the Arab Legion; a reliable source says that there are few men left at Latrun. It would seem to indicate that there is some sort of understanding between King Abdullah and Israel, but it is all very quiet. It can mean that the Israelis either are to come in, or have agreed not to do so. The end of the month should show which way the wind is blowing, and it may blow away rumours, too. One of our Armenian boys tells us that, according to their calendar, we will have another snow on 17 February. Can we go through another one?

[11 February] The teachers came down tonight for their usual Saturday night leisurely dessert. I served baked Alaska, since I had all the snow in the world for the freezer. The teachers were surprised to have ice-cream in winter, but enjoyed it. Only Mr Salim questioned it; he is quite sure that ice-cream was not meant to be eaten in winter! More bales of clothing having arrived yesterday made it possible for us to make up bundles for 137 families in one of the camps, about seven hundred people in all, and how they need them! I am learning a great deal about the clothing habits of the American people, especially the female of the species. But I do wish little boys did not wear out knees and elbows. The refugees remember the quilts they left in their homes; one friend left a lovely fur coat her husband had brought her from Italy in the winter of 1947. What we have to give to each one isn't much, nor is it easy for many to accept charity. The fact that we are not strangers is a help, for they know we understand, and so we all make the best of it.

We are often asked why the refugees cannot go to other Arab countries and be cared for there. That is not usually a question but an opinion couched in the terms of a question. In the many solutions propounded in our western lands, the word MUST is constantly used. The Arabs MUST do this and MUST do that. "They must accept the fact of the State of Israel and both Arabs and Jews must learn to live together" is the constant theme. Perhaps the Arabs should, for our peace of mind, but it is for them to decide what they must do. They are the ones who have lost their lands, their homes, their identity. As for the other Arab countries, they have done much for the refugees and continue to do so. Where are the refugees now?

By 1961, there were 142,670 refugees registered with United Nations Relief and Works Agency in Lebanon, 120,877 in Syria, 265,430 in the Gaza Strip, and 633,197 in Jordan, 146,000 of them in East Jordan. The remainder were in what was left to the Arabs of Palestine. Refugees in Egypt were not eligible for relief under the United Nations Relief and Works Agency, but there were at least 6,000 in Egypt on relief and 4,000 more who had found employment and were able to care for themselves. Not all refugees were registered with UNRWA. Many found work throughout the Arab World where their professional training and experience in education and government, as well as in business, was needed. Only one-third lived in the camps set up by the United Nations and they were mostly farmer folk, refugees from the fertile lands and orange groves of the plains. A tradesman or craftsman can be transplanted and find employment, but between a farmer and his land there is a mystical attachment that is not easily broken. Nor can he take his

land with him. The problem of the host countries in meeting such
an influx of needy people was great. They had to provide camp
sites, water, protection and education in the early days before the
relief agencies were set up, and to continue these services for the
following years. Egypt provided port and transport services for
food and clothing for the enormous number of refugees in the Gaza
Strip. In addition it carried on a large social welfare programme.
The Palestine Arab Refugee Institute in Syria had an extensive
social welfare programme as it had a large number of refugees not
on the relief rolls. Lebanon furnished port and transportation services. All host countries allowed all refugee relief commodities to
enter duty free. By 1960, it was estimated that almost all employ-
able refugees in Syria were able to find work and large numbers of
Palestinians were becoming well integrated into the life of both
Syria and Lebanon.

Most Arab countries have not ignored the needs of the refugees,
and if they do not grant full citizenship it is because the refugees
insist that the United Nations Resolution which grants them the
right of return must not be jeopardized. The refugees still cherish
that right and are not willing to give it up. The problem of the
West Bank of Jordan has been a great one. There, most of the
refugees simply fled from one part of Palestine to another; more
than 400,000 remained on the West Bank of the Jordan, and when
in 1950 it was joined to Transjordan, citizenship in the new state
was automatic. Palestinians have served in the government from
the beginning, and have represented Jordan abroad and in the UN.

In December 1957, when my husband and I went to Saudi Arabia,
Kuwait and Bahrein, we found Palestinians everywhere doing important work. In Kuwait alone, we were told, there were 25,000
Palestinians. They have not been sitting in tent doors counting
beads and being used as political pawns. It would have taken a
courageous politician, indeed, to tell the refugees that they were
going to be moved to another country permanently. One of our
last visitors in 1962 was one of our Old Boys who was back from
Kuwait on a visit. He was a graduate of an engineering college in
England and had found good work in Kuwait. But his exciting news
was that he had that day bought land between Jerusalem and
Ramallah and hoped soon to come back and build a house on it for
his family. That was the dream of all of them. I don't know if
Usama's dream will ever come true; I can only hope it will.

The most difficult aspect of the refugee problem as we saw it,
however, for the host countries was the presence in their midst of
large numbers of uprooted people, living under a great sense of

injustice, many of them excellent farmers now sitting idly in camps hoping daily for a chance to go home. Thousands could go back on foot, as they had come, without too much difficulty. Many of them could look across the borders and see their homes. They were an easy prey for the agitator and a threat to the security of these countries. The miracle is that there was no great breakdown in morals, but morale was hard to sustain. Initiative and enterprise cannot long survive years of charity, and these people did not accept charity easily. Nearness to their homes and lands and the seeming failure of their kinsmen to resolve their problems added to their frustrations. Syria and Lebanon, countries which suffered greatly during the First World War and had been under foreign control until 1942, had their own problems of economic stability and security.

When the Farouk Government in Egypt was overthrown in 1952, the young republic inherited not only great internal problems and the protection of the Gaza Strip with its quarter of a million refugees, but a hostile, expansionist Israel at its doors. Egypt did not annex the Gaza Strip but assumed administrative responsibility only. The flag of Palestine flew over the Parliament Building and Palestine was on their stamps. The Gaza people needed Egypt if Palestine was to continue to exist for them.

It may be hard to imagine what the problems were in the Gaza area. In a narrow strip, twenty-one miles long and four miles wide, a population swelled from 100,000 to approximately 300,000 almost overnight; and 221,000 of them on relief rolls was a Herculean task for any government to undertake. An added problem in Gaza was the fact that contact with the rest of Palestine and the world outside was practically gone. Gaza had been a busy place before 1948, serving a large hinterland to the east. It was famous for dates, oranges, lemons and water-melons, and was the port from which tons of barley were shipped to the beer-drinking countries of the West. The sea served the people in many ways. To the north and east was the country they considered their greatest enemy; their four-mile southern boundary was the desert; and the Great Sea, their western boundary, once a great source of income and a call to adventure. Now it was as confining and frustrating as the northern boundary and the Israeli-controlled Negeb. Even if one had money, it was not easy to get to other parts of the Arab World; and few people had money. If Gaza was to become one of the most difficult places for Israel to control during the Suez Crisis it was not surprising.

There is much misunderstanding in the West of the Arab people

and the Arab nations. In order to justify their aggression in the
Arab World, the Zionists have been unrestrained in painting them
as a degenerate people, ignorant and unimportant. Yet one old
Jewish settler in Palestine, Nathan Ghofshi, had this to say:

"We Jews forced the Arabs to leave their cities and villages . . .
some of them were driven out by force of arms, others were
made to leave by deceit, lying and false pretences. It is enough
to cite the cities of Jaffa, Lydda, Ramleh, Beersheba and Acre
from among the unnumbered others . . . here was a people who
lived on its own land for 1,300 years. We came and turned native
Arabs into tragic refugees. And still we dare to malign them,
besmirch their name. Instead of being deeply ashamed of what
we did and trying to undo some of the evil we committed by
helping those unfortunate refugees, we justify our terrible acts
and even attempt to glorify them." (Quoted from *Israeli Conflict*
pp. 21–22, by Ernest Fromm.)

Other Jews, equally sensitive, have tried to present a true picture,
but their voices are seldom heard.

William Ernest Hocking, in the foreword to *The Arab World*
by Nejla Izzeddin, says:

"There are peoples in the wide world whom it is our bounden
duty to know. There are also people whom it is a delight to
know. There are peoples whom it is both a duty and a delight to
know and such by all counts are the Arabs. Our Arab neighbours
for centuries have given character, meaning, and flavour to the
entire Middle East, a character never dull, never mean, never
quite obvious, which some have called a trifle enigmatic, with its
own dimensions of majesty and depth, its own capacities for
that union of reason and passion which is the life of history.
They hold the cross-roads of three continents, and their political
decisions will affect the course of world history, including our
own history, for years to come . . ."

My personal assessment of the Arabs is simply that their vices and
virtues may not be identical with ours but are comparable. We are
all members of the human family, and if we take time to understand each other we will find that fundamentally we are much
alike; environment and language and adjustment to our separate
cultures make us seem different, but one is not superior to the other.

When the United Nations met in its annual session in November
1948, it was faced with the tragic consequences of the recommendations of the year before. Set up with such high purpose after the

Second World War to prevent aggression and acquisition of land
by aggression, to be a community of nations wishing to live at peace
with one another, it was not getting off to a very good start. However, it went on record with the following resolution, a resolution
which was to be repeated regularly every year thereafter:

> "The refugees wishing to return to their homes and live in peace
> with their neighbours should be permitted to do so at the earliest
> practicable date, and compensation should be paid for the pro-
> perty of those not choosing to return and for loss or damage to
> property which, under principles of International Law or in
> equity, should be made good by the government or authorities
> responsible."

What they also failed to do was to resolve that there should be
no further immigration of Jews into the occupied territory until
the question of the refugees was settled. In 1972 it is still not
settled, and in the meantime the population of Israel has grown
from 600,000 in 1948 to 2,500,000 twenty-three years later.

One of the attempts of the UN to understand the problem and
to attain some sort of solution was the appointment of the Palestine
Conciliation Commission. In 1951, it reported to the UN that more
than two-thirds of Israel's cultivable land was abandoned by Arab
refugees in 1948, due to the war, that one third of the new immigrants were living on Arab "absentee" property, and practically
another third were living in urban areas such as Jaffa, Haifa and
Jerusalem from which the Arabs fled. In 1967, after the June War,
the daughter of Moshe Dayan in an article in *Look* magazine noted
that they were living in an Arab house. The Arab cultivable property, incidentally, was almost two and a half times the total area
of Jewish owned property on 15 May 1948 when the State of Israel
was announced to the world.

Agricultural settlements established in the next five years, as
stated by the Custodian of Enemy Property, numbered 370,350
people living on Arab property. At the same time, nearly all of the
olive groves, half of the citrus groves, and 10,000 shops and businesses belonged to Arab refugees. If the new state was able to more
than double its population in that same period, bringing in large
numbers of penniless Jews from other Arab countries, they could
thank the refugees. According to the *Israeli Year Book for 1951–52*,
Arab citrus groves alone earned the state ten per cent of its exports
income. One cannot go into all the details of that period and how
much there was to gain by refusal to allow refugees back, but it is
interesting to note that this "neglected and desert" land, which

was now "made to bloom like the rose", was formerly cultivated for the most part by Arabs on small holdings, and earned in 1944 $78,000,000 of a total $112,000,000 Palestinian income from agriculture alone. Much of that income was earned on the hills where farming was not easy. If those of us who lived to see this happen were anxious for the future peace of the area, it will be understandable.

In 1953, it was not difficult to see trouble ahead. Called on to do full-time relief work among the refugees, my husband and I were well aware of mounting bitterness and had little comfort to offer as we watched the tremendous material support the Zionists were getting from the United States and from some European countries, and the annual repetition of the 1948 Resolution in the United Nations completely ignored.

Victims of Partition

The story of the months following Count Bernadotte's assassination and the signing of the armistices has been briefly related, but one aspect of the Palestine Problem little known to the world outside Palestine has been that of the frontier villages, that line of humanity which separated Jordan from the Zionist State for eighteen years.

When on 18 July 1948 a truce was declared in the Arab-Israeli conflict, it established a 341 mile-long border between the two armies, an incredible frontier between what was to become the Hashemite Kingdom of Jordan and that part of Palestine then occupied by the Zionist State. Between 24 February and 23 April 1949, armistice agreements were signed between Egypt, Lebanon, Syria, Jordan and the almost twelve-months-old State of Israel, and open hostility ceased. The Israeli forces were at that time allowed to retain control of the territory beyond the UN Partition line which they had taken, pending the final settlement which would presumably follow soon. The Armistice Line was to follow the line where the opposing armies stood at the time of the truce; it was dictated by "military consideration . . . and was not to be construed in any sense as a political or territorial boundary."

However, this line was to remain until 1967. Beginning at Bardala in the north, south of Galilee, the line ran west and northwest, skirting Jenin, it then turned south touching Tul Karm, Qalqilya, Qibya, and numerous towns on its way. Proceeding further south, it suddenly indented at Bab-el-Wad eastward toward Jerusalem, cruelly bisecting the Holy City and pushing up like a probing thumb against its ancient walls. Then, west again past Bethlehem and Beit Jala and south-west bordering the Hebron district, curving east to the Dead Sea and ending at Aqaba.

When the Line was marked, no thought was given to the convenience of the people living in the villages on that Line, to their water supplies, or to their livelihood. For example, in Beit Safafa near Jerusalem, barbed-wire split the village in two, an ugly, threatening, heavily twisted roll of metal. Children played on both sides, cousins perhaps, but no longer with each other; they could not toss a ball across just for fun; women carrying their water jars on their heads, relatives and childhood playmates passed on either side with averted eyes without recognition, as that would break the truce and the Jordan Government was at great pains to maintain quiet and not provoke retaliation. In addition to separating families, children were separated from their schools, villages from their springs, but, more cruelly, a man from the lands on which he depended for his income. For, in every instance, it was the cultivable land that was gone, and what remained to the villagers were the stony hills, not easily ploughed and lacking the fertility of the land to the west, the land that could be irrigated.

There were 111 villages on that frontier line, with a population of 181,000 people, mostly farmers. They had built their homes on the high ground partly for health reasons but mostly to save for cultivation the land that sloped to the plains. Daily, these villagers viewed their land and their coast with the ports of Haifa and Jaffa, the latter since time immemorial their outlet to the great western world beyond. Through the centuries, from the time of the Phoenicians, the Greeks and the Romans to the present, galleys and ships had sailed to and from these shores. The barbed-wire could not shut the people off from the glory of a Mediterranean sunset, but upon its setting they had to shut themselves in their darkened houses, their safety in the hands of a small home-guard, young men of the village who kept watch by night. They knew that the truce at best was an uncertain one which had been violated with terrible consequences a number of times, reprisal attacks by the Israeli army leaving death and destruction in their wake. It was true that Jordanians sometimes broke the truce, but it was usually the desperate act of a farmer trying to get fruit from his own trees or a shepherd pasture for his sheep on his own land. There is no record at any time of a military foray from the Jordan side, and the Jordan government punished any individual who was caught attempting to cross the line. Israeli incursions were always military ones approved by the government. The Arabs are a sociable people, hospitality being one of their proudest traditions, and isolation may have been one of the hardest psychological problems for them, for military restrictions were severely maintained for their protection and for the peace of the whole area.

In October 1953, my husband was seconded to the Near East Christian Council Committee for Refugee Relief as Executive Secretary, and on the first day of January 1954 we moved from Ramallah to Jerusalem. The appointment was for two years, as it was thought the problem would be solved by then. We were to remain in

Jerusalem for the next nine years, and when we retired the problem was still as great as ever, with years of mounting bitterness and disillusionment for the refugees to presage critical times ahead. Although we had been active in relief work in and around Ramallah before we moved to Jerusalem, we were now to become involved in the frontier village relief programme, too. The NECCCRW, like the United Nations Committee for Relief, was primarily for refugees, people who had lost their homes and livelihood through the partition of Palestine. The people on the frontiers had not lost their homes, and so were not eligible for UN relief, and it was only later than 1948–49 that their desperate plight was brought to the attention of the relief agencies. Our committee had been doing modest work, but as time passed we saw that a great deal more was necessary. As a member of the area committee of the NECCCRW, called the International Christian Committee, and no longer tied to school duties, I soon found myself serving as a liaison between the frontier village people and the committee. As I visited the clinics, the schools, and the various programmes set up by the Committee and carried out with the help of capable, dedicated Arab teachers, doctors, agriculturists and social-workers, I never ceased to marvel at the courage it must have taken for the people who lived in the villages through suffering, deprivation, insecurity, uncertainty and isolation to hold so tenaciously to what remained. They had to watch aliens ploughing their land and patrolling their borders; hear shots in the night, not knowing which of their friends or kinsmen had rashly tried to cross the lines to see a parent or a brother, or perhaps to get a fig or an orange from his own trees.

In time, our committee and others were able to help with schools, school lunch programmes, seedlings that would grow in the stony soil, goats to provide milk for the cheese that was so much a part of their diet, chickens, and clothing and increased health services. Some of the relief was palliative, most of it of more permanent value, but what was needed most and what we couldn't give them was hope and security. However, I think the fact that we went to them from the outside world, so to speak, broke down their sense of isolation, and it gave them cheer to see something being done for their children. It was hard for us to look with them at their fair lands and to know that they longed to farm them again. This part of Palestine was so steeped in history that one could hardly believe so small an area of the earth had seen so much. Over it had marched the armies of the most ancient peoples and the most modern: Hittites, Ethiopians, Hebrews, Assyrians, Egyptians, Greeks,

Romans, Turks, French, Britons and Germans. The Queen of Sheba, Joshua, Sennacherib, Alexander, Titus, Abdul Malek, Saladin, Richard Coeur-de-lion, Napoleon, Allenby, all had played their parts and made their exits here; surely a country well within the stream of history and civilization.

George Adam Smith, writing in the 1890s, noted that Palestine "has never belonged to one nation and probably never will . . . the idea that it can ever belong to one nation, though they were Jews, is contrary to both Nature and Scripture."

Palestine, in our early days and until partition, had its Greek Colony, German, Moroccan, Armenian, Russian and Jewish Quarters, and people who retained some of the physical characteristics of the Crusaders: as cosmopolitan an area as one could find anywhere, with all faiths and denominations free to worship in their own way and follow their own way of life. George Adam Smith may have been prescient.

I not only marvelled at the courage of these village folk but I marvelled at the way they tried to meet their problems. Behind the miles of barbed-wire, the foxholes, the soldiers constantly on guard, they tried to carry on as normally as possible. When we went out to visit the work projects or to take relief, the traditional, gracious forms of hospitality were observed. We were assured "You honour us by your coming;" "My house is your house;" "May Allah bring you here in peace and may you go in peace." Sometimes it was coffee, sometimes delicious mint tea, but there were always refreshments. If I admired the flowers the teachers had raised under great difficulties in the school gardens, they were immediately cut for me to take home. I learned to admire them but always hastened to stop the headmaster from cutting them, as I could tell him that they would fade before I got back to Jerusalem and, pointing to my eyes and heart, assure him that I could keep the beauty of the flowers in my eyes and their kindness in my heart.

In 1967 that Line was wiped out, and thousands of those brave people who had withstood hardship for all the years were driven into exile and were added to the refugee rolls, their villages in many instances destroyed as they left. Willard talked with some of these people when he stood at the Allenby Bridge after the 1967 blitz, and could understand, as few of the foreign reporters could, the full extent of the tragedy they were witnessing.

The nine years during which I was in the villages some part of every week were a great lesson to me on how the human family can meet disaster. They were the descendants of people who had survived long centuries of war, of happiness and pain, and they were meeting the present catastrophe with a philosophy of life that was mature, and a faith in Allah that was deep. Love of home and land is strong in Arab countries; family records and traditions reach far back into antiquity; the earth is a challenge and the fruits of the land give them satisfaction, for they come from the Hand of Allah. In that confidence they endured the barbed-wire, the constant threat of attack, the poverty and isolation, sure that in time they would once again sit under their own trees, plough their lands, be surrounded by their children, and, who knows, even feel the sand of the Mediterranean shores between their toes. Their long years on the frontier, I feel, were a service to the rest of Palestine, and may have delayed the present crisis, giving the Arab World time to assess its responsibilities and resources.

When peace comes, as it must, Palestinians will owe a great debt to the frontier village folk who remained to show the world the depth of love people can have for their country, and the ability of the human family to endure infinite suffering to keep it.

"Before UNRWA, we were, and after UNRWA, we will be." With these words, Willard began a report to a representative assembly of relief agencies in Geneva in 1960. It is true that the church was the first organization to send relief for Palestinian refugees and it is probably also true that it will be there as long as the need exists and in the days when the refugees need help in rebuilding their lives.

We have told of the cables that were sent from Jerusalem by four Americans, one to the Federal Council of Churches in the United States, for relief and understanding of the problem, and one to the World Council of Churches meeting in Amsterdam "to examine the Palestine Problem in the light of principles of Christian justice with the view to recommend rectification of obvious wrongs." The response to the appeal to FCC for relief was immediate and generous. The second part of the cable was laid aside and an answer was to be long delayed. Three factors in the crisis at that time were possibly responsible for the seeming reluctance of either church or state to feel the necessity of action on the political aspects of the problem. In the first place, the world, particularly the Western World, was war-weary and only beginning to recover from the Second World War. In the second place, the United Nations was young and too recently organized for its inspired programme for world peace to make decisions of such great import as that in regard to Palestine, nor did it have the authority to implement these decisions; actually it was limited to recommendations rather than decisions. In the third place, the Church in 1948 was beginning to see the realization of its dream of ecumenism, as Christians from all over the world met in Amsterdam to form the World Council of Churches. Their programme was a full one and had to be carried out in a limited period of time. From reports which came to us from the meetings, we learned that, as with our reporters, it was generally felt that the situation was temporary, that we on the field were over-disturbed and emotional, even that we were indulging in "an orgy of sentimentalism." I suppose it was hard for that gathering to appreciate the urgency of our appeal. In the glow of ecumenism and the beauty and order and peace of Amsterdam, with plans for the future to be worked out in committees, the Jerusalem cable must have struck a harsh note indeed, although that was not intended. It was the call of the Jericho Road: "Who is my neighbour?" But the refugee problem was a world-wide one and the need for a department to meet the needs was great. The World Council of Churches soon set up a department for relief, and Palestinian refugees were to be a major concern for that department for years to come.

For three years, relief was distributed by committees in the "host countries", those countries to which Palestinians had fled in panic in 1948. They were Transjordan, Lebanon, Syria, the Gaza Strip, Egypt and that part of Palestine still held by the Arab population. In the Occupied Territory, there were also refugees. They were Palestinians who had tried to remain in their homes but had fled during the fighting and were not allowed to return. Some Palestinians also were removed from their villages for military reasons, as they were living in "sensitive" areas. Those active in relief work were missionaries already carrying on in their posts, and they simply took on this extra load. Overhead expenses were practically nil. The Presbyterian Mission, with headquarters in Beirut, placed its staff and facilities at the service of the relief agencies, thus providing a strategic location for receiving goods and funds and for distributing them to the other host countries. The office staff took on the added duties with selfless devotion as they handled endless paper work and kept in touch with government agencies. It was a great service, which eased our problems in countless ways, and the United Missionary Council which had been designated the agency to dispense relief for the ecumenical programme could hardly have functioned without it.

Other relief agencies were soon on the field with their own programmes. The larger ones were the Lutheran World Federation, the Pontifical Mission (later called Catholic Relief Services), the Mennonite Central Committee, the YMCA and the YWCA. We became

known as the Voluntary Agencies, to distinguish us from the United
Nations Relief and Works Agency, UNRWA.

When three years had passed and there was no change in the
refugee situation, the World Council of Churches decided the time
had come for the church to attempt a solution or at least to take
steps toward one. So it was that in co-operation with the International Missionary Council they decided to hold a conference in
the Near East on the subject, hoping that they might succeed
where governments had failed. Beirut was chosen for the place; the
time, 4–8 May 1951.

I must confess that the first reaction of our committee in Jerusalem to the proposal was negative. Through the years we had
seen commission after commission come to Palestine to study
causes of unrest. They had all made reports and recommendations
but nothing constructive had come from them. Eighteen in all had
come in thirty years, and if they had not succeeded it was not the
fault of the commissions, but of home governments. If we were
sceptical about another study, even a church one, it was understandable. Hope springs eternal, however, and we yearned for a
solution, too. If the Church was prepared to act, it was our duty to
co-operate. The only proposal we made was that delegates should
spend a few days before the conference visiting refugee camps and
in temporary homes, and meet with responsible Arab officials. This
we felt was absolutely necessary before they sat about a conference
table offering solutions. The local committee then worked out
schedules whereby the fifty delegates would be formed into small
working parties and assigned to special areas, so that by the time
they assembled in conference they could pool their findings. That
this was successful is shown by the report which finally came out.
Some of it is timely today.

> "The purpose of the conference as stated was: firstly, to show
> that Christians are concerned about the plight of the refugees;
> secondly, to call upon the churches in all countries, and especially
> those who can help, to take this need far more seriously than
> they have done and co-operate in the task; . . . we do not dream
> of restricting our help to those of our own religion . . . we have
> a sense of responsibility for the total problem."

When the sessions began, the delegates humbly admitted that
they had been guilty of sins of omission in the past and that they
were now aware of the magnitude and urgency of the problem.
After five days packed with lectures, reports and discussions, they
issued a report remarkable for its unanimity and understanding,

and they made practical suggestions for immediate action. Some excerpts from this report are of continuing interest. They confessed that they were "shocked by the plight of the refugees from Palestine . . . had our minds brought sharply back to the tragic chain of events which had caused this situation . . . in so far as Christians, by their action or inaction, have failed to influence in the right course the policy and decisions of their governments and of the United Nations, they too, are guilty . . . upon us therefore falls the greater responsibility to seek, in collaboration with all men of good will, a constructive solution for their problem . . . A great injustice has been inflicted upon them (the Palestinians), a measure of suffering they never deserved . . . We are convinced that there can be no permanent solution of the problem of the Palestine refugees until there is settlement of outstanding political differences between the Arab states and Israel . . . It is the duty of all governments, in co-operation with the UN, to press for and to facilitate an early and agreed settlement as an indispensable condition for achieving a lasting solution of the refugee problem . . . Finally, we appeal to all Christians to use their influence in persuading their governments and the UN as to the need for a definite political settlement and large scale schemes of relief and reconstruction . . . We would urge all Christians to give personally on a far more liberal scale to all activities of the Christian voluntary organizations engaged in the work of relief, rehabilitation, and resettlement in the Near East."

Needless to say, the conference gave us, in the field, tremendous encouragement and hope. The sense of isolation and frustration under which we had been working was dispelled. The presence of fifty consecrated people working together on a special task with open minds was in itself comforting. The past three years had been hard on us all and we needed the inspiration they brought. We had new hope as we thought of them fanning out into their own communities and organizations to carry out the recommendations they made.

They recommended expanding our programme to aid economic refugees, that is, those people who had not lost their homes and so were not eligible for UNRWA relief, but who had lost their livelihood; co-operation with UNRWA and the Voluntary Agencies also at work; the education of adolescents and adults; the release of Arab bank accounts in Occupied Palestine; and last, but not least, engaging a full-time Executive Secretary to help further the programme. Willard, a delegate to the conference, had no idea in May 1951 that in two years he would be called to serve in this capacity and end his service to Palestine in 1962 under the Near East Christian Council Committee for Refugee Work.

The Conference further recommended that the name of the local organization be changed from United Missionary Council to Near East Christian Council Committee for Refugee Work: NECCCRW. Dr Samuel A. Morrison, of the Church Missionary Society of Egypt, was appointed Executive Secretary and he established a programme of administration that gave the work a good foundation. Two years later he resigned, and Willard, then Principal of Friends' Boys' School in Ramallah, was called to take over by a committee locally appointed. The office was moved from Beirut to Jerusalem and became a centre for work which expanded in size and diversity each year, thanks to the continuing and growing concern on the part of churches in many lands. Also, as long as the churches were kept aware of the refugees, the larger issues of the Palestine Problem were kept alive.

The details of the refugee relief that was carried on for the following five years would fill volumes. Fortunately, with UNRWA to a certain extent filling the needs of nearly a million refugees for food, shelter, medical care, and to some extent schooling, our committees in East and West Jordan, Lebanon, the Gaza Strip, Egypt, and Occupied Palestine could turn to constructive self-help projects. It helped farmers make better use of the land that remained to them, established vocational training centres, increased grants for education, and gave loans to artisans and craftsmen to help them establish themselves as self-supporting members of society. Relief was only partly palliative; for the most part it was constructive. Programmes were adapted to the particular needs of each area and to the number of refugees involved. Flexibility was one marked aspect of the work, but, more than all else, the individual was made central, and his dignity respected.

Five busy years passed with added bitterness for the refugees and discouragement as there was not yet a solution to their problem. The brave words and wonderful hopes raised by the 1951 conference had not been realized. Relief had been increased, but the political solution so necessary was still pending. The determination of the refugees to insist on their rights to repatriation in the land of their fathers and their homes was hardening with the years, and they would continue to suffer rather than yield. Each year when Willard gave his report to the World Council of Churches on refugee relief, he ended with a plea for it to go beyond relief and seek that elusive political solution. In 1955, when he made his report to the NECC in Beirut, he urged that body to appeal to

Christian churches of the world to call for "a permanent, constructive solution to the long-standing tragedy of the Arab refugees."
The NECC agreed that the time had come to end the present state
and appointed a committee to draft such an appeal to be sent out
through the World Council of Churches and the International
Missionary Council. Both organizations agreed to consider it.

Following consultations with Arab representatives in the United
Nations and advisors and sponsors of the 1951 conference, the
WCC and the IMC finally announced that a second conference
would be timely and useful. This conference, therefore, convened
in Beirut on Friday, 25 May 1956 on the campus of the American
University of Beirut with the approval of His Excellency Camille
Chamoun, President of Lebanon, and with the gracious hospitality of
the University.

While recognizing the fact that the 1951 conference had "helped
materially to awaken the conscience of the world to the special
tragedy of this particular group of refugees . . . and had evoked a
vast amount of giving . . . it was forced to recognize the fact that
in the continued absence of a political settlement in the Near East,
the plight of the refugees and the problems they pose are as serious
today as they were in 1951."

The purpose of this conference then was: "first, to review the
position of the refugees in the continued absence of a political
settlement; to review current relief needs and programmes . . . and
to ensure in the West the continuance of concern for relief and
rehabilitation and to see greater understanding of the political
issues that must be faced." They stated that "Christians must
acquaint themselves thoroughly with the facts and make them
known, redouble their efforts to contribute to a just political settlement, and they must appeal to governments and individuals to provide adequate funds for the needs of the refugees." It was indeed
discouraging for them to face the fact that after eight years the
unhappy situation of nearly a million refugees was fundamentally
unchanged and they admitted that "the creation of the State of
Israel in 1948 had resulted in immeasurable misery for over
1,000,000 Arabs and this tragedy had not healed with time and
had created a serious menace not only for peace in the Middle East,
but for peace in the world . . . Speaking to the refugees, we must
confess the sin of Christian people and of governments which led
to their plight and its continuance," and they promised to labour
for a just and lasting solution to their problem.

Following this conference, as with the first one, relief contributions increased, and the service arm of the WCC stepped up

its contributions. With the passing of time, and with the Zionists filling Arab homes and Arab lands with immigrants from many lands, repatriation was becoming increasingly remote, and the need for constructive programmes increased. As a result, Willard's annual reports are filled with progress along these lines. Resourcefulness and imagination marked the work in every area. In order to keep down overheads and keep up many offices, the policy of the NECCCRW was to allocate funds to agencies already doing important work but without sufficient funds to do all they could with existing staff and facilities. For example, the Lutheran World Federation Trade School, a legacy from Schneller's Syrian Orphanage, which rendered signal service in Palestine for many years, was given a considerable monthly grant to train more craftsmen and artisans than its own budget allowed. The YMCA and YWCA centres in the Aqabat Jabr Camp in Jericho with its 70,000 refugees were helped to carry on notable and most important services beyond the possibilities of their grants from the International Committees with their world-wide responsibilities. Zerka Industries in East Jordan, under the management of Miss Winifred Coate, formerly principal of the Jerusalem Girls' College and missionary under the Church Missionary Society of England, was able to expand its many services with funds the NECCCRW could assure her annually. She has carried on a far-sighted and most important programme in all the years since then.

Meanwhile, its own committees in every area were branching out. Schools were maintained, clinics opened in border villages where medical services were almost negligible, seedlings, goats, chickens and young trees were sold to farmers at cost, and village people were helped to restore their homes damaged in the fighting. In one instance, a whole village was rebuilt, and new schoolhouses were built in co-operation with the villagers themselves.

When it was discovered that children in the border villages were beginning to suffer from serious malnutrition, a school-lunch programme was initiated along the border, which provided nourishing food each day for between 12,000 and 14,000 children. USA surplus flour, Christian Rural Overseas Programme (CROP) foods sent through Church World Service, UNICEF powdered milk, and considerable sums of money from the Oxford Committee for Famine Relief in England made this programme possible. It was not always easy for contributing agencies to appreciate our need of money to dispense their bounty, and the cash donations from OXFAM were a great blessing.

When one thinks of the numbers of people who shared in the

relief programme and the number of voluntary hours of service given both by Palestinians and by those of us who have been serving them through our Western churches, one's personal involvement seems small indeed. Yet we may get an appreciation of a relief programme to which thousands have contributed through such appeals as "One Great Hour of Sharing " by this brief report of the work of the NECCCRW with which I found myself called to serve as a member of the Jerusalem Committee. Although the committee was founded by four Americans in Jerusalem in 1948, it quickly became international as British and Palestinians were added to it. It also became international in a wider sense, as through it came financial and material aids from many countries, including Great Britain, Australia, New Zealand, Holland and Finland.

The Jerusalem Committee, called the International Christian Committee, was representative of all area committees. On it were churchmen, men of the law, doctors, teachers, social workers, and representatives of the YMCA and YWCA, combining ability, experience, wisdom and dedication in a remarkable way. They gave hours of valuable time and professional service each month and rose generously to emergencies between meetings. Through them, the NECCCRW was assured of responsible use of funds, and guidance in government and community relations. The Arab members interpreted the refugees to us and us to them, and the Westerners helped interpret the Arabs to the West. All together, we worked in happy association. My chief contribution was availability. No longer tied to the school, and Willard gone more than half the time, I was free to keep the committee and the workers in the various projects in close touch with each other. Before leaving the story of the Church and the Refugees, we should not omit some account of one of the biggest projects we were called on to undertake, for it was one which involved church women in many lands more directly than any other aspect of the refugee programme.

When the United Nations set up its own relief programme of food, shelter, and medical care for the refugees, it soon became evident that the provision of clothing was also necessary but the most difficult to meet. In the extremity, UNRWA turned to the Voluntary Agencies representing the churches. The organization offered to pay transport costs, to clear shipments through customs, to deliver assignments to the respective agencies, and, when possible, to distribute the clothing in the camps and centres, if the Voluntary Agencies would appeal to their churches at home. At first the request seemed too much even for the Voluntary Agencies to attempt, but in the face of the tremendous need a call went out to church people of many denominations in Western Churches. The response was quick and generous in quantity and quality. Soon tons of good used clothing were coming to us. In the field, the Voluntary Agencies met regularly to agree on areas of distribution and to prevent overlapping. It was also important to see that no area was overlooked. It would be too much to claim that we clothed the refugees, but we were able to give clothing to a people who needed supplementary relief, especially during the winter months.

One problem was that practically all the refugees were in the same condition of need, and since our clothing was of great variety and climatic conditions were different in areas of distribution, it was almost impossible to meet all locations equitably. Needs of hill-country people were different from the needs of people in Gaza, Egypt, or Jericho, for example. Our committees in agreement with UNRWA tried to distribute one family bundle a year and to give out as much as possible in addition to institutions and individual cases where people were not on UNRWA relief rolls but who had lost their income. That included people in frontier villages. In the part of Palestine remaining to the Arabs the chief agencies engaged in mass distribution were the Pontifical Mission, Lutheran World Federation, the Mennonite Central Committee and the Near East Christian Council for Refugee Work.

Our committee, the NECCCRW, started operations in an old Arab house which had been built in the late nineteenth century. When we went to Palestine in 1922 it had become the English College, as it was large, strongly built, with rooms for lectures, a large dining-room, and rooms for a few boarders. In 1948 the upper storey was so badly damaged that we never did try to repair it. The owners replaced windows and doors on the first floor when our committee rented it as it was the only place where we could find the space we needed for the clothing operation. We had no heat, and it was bitterly cold and damp in winter with the upper floor roofless and windowless, but we all accepted it gladly and the place hummed with activity five days a week. Incidentally, it was located at the Mandelbaum Gate, which, in the old days, was called the Saidi Quarter because the Said family home was there. This was where people crossed from the other side, so we never felt lonely.

UNRWA assigned to each Voluntary Agency a certain quota of refugee families, providing us with the number, ages, and sex of each, and with that before us we tried to make up the bundle. This was not an ideal way to give out, as we could only guess at sizes and weight, but with a list of 22,500 families and limited resources we could not investigate each family. We did the best we could.

In time, we secured an electric cutting-machine and were able to make thousands of school outfits for boys and girls. The garments were cut at the centre then given out to women who had sewing-machines and who were excellent seamstresses, and we were very proud of their work. We paid modest wages, but the women were only too glad of the opportunity to earn even a little money. When remnants of beautiful Scottish woollen material came, we made them into what the girls at the centre called Eisenhower jackets. And how grateful we were for the thousands of layettes that had been lovingly made by women throughout the United States. I used to wish the women could have seen the tears in the eyes of young mothers when they were given the attractive garments, many with handwork tastefully embroidered on them, and especially hand-knitted sweaters or blankets.

One operation which a friend said I had backed into was that of getting shoes, sweaters, and stockings for school-children. It all started when visitors to our refugee schools would leave a little money with me to "get something for the children." When I would ask the teachers what to get with twenty-five dollars, they usually advised me to save it until I had enough to get something meaningful for the 750 children we were at first trying to help.

What the children really needed most was shoes for our cold, rainy, wintry days. The committee could not give us money for them, so we could only pray that some day we might have enough saved up to get simple sandals. Then I learned that a refugee in Ramallah was making shoes from old automobile tyres. They were very cheap and in time we had money enough for them. They were not beautiful, nor did they fit well, but they kept small feet dry and off the cold stone floors of the classrooms. Visitors were touched by these efforts and increasingly more money was given to us for better shoes. These gifts helped us move into the sandal stage and we were very proud of them, but when the rains came open sandals were not much protection and we longed for sturdier shoes.

In the fullness of time, unsolicited gifts came to me earmarked for the refugee children in and around Jerusalem, and the day came when we graduated into Oxfords. A sympathetic Armenian shoemaker on Christian Street in Jerusalem, who had lost most of his business with the departure of the European community, was approached. He was glad to have work for his men and was willing to make shoes for little profit in order to give them work and to be available when our "troubles" would be over. He even came out to the schools, measured every child, and eventually was turning out hundreds of pairs of shoes for us. He not only measured but brought the shoes out to the schools and had the children put them on to be sure there had been no mistakes. We tried to have new stockings to go with the shoes, for that added comfort. The shoes were of good leather, and with care would last a child through the school year and at an average cost of $2.00 a pair.

So many people were interested in the children that in time we could branch out into sweaters. There were never enough warm clothes for children in the bales and we could not buy cloth for jackets, so we had to settle for sweaters. My good angel led me to a merchant on Christian Street, this one a Muslim, who in other days had brought in navy-blue sweaters which were part of the school uniform for one of the Jerusalem schools. His business had suffered, too, and he was glad to deal with me for marginal profit. These sweaters were made in Damascus from Scottish wool and were lovely. Like the shoes, I could get them for approximately $2.00.

The making of school uniforms, shoes, and the purchase of sweaters added in a modest way to the economy of the country, in addition to the blessing they were to the children. One particular stroke of good luck came through the Oxford Committee for Famine Relief in England. The Secretary combed English factories for seconds in children's sweaters on more than one occasion, and they were a godsend. This project which started out so modestly with shoes made from old rubber tyres for 750 boys and girls finally grew into a programme where three thousand children could be cared for each year with shoes and garments made to fit them and of good quality. It cost no more to make up good cloth than poor, and good cloth lasted longer so was cheaper in the end. There were times when I longed to be able to be more generous with cloth as I discovered that in the heart of every little girl there was a ballerina, and our garments were not *tutus* that would flow around them when in sheer happiness they tried to make them do so. We had thousands of pairs of shoes made through the year, bought thousands of sweaters and stockings, and in the Clothing Centre we could report 15,000 new garments made in one year.

As I review the reports of two important Church Conferences, I wonder how much is remembered. We watch the outpouring of Christian love and concern through the years with gratitude and were privileged to serve for Christians of many lands through the long years. We still look to the Church for leadership as it places on its members the responsibility of "not getting weary of well-doing" and working for justice. If we get discouraged, however, we may be forgiven, for the refugees are still with us.

At the end of his last report to the NECC and the WCC, Willard wrote the following:

"When I was called to begin this work in 1953 for a two-year assignment, we all hoped that the great problem which initiated the programme would be settled within that time. Failing the longed-for solution, we have tried to carry on as servants of the Church to minister to the more human aspects of the problem, mindful of the psychological and spiritual needs of the refugees as well as the physical.

"Neither the NECC nor the NECCCRW may ever fully know how well they have succeeded. Surely one could find many occasions when we have fallen short; perhaps we should not worry about all the statistics, interesting and heart-warming as they are, but pray that all the loving Christian concern behind them may have touched the lives of the people we have tried to serve. That is the final criterion and only the Heavenly Father can pronounce judgment.

"It has been a rich and rewarding experience to have been associated with an ecumenical movement of such an international character during the past nine years, but even more than all this has been the joy of working with so many dedicated people here and abroad and an awareness of the vast amount of love and goodwill which is available everywhere and which responds to human need so generously."

The year 1953 was typical of all the years between 1948 and 1962 when we left Jerusalem, and apparently until 1967. Tension was our daily food, with frequent border eruptions, many violent and bloody, and there never was a time when we did not feel that the Zionists would make another attempt to take all of Palestine with the Jordan River for a boundary. We all thought they would seize a moment when the world was much preoccupied elsewhere, particularly a time when the United States was involved either at home or abroad. We also knew that when it happened the West would be led to believe that the Arabs were to blame. In his book *Violent Truce*, Commander Elmo Hutchison tells the story of the three years he served on the United Nations Truce Supervision Organization, and it is solemn reading, proof of the fact that while the world cried "peace" there was no peace in Palestine. We soon became familiar with the white jeeps of the UN Truce Observers flying the blue flag of the UN as they travelled from one zone of trouble to another at all hours. Their task was an almost impossible one. A Mixed Armistice Commission was set up to judge border incidents, and the Truce Observers were required to maintain the strictest neutrality as they met with two Israelis and two Arabs to decide where guilt for the incidents lay. The Truce Observers, an international group, and as representatives of the United Nations to be honoured and respected, often moved at great risk on the Israeli side of the line. Those we saw at work were men of the highest integrity, and they represented their countries well.

While the records contain many reports of military forays into Jordan by the Zionists, one of the most serious in 1953 was the savage attack on the village of Qibya, about fifteen miles north-west of Ramallah, during the night of 15–16 October. The news reached Ramallah during the early hours of the morning, and Willard drove out immediately to see what relief our committee could give. He returned, troubled and shaken by what he had seen. Fifty-three men, women and children had been killed as they slept in their beds, and fifteen wounded. The people were still almost too stunned to speak but the evidence was all too plain of whole families wiped out. In one instance a mother of six survived alone. Bodies were still in the rubble of their homes blown up while they were in them, the school-building and the water-tank destroyed, and survivors were begging for help to bury their dead. Willard thought it had all the appearance of an Israeli demolition practice manœuvre, it had been carried out so swiftly and systematically.

A few days before this incident, a hand-grenade had been thrown into a house well inside Israel, killing a woman and her two children. There was evidence that it was the work of infiltrators, and when the Jordan authorities were informed of this, they agreed at once to track down the culprits. There was no reason to believe that the people of Qibya were responsible, but before the Jordan authorities had time to investigate the Israelis moved in. One thing the Truce Observers were agreed upon was that the Jordan government was making every effort to avoid border incidents, as they were not ready to invite the Israeli type of retaliatory methods nor were they ready for full-scale war. Israel was condemned for this incident in the Security Council, but many border raids were carried out on a smaller scale that were not taken to the Council. The border villages were a daily challenge, as well as an irritant, to the expansionist state, and there was continual harassment. I went to Qibya often in the years we lived in Jerusalem, as our committee joined with others in the task of restoring the village, and I never ceased to wonder at the courage of those who survived, for there was no exodus from Qibya even after so dreadful an experience. When the Security Council condemned the Arabs for border incidents, it was condemning individuals who acted at the risk of imprisonment by their own government; when it condemned Israel it was condemning planned, military, government-approved action. To live within ten or fifteen miles of such incidents as Deir Yasin and Qibya and to see the survivors rebuild their lives is an experience one never forgets.

Later, Moshe Brilliant was to write: "Those bloody 'border incidents' are seldom accidental . . . they are retaliation, part of a deliberate plan to force the Arabs to the peace table. Some call it 'realistic', others 'cynical'—but it promises to be effective." (*Harper's Magazine*, March 1955.) Was he being overly optimistic, we ask?

An important event of 1953, one which we hoped would clear the air, was the visit in June of John Foster Dulles, Secretary of State for the United States. When we heard of it, we were hopeful that some constructive policies might come from it. He was to visit hurriedly several capitals in the Arab World, but whether his visit was simply a gesture of an earnest attempt to understand the situation at first-hand was problematical. We do not know what happened elsewhere, but the moments he spent in Arab Jerusalem did not improve the situation. Several important Arab officials were at Mandelbaum Gate to greet him, but he had allowed only twenty minutes for the West Bank. Our friend, Aref el Aref, told us what happened. Ignoring the Arabs, Mr Dulles got into conversation with Ambassador Green. Aref el Aref, former official in the Mandate Government, former Mayor of Jerusalem, and a historian, said he broke the rules of courtesy and tried to present the Arab case to Dulles. He was brushed aside and Dulles sped on to Amman. This incident caused unhappy repercussions in Jerusalem. Dulles would have been well advised to reach Amman in some other way if he could do no more in Jerusalem. He was the only Secretary of State to visit Palestine from then until 1971.

On 7 October 1953, we were invited to the American Consulate to a reception to meet five US Congressmen on a fact-finding tour. They arrived late. Willard was in Beirut so I went with Mr and Mrs Daoud of Ramallah. There was little chance to talk with the visitors, but I did have a few words with Mr Jensen of Iowa, an important member of some committee, and Mr Laird, a congressman from Minnesota. I don't know how much they learn on these hurried trips and am inclined to think they feel that they are already well informed and mostly want to confirm their views and be able to say they have been on "both sides". I wish I could have felt that the visit of these five, and that of John Foster Dulles, would bring about more unbiased decisions and ease the pressures on our government in the United Nations.

Crises and Portents

The year 1955 was to be one of almost constant crises, beginning with Israeli raids in the Gaza Strip in February and ending with the repercussions of the Baghdad Pact in Jordan in December. We thought the latter was the most serious incident of the year, perhaps because we were in the midst of it, but it was the former that was to set up a chain reaction which is still unresolved and fraught with danger far beyond the reaches of the Gaza Strip. The violent reaction in Jordan to the Baghdad Pact was but another incident in the sad story of the Partition of Palestine, and was to sink into relative insignificance before the events of 1956, which were to spread the area of conflict east and west and to bring the rest of the world to the brink of war. I must confess, though, that the Baghdad Pact Crisis was no simple matter in Jordan, and it did have the effect of letting the international forces know that seven years had not lessened the determination of the refugees to be heard and that they mattered. Rightly or wrongly, they feared the Pact was a way to get their government to recognize Israel.

We were in Beirut during the last week in February on committee business. Willard came up from Gaza on 24 February, and reported good meetings and progress in the relief programme. The Gaza Strip, administered but never annexed by Egypt, had been relatively quiet since the armistice. Two-thirds of the population were refugees, yet the city of Gaza was making great strides in modernization of streets, businesses, homes and agriculture. The United Nations Relief and Works Agency and the Voluntary Agencies were serving the 225,000 refugees in many constructive ways. Hundreds of young people from Gaza were working in other areas of the Arab World and were sending money back to their parents to help them restore their homes or build new ones. However, it was a vulnerable area and only the fact of an enormous refugee population may have kept Israel from attempting to annex it up to this time. Now that seven years had passed and Israel was in need of space for the immigrants she was bringing in from all over the world, we should not have been surprised when a new turn in events seemed to be taking place. But we were not prepared for the ferocity of the attacks nor for the speed-up of the new strategy. We were in the beautiful airport in Beirut when the first news of the Gaza raids reached us.

[1 March] Up early as we were to be called for at half-past seven to get the UN plane for Jerusalem. We arrived at the airport in good time, formalities were quickly cared for, and we boarded the plane about half-past eight. We set off, happy to be on our way home, but when we reached the end of the runway the pilot, instead of flying out over the Mediterranean, turned around and headed back to the airport. Something wrong? "Engine trouble" the pilot said, but not convincingly, and no crew was rushing out to find out what the trouble was. Finally we were told that there would be no flight. In a little while we were told that there was "trouble" in Gaza and they could not land there today, so the whole schedule was postponed. We had to wait until the afternoon Air Jordan flight, and as we waited about, news filtered through. We were not told much, but from the air of suppressed excitement and concern of officials who were getting the news, we guessed it was serious . . . Much anxiety in Jerusalem tonight; we never know who or what area will be next. We know Jerusalem is on the list and timing is important.

During the next few days, we learned the extent of the Gaza raids. On Monday night, Israeli paratroopers crossed the Armistice Line east of Gaza and attacked an Egyptian military camp near the railway station. Using heavy explosive charges, they completely destroyed the building, some Nissen huts, and a pump-house which supplied water for at least one-third of Gaza residents. At least fourteen Egyptian and Palestinian soldiers were killed, sixteen wounded, two civilians killed, one a small boy, and two civilians were wounded.

While that operation was going on in the east, another Israeli force entered the Gaza Strip, six kilometres south of the town, and ambushed a truck carrying thirty-five soldiers and an officer. They set fire to the truck, then attacked with machine-gun fire and grenades. The officer and twenty-two soldiers were killed and twelve were wounded.

These incursions by the military were the most alarming incidents on the Armistice Line in the Gaza area since the Armistice in 1949, and caused considerable conjecture in all areas. For the refugees, unarmed and helpless in the camps, it increased their fears and their insecurity. For President Nasser, it was a crisis he had not anticipated and he knew his army was not prepared to meet the well-equipped and well-trained army of the Israelis. He had been less than a year the official head of his government and, with his council, was trying to solve some of the many domestic problems of Egypt. There had been relative quiet along the Armistice Line in the past years and there was the conviction that the Palestine Problem, being a political one, would finally have a political settlement. Nasser needed money for hospitals, schools, industry and agricultural developments among other things, and there was not enough for all these things and arms, too. Now his army was pressing him for arms for defence against further such attacks, and the refugees were crying: "Give us arms to protect ourselves." In the end, he was forced to admit that Egypt must arm, and that decision was the first in a series that would change the political climate of the Mediterranean World for some time to come.

Charles Malik, speaking to the World Council of Churches Conference, held in Beirut in 1956, predicted that Egypt would play a leading role in the future of the Middle East. And I remember that an Arab refugee living in Beirut in the days of Farouk, one whose losses were heavy, remarked that the leadership of the Arab World might come out of Egypt as it had come in times past. Could it be that the decision forced on Nasser, by Israeli attacks on Gaza, might be the turning point in the Middle East stalemate? Observers close to President Nasser were always impressed by his desire for a peaceful settlement. Unlike Ben Gurion, he did not think war had to precede a political settlement. Now, he would have to set aside some of his cherished hopes for his people at home and concentrate on defence. His hospitals, schools, industries, would have to wait.

Willard went to Egypt frequently in the course of his refugee work and always came home impressed with the efforts of government to improve the life of the farming class especially. He visited the model village in the Liberation Province, Tahrir, where a thoroughly modern experiment of reclamation, education, and population control was being carried on. He found great enthusiasm in many projects on behalf of social welfare among Egyptians generally, long overdue. I can remember in our early days in Palestine, long before Nasser, that we got our charts on health projects for our clinics from Egypt, but Nasser was carrying his programme forward much more energetically and scientifically than it had ever been done.

President Nasser, in this moment of crisis, could not ignore the cry of the refugees in the Gaza Strip for protection or of his army for the weapons to provide it. We wondered at the time if the raids were an attempt to test Nasser's leadership. This phase ended with Israel being condemned in the Security Council for: "a pre-arranged and planned attack ordered by Israeli authorities, committed by Israeli regular forces against the Egyptian regular army forces." Like all such condemnations, it was put on the books and left there for the historians of the future.

During the year, tension along the Strip continued, and appeared to be a studied plan of harassment. Israel complained that she was denied use of the Suez Canal, which was good propaganda abroad. What was forgotten was that the Suez Canal was in Egypt, not on a border, and that by the Constantinople Convention she was responsible for the safety of the Canal for passage and against sabotage. Also, since no peace settlement had been made, a state of war existed between the two countries. One other feature we forget is that the Palestinians remaining in their country were cut off from their Mediterranean ports and one cannot think of a time in its long history when that condition existed. Israel acquired Palestinian territory by aggression but was still allowed to remain in the UN. When a small ten-man crew Israeli ship was denied passage through the Canal, it created intense emotional reactions in our Congress, but the plight of a million Palestinian refugees hardly raised a flutter. President Nasser maintained that if Israel would obey the UN resolutions on the refugees, the matter of the Suez Canal would be no problem at all.

During the summer there was stepped up a spate of anti-Nasser propaganda that should have shamed the American press. An Egyptian friend, a graduate of Bryn Mawr with a doctorate from Cornell University, told me that when these blasts were printed in our papers, it was not Nasser that was being attacked but every Egyptian, and she felt that every time there seemed to be some kind of rapprochement with the West new attacks were made to prevent it from flowering. She reminded me that Egypt had almost always faced west, in ancient as well as in modern times. She, like most of the Arab World, loved America and had been happy while a student there and longed to see the two countries friendly.

Following the Gaza raids, there was a great flurry of attempted peace negotiations by the British, the USA, and the UN, but sadly they all seemed to create only more trouble. The Palestinians were constantly afraid that each move was to make them accept Israel and be willing to settle somewhere else, and were suspicious of all the activity. We, too, lived in a state of unease. It was not until the end of the year, however, that the storm broke when an attempt was made to get Jordan to join the Baghdad Pact.

Very briefly, the Baghdad Pact was a plan of Western governments to create a tier of pro-Western countries on the southern
borders of Russia, from Turkey to Pakistan. The USA did not become a signatory to the Pact but is credited with thinking it up.
Great Britain joined early in the year with Iraq and Turkey. It was
a treaty of alliance "for the purpose of defence against possible
Russian aggression and Communist subversion." Some Arab states
refused to join as they feared that it was simply new evidence of
Western Imperialism. I doubt if any of the other countries realized
that it would be the little country of Jordan that would be the
greatest challenge to the Pact; nor did we, as we went about our
work, appreciate the smouldering resentments that were ready to
flare into violence before the matter was settled for Jordan.

Matters came to a head early in December with the arrival of no
less a personage than Sir Gerald Templer, Chief of the General Staff
of the British Army. His mission was to persuade Jordan to extend
the Anglo-Jordanian Treaty to include membership in the Baghdad
Pact. Many factors probably entered into the violent reaction of
the Jordanians, but it must have been a surprise to King Hussein
himself that it took the course it did. The entire government resigned following the resignation of three ministers. Another
government was formed that lasted only a few days, and finally
stability was restored under Ibrahim Hashim. The above is an all
too simple explanation of so important a crisis, but it will serve
to show how close we were to upheaval all the time.

The storm broke in all its rage on Saturday morning, 17 December, and it was a day when I had plans to go to a camp to distribute
sweaters at the girls' school there. Deir Ammar Camp was one of the
lonely ones in Palestine. Most of the camps were set up near
population centres, but this one was off to the north-west on a hill
quite far from towns. The refugees there could look down on the
fertile fields below that were their heritage and which they had
farmed well. During the fighting of 1948, they had fled for temporary security to the hill country and, like all the others, expected
to go home when the fighting was over. They could have gone
home easily without the aid of cars. I have stood beside older men
of the camp as they looked down on their land and pointed out
landmarks to me: the smoke from the cement factory, for example,
clearly visible. The United Nations officials were aware of the
suffering of these people cut off from both land and countrymen.
So our committee and UNRWA tried to get out to them as often as
possible. There were two schools in the camp with about 750 boys
and girls in all. Since UNRWA did not provide clothes, our com-

mittee tried to get school uniforms and shoes, and sweaters for the girls made from Scottish wool in Damascus. Coats would have been better but we had not enough money to buy them. I was to go out that morning in the UN jeep and Willard was to come to get me later, as the UN jeep could not wait for me. Before going to bed on Friday night I noted in my diary: "No buses to Ramallah as there is rioting over the Baghdad treaty. We hear that new ministers have been put in who will sign it. I hope we won't have more trouble." Alas!

[17 December] Left at eight o'clock this morning for Deir Ammar in the UN jeep. All was quiet and I started out happily as the air was chill and I knew the sweaters would be most welcome. A lovely morning; the rains have come, making the hills green and colourful with the first wild flowers. We drove through Ramallah quickly and found it unusually quiet. We speeded past groups of young men and boys standing about talking, as UN jeeps are not always popular when troubles arise and might be attacked. Strangely enough, in spite of rumours, I had no feeling that we might run into difficulties. When we arrived, we found Mr Carver, Deputy Director of UNRWA, and Mrs Carver, and an Independent Labour Organisation VIP and his wife there, and, although they could not have been there long, they were on the point of departure. I went at once to the school and the distribution went off speedily as I had the girls' sizes in detail. The girls looked sweet in their blue sweaters and I think I shared the feeling of warmth with them as they sat there pleased to have something new, the right size, and cosy. Since Willard had not arrived, I was taken to the office of the camp leader and was served the traditional coffee and sweets. There was a good deal of coming and going and voices were low, but so far all was quiet in the camp. But I began to sense that the camp leader was anxious, and I was not surprised when Willard finally arrived to have him eager to see me off. Of course, they offered Willard coffee but did not press him when he said he thought we should be getting home. As we left the camp, Willard said there was plenty of trouble in Jerusalem and we must get to the house as quickly as possible.

When we reached Ramallah, the streets were cleared and shops were closed. We had just missed a big demonstration! Willard decided to stop at the home of Samaan Effendi Daoud, one of the three ministers who had resigned from the cabinet, to find out what he could tell us about the situation. He talked

freely, said that he had told Sir Gerald that Jordan did not need
more pacts, that its treaty with Great Britain was all they needed.
Samaan Effendi had served as a judge in the Mandate Days, was,
of course, a Palestinian, and so understood the refugees and their
fears. We did not stay long and were soon back in Jerusalem
in our own home on the hill where several consulates are
located. We learned that the British, American, French and
Turkish consulates had been attacked in Jerusalem. In Jericho,
the Musa el-Alami farm had suffered great damage and the
Mennonite stores were set on fire and their house attacked while
some of the women were in it. The rioters seem to have been
school-children, not the youngest, but secondary school ages. We
called the Mennonites at once and offered what help we could
give them, and Mr and Mrs Rutt came to stay with us for a few
days. The country is in a state of emergency. Much trouble in
Amman. Egypt is being accused of fomenting and encouraging
the rioting.

[19 December] Willard prepared to leave on the UN plane for Gaza
this morning. He even got on it but decided to remain here when
he learned that the Turkish Consulate was being attacked again.
This building practically backs up to our house. Slater Blakiston,
from the American Consulate, hurried in about eleven o'clock
and asked us to go to the City Hotel as he was afraid for us as
bullets were flying and the mob might remember we were
Americans. We found the hotel lobby full of Europeans, many
of them UN personnel. The plane from Cairo did not stop,
simply flew right back to Cairo with its passengers. Mobs were
all over the city, mostly young people. All UN families have
moved away, so we are alone on the hill tonight. A curfew has
been imposed and the Legion is in control.

Willard had to go to Egypt for meetings on the 23rd so
suggested that I go with him. He thought the change would do
me good! It had been an exciting time. But before then he had
a cable to go to Lebanon for another disaster. This time it was to
help flood victims. An unusual rain had fallen, causing great
destruction, and many were homeless. So he went north and I
went to Egypt alone, hoping he would join me soon, perhaps by
Christmas. Fortunately, we had many friends in Cairo and I was
well cared for until Willard arrived on the afternoon of Christmas Day. He spent the last day of the year in conference with
Egyptian officials. Colonel Gohar, recently returned from the
USA, had the latest news on the UN relief proposals. One wishes

the UN could do more than talk relief! This year has proved beyond doubt that we live in an area of smouldering fires, some call it a volcano, which can burst into flames at any moment. And this, as time passed, was merely the prologue to an even more dangerous year culminating in the Suez Crisis.

On 3 January 1956, we were luncheon guests of Bishop and Mrs Johnson in their lovely home on the Nile. As we talked about the growing tensions in the Middle East, Bishop Johnson laughingly told a story of an experience he had during the Second World War, and as I begin the record of this year, it describes it well. Bishop Johnson had occasion to call on an American captain in North Africa one morning during World War II in connection with his services as a chaplain. As the two men chatted, there were frequent interruptions by phone calls and messengers bringing in dispatches. As he rose to go, Bishop Johnson remarked that the Captain had a good deal of work ahead of him. Glancing down at the pile of dispatches and notes on his desk, the Captain replied: "There's a lot of hell in that pile of papers and only your Boss knows the answers." As I look back over the years, I have thought of that story quite a lot. Surely this has been one of the most difficult and puzzling years yet.

I returned to Jerusalem on 4 January, refreshed and rested; it had been good to be with friends of long years, many of them, and Egypt always had a fascination for me. I loved going to the museum and out to the Pyramids, lost in wonder at what these ancient people had created of massive buildings and beauty of the most delicate design. Willard and I liked to walk out in the evening to "smell the air"; it was the time of day when the people of Cairo went out into the streets to enjoy the cool night breezes, too. But we returned to a city not yet recovered from the violence of the past weeks or from the fears that had been kindled by the play of international politics beyond their understanding. There was unease and foreboding. Mr Blakiston, of the American Consulate, let us know at once that if trouble came we were to go to the American Colony, which would be a protected area. We learned that although Jerusalem was quiet, Amman, Nablus, and Jericho were still unsettled. On Saturday, 6 January, the American Consulate was attacked and much damage was done before relief arrived. We are told tear-gas was used to protect the consulate, which was understandable as Mrs Blakiston was there with her young children. The flag which flew outside the gate of the consulate was torn down. Mr and Mrs Rutt, who were still with us and had been advised not to try to return to Jericho yet, felt that they should go to Lebanon. They needed a change.

[8 January] While we were at breakfast, Slater Blakiston called to tell us that law and order had broken down completely, and strongly advised us to go to the American Colony for the day. Willard went down to see what had happened at the consulate and reported that it was "pretty bad". He took Walter and Gladys Rutt down to the Colony but we decided to remain in the house. With Willard's office in the house, we do not like to leave it unguarded. I worked off my anxieties on cupboards. Later in the morning Mr Wrangel, son of the famous White Russian General of First World War, came to see Willard on refugee affairs. He is with the Tolstoi Foundation, an organization which aids Russian refugees, some of whom are in Jerusalem. Naturally, we talked about the present situation. He said, among other things, that as far as Russia was concerned, the real leader was Kaganovitch, a Russian of the Jewish faith, but he kept behind the scenes and remained at home while others went abroad. Mr Wrangel wondered if Russia had a deal with Israel. He remembered that Russia had voted for the Partition of Palestine and was among the first to set up an embassy in Tel Aviv in 1948. So many speculations these days. We will remember that Ben Gurion thanked Russia for helping them at that time.

On Monday, Mr Blakiston came again to tell us that all foreigners should consider their position here as the situation was grave. The curfew was lifted for two hours to enable us to get food, and meantime the Arab Legion was protecting any of the foreign community who needed to get to a plane or any other place. We had some excitement on Wednesday that lightened our spirits because it ended amusingly after a few hours of frustration. Mr Blakiston came again to the house soon after nine o'clock with the news that Walter and Gladys Rutt could go on a plane to Beirut at half-past ten. When we were all ready to take them to the plane, Walter was missing. For some reason unknown to his wife, he had gone off and could not be located. Mr Joury of the Tourist office and Willard began a search, fearing Walter had wandered into a forbidden area and, not having the language, would not be able to extricate himself. We were all anxious. Finally, at one o'clock Willard rushed into the house, filled a bag with fruit and dashed off without explanation. Meanwhile, Gladys had gone to the airport to wait for Walter there. Willard got back in an hour and was able to tell us that Walter had been going from office to office trying to get a permanent visa on his new passport. Willard had followed his trail to the Lebanese consulate and people there thought he had returned to the house. To everyone's relief, the plane was late and he got on it with a bag of fruit to keep him alive. We all heaved a great sigh of relief.

[13 January] Curfew was lifted this morning and we are all relieved. Two Arab Legion officers came to the house this morning to find out how we were and what protection we felt we needed. We told them we felt quite safe but would like to have telephone connection with the American Consulate or one of their offices. They thought regular telephone service would be established soon. One was Major Khaldi, of an old and honoured Jerusalem family and formerly *aide-de-camp* to the King. Both were friendly, stayed for coffee and sweets, and seemed glad we were not worried. We have no fear of people like that; it is the mob of irresponsible youngsters completely out of control that is to be feared. We did appreciate the call.

[14 January] It is good to be almost back to normal. We had a succession of visitors; some had morning coffee with us; two remained for lunch; an American from the Mennonite Services was with us for dinner. Just like the good old days!

The first two weeks of January had their moments, fortunately some lighter ones. Ruth Black came in one day with the latest tourist story. One of the more recent Christian shrines in Jerusalem is the Garden Tomb at the foot of a hill which from certain points of view resembles a skull. It is often called Gordon's Calvary because General Gordon, sitting in the garden of the American Colony home, now a hospital, in the Old City many years ago, thought it fitted the description of Calvary. It is a highly controversial site; archaeologists generally do not accept it, but it is a garden and there is an empty tomb in it with this skull-like hill above, so it has an appeal to the tourists as well as to some scholars. Ruth told of the tourist, notebook in hand and camera over his shoulder, turning to the guide as he was leaving to ask: "Now is this really the place where General Gordon is buried?"

We now could get on with our refugee work and even began to think there was a miracle as far as we were concerned. For some reason the Israelis had gone to Egypt and were leaving us alone for a bit.

As the days passed, more and more rumours were spread abroad.

On 14 February, we drove down to Hebron to see Ada and Ida Stoltzfus, twin sisters loaned to our committee by the Mennonites, who were responsible for the work of our committee in that area. They had been able to remain all through the disturbances and we had no fears for their personal safety, but we wondered what they felt about the future of the programme. The trip to Hebron was lovely, the country so beautifully green after the rains. Almond trees near Bethlehem were a cloud of pink blossoms, farmers were ploughing, grape vines were being trimmed, and hundreds of olive trees were coming alive again. I love this time of year in Palestine. We found the twins and the American doctor and his family well, but considerably perturbed over certain aspects of the riot. One rumour was that two young men were each given fifty pounds to burn the stores and the house where the twins lived. The plot failed and the money was returned to the two ministers who had hired them. Whether or not there was any foundation to the rumour, the riots had puzzling aspects and we wondered who was behind them. By the end of the month, noting the peace efforts of the West, I was cynically ready to record: "The West seems determined to make peace or force one; let us hope they don't precipitate a war!"

[2 March] Just when we thought we were in a period of quiet, the unexpected happened again. Grace Whiting came to the house this morning in tears. Her news was that Glubb Pasha had been dismissed from command of the Arab Legion and was already on his way to England in a special plane accompanied by Sir Patrick Coghill of the CID and an important British colonel. This really stunned us as we had felt Sir John Glubb's place was absolutely assured for all time. No one knows why this abrupt action has been taken. Glubb's mother, Lady Glubb, lives at the American Colony. Grace said that Glubb Pasha had been able to talk with her and make arrangements for her return to England as soon as possible. Lady Glubb is a doughty person and when she was told of this sudden dismissal of her son, she sat up and proudly said: "I am the daughter of a soldier, I was the wife of a soldier, I am the mother of a soldier and I can face this." The country is quite disturbed by this news and it will no doubt stir up a great furore in England. What the repercussions will be is yet to be known.

A few days later we learned of one amusing incident connected with the dismissal of Glubb Pasha. An English friend told us that Sir Patrick Coghill was not in Amman on the afternoon Glubb

Pasha was notified that he must go, and no one knew where he was. Since he was to leave with Glubb Pasha, it was important to find him as quickly as possible. He was finally located in Jericho in the house of a friend at two o'clock in the morning fast asleep. The messenger awakened him and, not being too well versed in English, told a sleepy Sir Patrick that his services were "extended". Puzzled, but too sleepy to wonder why this message had to be delivered at this unearthly hour, Sir Patrick simply turned over in bed and fell asleep again.

This new step in the diplomatic story started another wave of demonstrations, happy ones for the most part. The people are weary of the play of politics which has pushed the fundamental problem of the Middle East into the background, and this gives them hope that their problem might be solved by their own people. Some few were anxious, as Israeli aggression is always imminent, and they leaned strongly on the Arab Legion. They did not know how Glubb's dismissal would affect it nor was it clear why he had been relieved of his command so suddenly. His position was difficult. In noting the rumours that went the rounds at the time, I learned that one was that there had been a plot to assassinate Glubb Pasha; if that were so, then the King had taken the action he did to protect him. Another was that America was behind the dismissal and that Britain was behind the riots. It was true that America was filling the vacuum in the Middle East created by the end of the British Mandate and the end of her occupation in Egypt in the near future. America's entry into the Middle East was to keep Russia from coming in to take Britain's place. Hussein's reasons were to become known later, so we lived on speculations for some time. Sir John Bagot Glubb has never in the press or in public utterances expressed bitterness, and he has maintained his deep love for the young king and the Arab people in a spirit of nobility not too common.

Willard was in Gaza early in April for his usual committee meetings. He left on the morning of the fifth and reported when he came home that as the UN plane was leaving, they could hear the sound of heavy mortar firing near the town. The next day we learned that the Israelis had bombarded the town almost all day, the second such incident in two months. It was market day in Gaza and the streets were filled with shoppers. When night came, sixty-three Gaza residents were dead and one hundred wounded, more than ninety per cent of them being townsmen, women and children. As only four soldiers were killed, the market-place was clearly not a military target. Egypt retaliated by sending *fedayeen* into Israel and claimed heavy casualties. The fact that this happened in Gaza did not quell fears in Jordan and emergency action was taken.

We did not realize it at the time, but this raid on the Gaza Strip was to have far-reaching consequences. In the first place, it was evident that Egypt was to be the centre of Israeli propaganda and aggression in the coming months. This would have the effect of diverting attention from Palestine and the refugee problem and be an opening to the campaign in Sinai and Suez, a part of the strategy of the Israelis. On the other hand, President Nasser was now faced with the fact that the people of Egypt must be prepared to defend themselves. Ever since the first big raid in February, his army had been pressing him to get arms for them, and with this latest attack on Gaza the refugees were demonstrating and demanding arms for themselves if Egypt could not protect them. Nasser's dreams of building up his country and not using its resources for weapons of war were not to be realized in the near future. Now, he had to face the fact that as head of the government, and responsible for its defence, survival must come first, and he turned to the Western Powers for arms. When they refused to sell them to him, as a last resort he went to the Soviet Union and was able to buy arms from them. This action brought bitter denunciations of Nasser in the Western press and from governments, although one cannot but wonder what they expected a country threatened by aggression to do. Nasser asked for defence weapons only, which he needed desperately. In the emotional atmosphere in the West, it was forgotten that communist arms had been given to the Israelis in 1948 and that Israel was the only state in that part of the world that had a recognized Communist Party. Later it was reported that asking Russia for arms led to Dulles making one of the most unhappy decisions of his career, one which in turn led to the Suez Crisis, which has cost the Western World vast sums of money and loss of prestige in the Arab World. Dulles' decision was to be made before the year was out, and in the meantime, the reaction to Egypt's plea for arms was to step up arms aid to Israel!

The next crisis of the year was connected with the High Dam. The building of a dam to utilize the waters of the Nile was not a new idea of the leaders of the new republic, but it was to take the courage of the young members of the Revolutionary Party to attempt it. This was a peaceful project for the good of the people of Egypt to provide food for the growing population and to improve the economy of the country. Egypt would need a loan for this great scheme and submitted a request for one through the World Bank. Britain and America were friendly to the idea at first and the World

Bank, after carefully studying Egypt's economy, endorsed it. Egypt was jubilant. Early in July the way seemed clear for final arrangements and only the official endorsement of Britain and the USA were required, particularly that of the latter. Then, to the astonishment of those who had been following the developments in regard to the High Dam, and the astonishment of Nasser, Dulles announced a surprise decision that was to strain, to put it mildly, relations between Egypt and the USA for some time to come.

The United States had decided to withdraw its support for the High Dam. We were in the United States at the time and were as shocked as were all who longed for better relations between America and the Middle East. We learned later that it was not only the fact of withdrawal that angered Egypt, but the undiplomatic method Mr Dulles used, to the point of rudeness when he announced the decision to the Egyptian representatives, that added fuel to the flame. Britain followed America's lead, claiming lamely that the American Congress was against it. Nasser had asked for a loan which the World Bank reported Egypt was able to carry, but that aspect was lost in the emotional climate of the moment. It was sad too, that we did not remember how humanely the Egyptian Revolution was carried out and the country rid of the Albanian Dynasty which had ruled Egypt for so long and in later years so corruptly. Nor did they note the fact that the new regime had inherited the war with Israel and had kept the Armistice Line quiet since taking over. Still more important, they did not stop to think of the millions in Egypt who were to be helped by the Dam, nor remembered that they had refused the sale of defensive weapons to Egypt while they were stepping up more offensive arms to Israel. It seemed to us more like a petulant rebuff because Nasser had turned to Russia for arms.

If Egypt's reaction to the Dulles snub was drastic, it should not surprise us too much. And it came quickly. On 26 July, word flashed around the world that Egypt had nationalized the Suez Canal. It was a bold step with international repercussions, but Nasser had weighed the problem carefully and it was executed skilfully, and again without bloodshed. He was vilified in the Western press beyond belief but there was not much the Big Powers could do. The Canal was in Egypt; and there were other important canals in the world, the Panama for example, and precedents could be dangerous. An American friend we were visiting soon after told us that an American expert on the Middle East had written to Mr Dulles: "You know you can't do a damn thing about it. I would advise you to give Egypt money to widen the Canal."

We returned to Jerusalem on 6 September, to find many changes in the three months we had been away; the Kalendia airport was being enlarged, new buildings were going up and more homes were being built between Jerusalem and Ramallah. It was good to be at home again, away from the confusion of the USA. Old friends met us at the plane, there were flowers in every room in the house, the garden was standing the summer well, and we were breathing the healing air of the hill-country of our beloved Palestine. The sad note was that so many of our friends had left the country on advice of their governments and those who remained were under considerable strain and were pessimistic about the future. John Barwick, with the American Friends of the Middle East, thought we should get our possessions out of the country at once as storm clouds were gathering. He and Laura expected to go soon. But we did not want to present a picture of people ready for flight, so decided we would carry on as usual. If the situation became so bad that we had to leave suddenly, then possessions would not be important. We had seen many of our Arab neighbours lose a great deal more than we would ever have to lose, and we did not want our neighbours to think for a moment that we knew what was ahead. We were as ignorant as they, and as uncertain of the future as they. So we carried on normally, painting cupboards, tending the garden, working on refugee programmes, taking visitors to the Holy Places, having friends in to tea and riding in the bus to Ramallah when necessary while the crisis steadily worsened. How soon the storm would break we could not foresee.

[13 September] The High Priest of the Samaritans called today to welcome us back and hopefully get a Parker fountain pen he had asked me to bring him. He had asked for one when we made a brief visit to the USA in 1949 and I failed him then, although I did give him a rather nice English one which was a gift from my brother and was still in its box. He was disappointed but apparently had not given up hopes of having a Parker some day. I appreciated his admiration of the Parker pen and wished I could have afforded one for myself. I pretended that he was not really serious about it, in fact I had hoped he had forgotten, but almost at once he asked if I had one for him. I compromised this time by giving him a set of fruit knives I had bought in Germany on the way home, and he was quite pleased as they would be more useful to him than the pen. We had a good visit over coffee and sweets.

The Coptic bishop followed next, greeting us warmly, and

proceeded to ask Willard for help with food and supplies for his schools. He was followed by Mr Basri Allah-ud-Din, Minister of Social Welfare, with whom Willard had close association. He was cordial but rather reflected the disillusion of the younger Arab officials with American policies, they say they are "fed up". Later, Gene Bird, the new American Vice-Consul on his first assignment, stopped by. He was not encouraging about the outcome of the present crisis, which made us think our previous visitor knew what he was talking about. We liked Mr Bird and are glad he will be our neighbour on the hill, but thought he had been given a tough post at the beginning of his diplomatic career. The afternoon ended with callers from Ramallah, also anxious people who hoped we could enlighten them on American opinion in regard to the Middle East. We wished we could give them some hope but we had come back almost fearful of the pressures that were being put on our senators and representatives to aid Israel and of so much ignorance where we should have expected to find understanding. A British friend came in time for tea, one of the two British women still on the UN staff. Then Malcolm McCallum arrived from Egypt for committee meetings tomorrow and he stayed to have supper with us. As I think of the visitors of the day, I realize it gives a picture of the Jerusalem that means so much to us: Samaritan, Copt, Palestinian, Muslim and Christian, American and British, all coming and going and mingling in normal association.

By October, there was no doubt in our minds that the portents of more serious crises were becoming clear. I met Colonel Eddy at the American Colony next day and he was full of foreboding.

On the 18th I had a call from Ellen Mansur in Ramallah asking for cloth for a dressmaking class our committee operated there. Ellen, who gave so generously of her time and talents to help us with the project, would not have telephoned if the need had not been urgent so I hurried out. On the way home, I stopped to see Mrs Rodenko, also a dedicated helper. She and her husband and five children were refugees from Jaffa. Her husband, a doctor, had fled from Russia to Lebanon during the First World War. Their home was on Radio Road, from which they could daily look down on Jaffa, where their home and possessions were. She was troubled and asked if we had been warned of impending danger. I assured her we had not, but I asked why she had asked. Well, she said, Britain was flying planes into Israel. They could see them from their home. I could give her neither information nor comfort but sympathized with her anxiety.

I returned to Jerusalem a little late for lunch, and as I neared the house I met Mr Dawson of the British Consulate returning to his office from lunch. Rather flippantly I asked him what the British were up to now. He was startled, assuming I was serious, and wanted to know what I meant. I told him that people in Ramallah were watching British planes flying into Israel and that they were worried. He hurried off and, to my complete surprise, he returned soon to tell me they were not British planes that were flying into Israel. I must believe that . . . and he was off again. Did he know whose planes they were? And why should he go to all that bother to come all the way back from the consulate to tell me? I don't yet know how much the British Consular Staff in Jerusalem knew of the impending Suez attack or how useful I had inadvertently been to them. If they knew, they could alert the government to the fact that the Arabs were aware of reinforcements to Israel; if they did not, they had reason to ask their government what was happening. As events proved, sooner than we expected, Mr Dawson was telling me the truth all right; the planes were not British but were French Mystère IVs, which were to be the mainstay of the Israeli thrust into Sinai within not many days.

Because Jerusalem was a divided city, there was an American Consulate on each side. Consular people, including wives, could cross from side to side freely within certain hours each day and the wives loved to come over to shop and walk about on the Arab side. On Monday morning, 25 October, as I was on my way to the Clothing Centre, I met the wife of one of the Consular staff near the Consulate, which almost adjoined the Centre. We chatted a few minutes, then I told her that some of the neighbours were coming in for coffee on Wednesday morning and I hoped she might be able to come over to join us. She accepted with such pleasure that I was surprised, not expecting such grateful thanks for so modest an invitation: "I would love to come. It is dreadful over there. No one is talking to us, we are isolated; of course I will come." And she did, and we had a delightful hour with neighbours, Arab, British and American with much in common. I had rarely taken time for morning coffee and shall always be glad for the kind angel who directed me to have a coffee on that particular date, for it was to be the last one of the kind we would have for a long time. The full significance of this simple incident was not borne in on me until long after, as the story of the Suez Crisis began to come through.

Comfort and Hope:
Grandfather and grand-
daughter in a refugee camp

Refugee Camp

Poultry Project at Gaza:
"Human thermometer" shows a
Rhode Island Red to the author

Refugee Camp

New Shoes

New Shoes: the boy was born in
the flight in 1948.
Still a refugee

Bedouin of the Azazma tribe, at Jerusalem.
The sheep were provided by the Relief Council

Bedouin Women: Refugees in Samaria

"Reprisal incidents" in the Hebron area created increasing fears among the Arabs on the West Bank, for such incidents usually preceded a violent strike and, always fearing the loss of the whole of Palestine, the people thought that might be the next step. This growing fear made it important for our refugee committee to make emergency plans so that if the British and American members of the committee had to leave suddenly, the funds and material for the refugees would be in capable hands and available. Little did we dream that the emergency was almost on us and the fire already kindled that would burst into flame with startling suddenness. Bishop Stewart of the Anglican Community was Chairman and I, Vice-Chairman. Fortunately, the treasurer was Mr Labib Nasir, General-Secretary of the YMCA, Jordan, and he was thoroughly familiar with committee programmes. Mr Hanna Atalla, judge, banker, a man who had held responsible positions in the Mandate Days and later in the Jordan Government, was asked to be Chairman and to take the bishop's place; mine was left pending further organization. It was good that there were several Palestinians on the committee who were dedicated and able so that we did not have the problem of an entirely new group. The new chairman had not served on the committee but he was a prominent member of the Arab Orthodox congregation and would steer the committee wisely should troubled times come.

Willard was in Cairo late in October and returned to Jerusalem on the 27th. He reported that on the surface all was quiet but the city was full of rumours. In the evening Dr Majaj, a specialist in children's diseases, and doing special research on anaemia in children which was developing in Jordan, came in to tell us that there would be a demonstration the next day to protest against the kidnapping of Ben Bella and four Algerians by the French as they were on their way to a conference in Tunis. So reassured, we were not prepared for what followed.

Sunday morning was peaceful enough. The Bird family stopped in on their way to the other side of Jerusalem to have dinner with friends. They were our near neighbours but they did not usually feel that they had to keep us informed of their movements. I invited them to have tea with us when they returned. All was quiet until half-past one, when we heard shooting near us. Soon bullets began to fly over our house and it was then we knew that the French Consulate, practically at our back door, was being attacked. Police and Arab Legion soldiers filled the street in front of our house. We closed the iron shutters of our house but peered through slits lest we might be needed to go to the rescue of the wounded.

The soldiers ducked beside our garden wall to avoid the bullets, which were not being directed at the house but merely coming from wild shots. The Legion tried to leave it to the police to dispel the mob and moved in only when the police failed. We learned of great damage to the consulate, which was also the home of the French Consul-General, and the young wife of the Consul and their children were in the building. It was a terrifying experience for them. Willard talked with a reporter for *Falastin* later who said that the French guards tried to defend the building with smoke bombs and rifles but were unable to keep the mob from getting inside. Egypt was blamed for this, as she was for every disturbance we had at that time. One Arab was killed and nine wounded and two French officers wounded, one seriously. Regardless of who was to blame, it was a tragic and irresponsible protest and another link in the chain of the whole unhappy story going back almost fifty years. The Arabs generally deplored the incident and the Governor of Jerusalem was severely censured for not providing adequate protection for the French Consulate. We all felt deeply distressed for the Consul's wife, who was but a few days in Jerusalem when this happened. The city quietened down by teatime, but it would take some time for us to forget the violence of the afternoon.

Monday, 29 October, was to be another of those days! It started with a rumour that the State Department was ordering all Americans out of the Middle East. Before it was confirmed, I hastened out to Ramallah to settle refugee accounts and plan with Ellen lest we should have to go. I returned in time for lunch to more rumours, but so far we had no official notice. Around two o'clock I went out to work in the garden, too restless to do anything else, and while I was picking off dead geraniums, Gerri Bird stopped on her way home. She was bitter about yesterday's mob action, and nervous. In a vague way, she indicated that we would be getting official notice of evacuation, and she urged us to go; that there was sufficient activity on the other side of the lines to make evacuation necessary. Willard was busy in the office with his Armenian secretary at the time and as I did not want to give Willard the news in front of him, I wrote a note and dropped it on his desk and went back to the garden. Willard joined me soon and we talked it over. Our decision was to stay as long as we could. In less than an hour the following notice was delivered:

"Because of increased tension in the Middle East area the United States Government considers it advisable for American citizens to leave Jordan without delay. It is suggested therefore that you place your passports in order at once, making sure that they are valid for travel, and make immediate commercial transportation arrangements for your departure. Please inform the American Consulate-General, Jerusalem, of travel plans whenever possible."

The radio that night had a good deal of news about the revolution in Hungary and reported that Israel was massing troops on the border. And so to bed on that note.

Next morning we had a message that the American Consul wanted to see us. Since we had no telephone connections, we had no choice but to go down to the American Consulate. We did not know what pressures there might be to get us out but we were still firm in our conviction that we would stay. Very few British people were left in Jerusalem and all French people were gone save for the nurses in the French hospital. There were not many Americans left either. The Consul-General was kind but advised us to leave. He told us the plane would go at two o'clock in the afternoon, places were reserved on it for us and we could each take one suitcase. Willard asked, "Is this an order?"

"No, it is not an order but our advice is to go. If you refuse to go, we cannot promise to protect you."

We looked at each other again; we had not changed our minds and Willard thanked the Consul-General for his provision for us, but we would remain, understanding fully that we did so on our own responsibility. Willard then returned to his office and I went to the Clothing Centre to talk with Olga, the supervisor. From there I went into the Old City to shop for supplies for the sewing classes and to Mr Najarian's on the Via Dolorosa to order Jerusalem handicrafts for friends in America. I called on Katy Nimr Antonius on the way home. Katy is the daughter of Dr Faris Nimr Pasha, a Lebanese, one of the founders of *Al-Muqattam*, a well-known Arab daily newspaper published in Cairo. Dr Nimr, as a young student in Lebanon, helped form a secret society in Beirut representing the enlightened elite of the country which was the first organized effort in the Arab National Movement. She is also the widow of George Antonius, author of *The Arab Awakening*, a book essential for one who would understand the background of the Palestine Problem. Katy grew up in Cairo but lived in Jerusalem after her marriage. Latest news from Katy was that she was back in Cairo living in her old home. She was a hostess *par excellence* in Jerusalem and carried on her father's and her husband's concern for the future of the Arab World. She was terribly upset over Sunday's demonstration and said that there was a rumour that the Governor of Jerusalem might be taken before the Ministry for negligence. She was also distressed over the evacuation order and seemed glad to know we would stay. After lunch, Willard and I went out to Ramallah and found the Americans at the schools on their way out. We saw some of our friends but hurried back as a curfew was to go on at five o'clock in the evening. The evening news was that the British and French had decided to send troops to strategic points on the canal but that Egypt said she could not accept such a condition. Eugene Bird had a truly hectic day helping Americans get off.

The next days were days of uncertainty. We knew serious events were taking place around us but did not know yet if Israel was coming our way. We did not know that Israel even then had moved into Sinai. The Cyprus radio continued to broadcast movements of the British troops towards Egypt but the American Consulate was still apparently in the dark about British and French plans. The atmosphere was one of secrecy, which increased the unease and speculation. A few notes from my diary of these days will indicate the situation in Jerusalem and how little we knew.

[1 November] Gene Bird came to the house this afternoon and asked us to go to the American Colony tonight as it was important for the American Consulate to know where all Americans were. He may have fears of anti-Western demonstrations as feeling over the Suez affair runs high and the Arabs suspect that America must be party to it also. He may have even greater fears if rumours have any substance at all. So we are spending the night at the American Colony. We came down before the curfew was to begin at five o'clock. On the way down, we met a United Nations Truce Observer who greeted us with surprise as he thought we must have been evacuated. We assured him we were remaining on our own responsibility, that, as the Arabs would say, it was on our own heads if we had difficulties. He was silent a moment, then glancing over towards occupied Jerusalem, so near yet so very, very far, he said: "I would hate like hell to see them come over here." The British are terribly upset and ashamed, painfully so. Miss Moore, a long-serving teacher in the English College for Girls, has sent a cable to London demanding the fall of the government! I think we are all puzzled over the "un-Eden like" action. The French here share the British humiliation. Madame Vigier, charming wife of the French political adviser to the United Nations Mission in Palestine, could only say: "What has happened to my country?" We hope America is not in it.

[2 November] Got up early and went back to the house. We did not want word to get around that we had gone and thought it would be good to be there when the milk-woman arrived. Her eyes lighted when she found us, as she had walked miles to bring the milk and had been afraid we would be gone. When we were eating breakfast we had another visitor. This time it was Abou Ahmed, the *bawab* (door-man) for the Lebanese Consulate. Our garden adjoined the Consulate garden and Abou Ahmed often kept his eye on our place when we were gone. We had never asked him to do this, he simply liked doing it, for he had known Willard before we moved to Jerusalem. He told us he thought we had been evacuated and was surprised to see our house open when he got up, so he came bringing in one hand a soup-plate filled with jasmine blossoms and in the other a live rabbit. The jasmine blossoms filled the house with their fragrance. He explained that he had brought the rabbit lest we were shut in and would need food. I was glad to show him that we had food for a few days and asked if he would just keep the rabbit in case we should need it later. I don't know when anything ever touched us so deeply, and I am sure we will never forget the picture Abou Ahmed presented as he entered the house with blossoms and rabbit. It lifted our hearts. "So shines a good deed in a naughty world!" We served him coffee and told him he gave us a wonderful feeling of security. Later this morning, the Emergency Committee of the ICC called a meeting and invited me to attend. Since they felt that as long as the British were attacking Egypt they could not invite any of the English people at the cathedral, I thought they should not feel it necessary to invite me either. They insisted that as I had been so long on the committee and the new chairman-to-be had never been on it, my presence there would be helpful. Actually they wanted me to chair the meeting. We are lucky to have Mr Hanna Atalla as our new chairman and we will need his guidance. The meeting went well, for the committee is an able one. We are spending the night in our own home; curfew is on, the windows are blacked out, but the radio keeps us in touch with the world. We gather that England plans to "make over" the Middle East to suit her and doesn't mind all the condemnation that is being heaped on her. We are still in the dark about the future of Jordan.

[3 November] Went out to Ramallah this morning and found the people there in great distress as news comes through, some of it contradictory, some of it full of foreboding. They feel that if they could only know what to expect, they would know what to do. But what can they do? The latest news is that King Hussein has asked Iraq to come in. Curfew still in force beginning at five o'clock.

[4 November] Another day of waiting and wondering. We hear of a UN police force for the Middle East. The radio also tells of troops leaving Cyprus for Egypt. Can the UN survive all this aggression? This British and French "police action", if carried out, takes us back rather than forward in international relations. We had several Arab friends in to see us in the afternoon. I am sure they think we may be informed on what to expect, but we are as much in the dark as they.

[5 November] We listened to a recast of Gaitskell's speech in Parliament yesterday as we ate breakfast this morning. It was a blunt, strong condemnation of Eden. Britain and France have landed troops in Egypt and tonight the news is that Egyptians are surrendering at Port Said. I'm afraid this fire will not be put out soon. And in Hungary tragic events are happening, too. One other item is that Syria has damaged the pipe-line which carries precious oil from Arabia to the West, this to show sympathy with Egypt's problem. As the story builds up France and Britain are being accused of collusion with Israel and they deny it. Seems stupid for them to deny it; such a concerted assault on Egypt looks far from being merely coincidental. If it is true that there has been collusion, how can we expect the Middle East to have faith in the Great Powers of the West? The papers indicate that the American Consulate expected Israel to attack Jordan last Saturday night. I rather think they expected it sooner, perhaps the night they wanted us all at the American Colony. The Allies must be given credit for choosing a good time for their joint action against Egypt, for Russia has her hands full of Hungarian troubles and America has an election tomorrow.

[6 November] American elections today and all praying that Eisenhower will be in again. I possessed my soul by working at the Clothing Centre for some hours in the morning. We took baby clothes to the Arab Women's Union clinic, shirts and socks to Dar-ul-Awlad, a boys' school sponsored by Katy Antonius, and prepared layettes for refugee babies in Ramallah. I went out to Ramallah with Olga to help distribute the layettes in the afternoon. The news on the radio is so disturbing that I telephoned Laura Barwick in Beirut tonight to ask her to write to our son to let him know we are all right so far and were able to get about freely. Tonight several friends braved the curfew and came to see us. Our talk was of the crisis and the mixed news we are getting; but mostly we talked of the election. They are as concerned as Americans at home must be. News had come earlier in the day that a cease-fire was to go into effect at midnight. Eisenhower had come out so boldly against the tripartite attack on Egypt and the secrecy with which Britain and France and Israel had carried it out that we wondered if the Jewish vote which they talk about so much would defeat him. We were quite touched when Mrs Said, of an old Jerusalem family and a good friend, spoke up: "We hope and pray that President Eisenhower will be elected. But you mustn't worry if he isn't. He may lose the election, but he has won the respect of the world."

[7 November] The first good rain of the season and Eisenhower is in again, bringing a ray of hope at last that the crisis may be over soon! People smiling over the happy combination of the rain and the result of the election. We hope and pray that Eisenhower can maintain the high standard of statesmanship that he has shown so far. Mrs Vester invited us to dinner at the Colony to celebrate. Surprisingly, the British Consul-General was there and seemed to be happy, too, over the election. We sat at the same small table and in the course of the conversation he told me that he had a Scottish mother. Since I had one too, we had something in common. There was talk of the situation in England over the Eden policies: how the country is divided as it has not been in years, and violently so. They say Nutting has resigned from the cabinet. The Arab Legion took special pains to protect the Israeli convoy to Mount Scopus today. By shutting off the streets and interurban traffic, all went well. I was held up by it as I was on my way to the Clothing Centre, and I marvelled to see how well Jordan has observed the agreements in regard to this convoy ever since 1949.

[8 November] We had planned to spend my birthday at Aqaba today: it seems such a long time ago that we made this plan! The moon is nearer. So, I celebrated by working on committee affairs. Willard thinks we should go to Beirut on Monday for the regular meetings of the NECCCRW and CCCVA, Central Co-ordinating Committee of the Voluntary Agencies. He thinks we can get places in a taxi, and that travel to Amman, Damascus and Beirut will be possible. Friends think it is a wild plan and word has come that the American Consul in Beirut is invalidating all American re-entry permits to Jordan. Willard reminds me that when we go to Lebanon our official dealings are with the Lebanese Government, so is determined to go ahead with plans. "The show must go on!" We must go ahead normally for the sake of the many in other countries who support our work as well as for the people we are trying to help here; and it will cheer people to see that the work goes on. So we will be off early Monday. Willard remembers that the International Red Cross gave him their flag for the station-wagon-ambulance in 1948, and he hopes the UNRWA would speak for us if difficulties arise about re-entry.

And so life went on. We heard that a UN force was on the way to Egypt and hoped it was not going to mean a second Korea. The Arabs, weary of eight years of tensions and incidents and continued threats of aggression, would like to get the problem of the refugees settled, and fear that with focus on Egypt now, they will continue to be forgotten. One hope is that Nasser has reiterated the fact that if Israel will carry out Security Council resolutions on the refugees, the question of Israel using the Canal is settled. It was Farouk who closed it to them in 1948 and the refugee situation has not changed. No matter where discussion on the Middle East begins, the trail leads back to the *fact* of Israel.

We left Jerusalem at half-past six on Monday morning in our own car, and had a pleasant trip to Beirut. Officials at border points in Syria and Lebanon were more than friendly, the former even serving us coffee while we waited for the usual border formalities. And when they sent us on with "*Maa Salaami*—Go in peace", this customary good-bye had special meaning for us that day.

Arriving in Beirut in the afternoon, we were surrounded by Palestinians and British and American evacuees wanting to know what was really happening in Jordan. We were happy to report that all was well so far. In the evening we drove out to the Women's College to see our Palestine students to assure them that their fathers and mothers were well. What a warm welcome we had, and when they told us that they had said from the beginning that we would not leave, we knew that our decision had been right. The heads of Arab States were having a meeting in Beirut to discuss recent developments, so we had the experience of seeing them enter

the UNESCO building next morning amidst much pomp and ceremony.

The meetings of the committees went as usual, everything quite
normal, but it was the excellent and moving report of Michael
Hocking, an English official with UNRWA, on Gaza, that made us
see the crisis in all its depth. Already, hundreds had died, and
young men, marked as *fedayeen*, were fleeing. The Israelis were
liquidating them and anyone suspected of having the least association with them. He said that there was desperate need of doctors
and nurses in the camps. Two women doctors at the meeting
volunteered; but we learned that they could not get clearance to go
in.

We returned to Jerusalem on Friday, again leaving at half-past
six in the morning. The Arab kings, princes and heads of state were
returning to their respective countries, too, so progress was slow for
us because of their convoys. At the Lebanese border they had a big
send-off, and a few metres beyond, the Syrians waited to welcome
them with bands and flags and a big crowd. It was all colourful and
we enjoyed being onlookers.

The tone of the country was decidedly more cheerful when we
returned. On Sunday we learned that an Air Jordan plane would
leave for Cairo on Monday; this was the first plane for Egypt since
the beginning of the crisis and Willard immediately applied for a
place on it. They also announced that planes would be going again
to Beirut. Mr Dawson of the British Consulate told us that he
thought evacuees would be able to return soon and that Bishop
Stewart was already on his way back. No wonder the atmosphere
had changed, and so quickly. On Tuesday morning, young Dr Kal-
bian came to tell us with understandable pride that his first child,
a boy, had just arrived and mother and child were in the almost
deserted French Hospital a block from us. Such a happy note in our
unhappy world. God was still in His heaven and a baby brought
hope. We needed the happy news, for before night we received a
call for clothing for hundreds of young men who had fled from
Gaza and were in great need. Also, news from Britain was that the
country was still split over Suez and that Eden was ill.

Willard remained in Egypt for a week and I busied myself with
work at the Clothing Centre and other committee business. Friends
were thoughtful and many called; some were surprised that I was
staying alone in the house, but it hadn't occurred either to Willard
or to me that there was any need for me to be afraid. I was used
to staying alone when he had to attend meetings and the times
seemed all right now. Thanksgiving Day was celebrated at the

Cathedral on 22 November. Canon Every led the service and the American Consul-General read the President's proclamation, which was hardly realistic in our situation. But we could be thankful that the fighting had ceased and we could pray that a sincere, concerted effort might be made toward a speedy peace for all the countries of the Middle East, and especially for the dispossessed Palestinians. The British Consul-General invited the few Americans in Jerusalem to a Thanksgiving dinner in the evening, served buffet style. The Americans were in the minority and dinner was quite international in the end, for our host had invited some UN personnel to swell the crowd. This occasion was delightful and added to the general feeling that things were getting better. And how we were needing just such an affair! I was sorry Willard had to miss it.

Willard's report from Cairo was encouraging. He thought the morale of the people was wonderful. Instead of bringing Nasser down, the invasion had strengthened him and the people were solidly behind him. The government had set up centres for Port Said refugees and were caring for 60,000. They allowed ten piastres a day per person, and teachers, social workers, and other professional people were giving fine volunteer service. He had met with his committee and other vountary agencies and they had formed a special committee to co-ordinate relief efforts. They had also made a special appeal to World Council of Churches members and Church World Service was already preparing to send help. Willard went again in December and this time spent ten days. He was able to get to Port Said and found the devastation much worse than the press had reported. In fact, he felt that it had been deliberately played down. He met Senator Douglas and other American VIPs but they were getting a "supervised" tour and not the true picture. Britain and France were now trying to justify their invasion and still trying to claim that there was no collusion with Israel. (Now that the story of the collusion is well documented and told in the books, we cannot imagine why they expected the public to believe them in the first place.) One incident pleased Willard. When he was in a refugee camp, in a school-house, the leader introduced Willard as an American and the people immediately cheered for Eisenhower and then for Nasser. They felt that they owed it to Eisenhower that the cease-fire had come so quickly.

Work on refugee clothing speeded up in the next few weeks, and we were glad to provide clothing for 250 Gaza refugees in addition to our own families. By early December we were beginning to think that the emergency was over. It was, in the country as a whole, but a delicate situation had arisen in our Emergency Committee. The British were still in Port Said when they had to call a committee meeting and asked to have it at our house. However, the Executive Committee felt that the time had not yet come to invite any of the British members of the committee to meet with us as long as Britain was technically occupying Port Said. They consulted Willard and he tried to point out that our work transcended politics and hoped they would invite the Bishop and Mrs Stewart. They assured Willard it was not a personal matter and they thought the Bishop would understand the embarrassment his presence might cause, and bring criticism on them. Willard went to the Bishop and Mrs Stewart and explained the whole situation to them and they were understanding, though perhaps a little hurt. So we met at our house with Mr Hanna Atalla in the chair. The meeting went well until nearly the end when Mrs Vester, who had not approved the committee's action, could hold back no longer and spoke angrily about the exclusion of the British members of the old committee. She said she was shocked beyond words, although she was not sparing of them at the moment, and accused the present committee of lack of Christian love. Since two Christian nations were presently in Egypt and had killed and wounded many and destroyed a great part of one of Egypt's larger cities, the Arab members of the committee, all Christians, felt that we had not presented a very good example of Christianity in the Muslim World. They thought the British members understood how the Arab people felt in the present crisis. Mr Atalla was upset, but he summed up the Arab Christian point of view in a fine spirit which cleared the air. The meeting ended amicably over cups of tea and cakes, and another crisis was over. In all the years I was on the committee, I think this was the only time there had been such a scene and I was more than thankful Mr Atalla was in the chair.

The year ended with the Western Powers trying to extricate themselves from the Suez Crisis. France and England were getting out of Egypt, but getting Israel out of the Gaza Strip was a bigger problem. However, Jerusalem was getting back to normal, or as normal as a divided city could get, and we welcomed the coming of the New Year, hoping that solutions would be worked out for a permanent peace. A vain wish and we knew it, but it was important not to be too pessimistic.

I spent most of the last day of the year at the Clothing Centre. The few weeks we had spent in the USA in the summer were almost forgotten in the exciting events in the Middle East which came so close to us. We were glad we had remained throughout the crisis.

[31 December] The Old Year goes out more quietly than we had dared hope or expect, with the Middle East holding the centre of the World stage. We watch America's policies with apprehension . . . but continue to pray for the peace of Jerusalem and the whole Middle East.

Suez Crises

The Suez Crisis was not to end with the Old Year as we had hoped. France and Britain had withdrawn early in December, but despite UN resolutions demanding withdrawal, the Israelis had stubbornly refused to leave the Gaza Strip and reports from there were most distressing. Living as we did in a small country, and meeting people closely involved with the political life of the country, we knew that no one doubted the collusion of the three countries that were involved in the crisis, but it would be some time before we were to know the whole sorry story. The incredible deception practised by France and Britain was hard to understand. What these two countries hoped to accomplish by getting rid of Nasser was hard for us to fathom. Furthermore, in 1950, France, Britain and the United States had issued a Tripartite Declaration which was an agreement to act within or outside the United Nations to prevent violation of the Armistice Lines established in 1949. There was a United Nations Truce Supervision Organization, UNTSO, at that time, but it needed support as violations were frequent and the Tripartite Declaration was to strengthen it. Now, two parties to the Declaration had acted independently and secretly and had aided Israel in a violation of the Armistice to the extent of allowing it to be a military aggressor, too. If the lines between Washington and London were so hot as to become almost aflame, according to reports, it was not surprising.

If that was not enough, the tragic story of Kafr Kasseem added to the painful combination of events of the sad end of the year. Kafr Kasseem was an Arab village in Israel close to the Armistice Line, with a population of approximately two thousand Palestinians. It had the reputation of being co-operative with the Occupying Government. We had heard vague rumours about the massacre that had taken place there at the end of October, but in time the whole story came out. On 29 October 1956, on the eve of the invasion into the Sinai Peninsula and Egypt, the *mukhtar* (head) of the village was told that a curfew would be imposed at five o'clock in the evening. It was then half-past four and many of the villagers were in their fields; some were working in other places, and as it was the olive season whole families were in the groves picking olives. The *mukhtar* protested that it was impossible to notify them all and begged to have the curfew go on later. The officer in charge refused and set up road blocks into the village. Soon after five o'clock the workers began to come home: men, women and children, in automobiles, trucks, and on bicycles. As they tried to enter the village they were machine-gunned. By six o'clock forty-seven civilians were dead and thirteen survived by feigning death. Of sixteen olive-pickers in one truck, fourteen of them women, only one young girl survived. This incident recalled to our Arab neighbours Deir Yasin and Qibya among other atrocities, and it aroused the old fears. The news of this massacre was suppressed for some time, even in Israel, but was eventually admitted in the Knesset, where it must have shocked many troubled Israeli citizens.

An incident on 23 January brought the tragedy of the Gaza Occupation to us distressingly. That morning, the headmaster of the Hashemeyeh College called us at the Clothing Centre to ask for some clothing for fifteen young men from Gaza who had fled from the Strip and had arrived with nothing but the clothes on their backs. I hurried down to the Centre to help prepare bundles of clothing for them after getting as much information about their ages and sizes as we could. They were all young but had feared for their lives. Mr Suleiman took us to the hostel where they were put up so that we could see them and talk with them. It was a harrowing story which they hardly needed to tell, as their appearance, their state of exhaustion, and their nervousness indicated all too well what they had suffered. They told us of the difficulty of getting away from Gaza, actually fleeing without time to stop for food, how they had travelled in the night and slept in caves during the day and how it had taken four days to come the relatively short distance. Stories which they told of life in the Gaza Strip were later confirmed by responsible Western observers.

The Israelis had determined to wipe out the *fedayeen* and all suspected of helping them, as long as they were in Gaza, and these young men had seen many of their friends killed in the camps and in homes in the town. Raids were made in the night and men of all ages were torn from their families, many young husbands with young children, and were not seen again. Mr Labouisse, who was Director of the United Nations Relief and Works Programme, reported to the UN soon after the occupation that at least 275 persons had been killed. Another report was that at a refugee camp in Rafah, at a round-up of refugees, Israeli soldiers fired on the crowd, killing more than one hundred. When I was in Gaza four years later, I

was told that recently, when a family was excavating a plot of
land for a new house, they came on a grave with twenty-eight
bodies in it. The Suez Crisis was to plague us for a long, long time.
As I recalled the hour we spent with these young men, hearing their
story, I jotted down in my diary that night: "They were a pathetic
lot. These and thousands like them are more to be feared by the
Israelis in the future than the Nasser they are so strongly against."
As I write this many years later, I am not surprised that Israel
finds the Gaza Strip so hard to govern and the people so resist-
ant.

The whole Egyptian affair had created tensions all around us and
we found it particularly so among the older boys in schools. I
visited schools in camps with clothing quite often and I soon
learned from the attitude of the older boys when some new crisis
had arisen. It was never against me personally, but one sensed
undercurrents of resentment against America over their lot and
over the inability of the UN to face their problem squarely.

This was brought home to me in a rather unhappy incident on
30 January 1957 when I went out to Deir Ammar Camp to distribute shoes to more than seven hundred boys and girls in the refugee
schools. I had been particularly happy about going, for it was a
bitterly cold day and the shoes and new stockings to go with them
would be a comfort. This was not a United Nations Relief project,
but the UNRWA team learned about the distribution and the publicity department asked if they might take pictures. Our committee
had never emphasized picture-taking and had tried to keep it within
bounds, enough only to let donors see some of the fruits of their
giving. However, there seemed no reason to object to the team's
request.

All went well at the Girls' School, but when we went to the
Boys' School the older boys staged a demonstration and created
quite a disturbance, almost stopping the distribution. UNRWA is
associated in their minds with the Partition of Palestine, and it did
not make for love of the United Nations. The publicity-team finally
got some footage, but under great difficulty. The *mukhtar* took me
aside and told me that the elders of the village would consent to
pictures for Mr Jones or Mrs Jones, but this big affair had been too
much for the boys. I appreciated the point of view of the boys. I
was very sensitive about it myself and I had not asked for the
pictures! I realized that ten years of living within easy walking
distance of their homes had not softened the bitterness and frustration that was the daily lot of the elders. Now the older boys in
school were growing increasingly rebellious at the failure of their

fathers to better their condition and at the play of politics that kept their government from getting them back to their homes. The older teenagers had memories of life on the plains where there was sunshine and food, homes and happy boyhood. It was indeed sad to see a whole generation growing up in a camp. They were keen students and aware of what was going on in the world about them, and of international events. I happened to go out to the camp a day or so after the mayor of New York insulted the King of Saudi Arabia, who was in the United States as the guest of the government. The governor of New York refused to attend a reception for him. The older boys surrounded me to protest. I was fortunately able to ask them how he was greeted when he went to Washington, and they admitted that there the welcome was according to the rules. Was the mayor of New York more important than the President of the United States? News travels fast these days and reaches even remote, isolated places in minutes, and radios were the chief diversion of camp-life. The next day I was to write:

[31 January] More rain with high winds and rain turning to sleet has chilled us all to the bone. I could weep when I remember Deir Ammar as it was yesterday, its sodden tents and the people looking down on their old homes in the milder climate of the coastal plain. So glad the children have shoes, and so glad we measured children in Ramallah for shoes this afternoon. How they need them!

[2 February] We woke to a white world. Jerusalem is blanketed and looks lovely, serene and ageless. If it were only at peace! The snow began yesterday accompanied by hail, thunder and lightning. Travel is now impossible. When I woke up I was glad it was Saturday, as the Clothing Centre is closed on Saturday and the workers would be safely at home.

But my relief was short-lived, for soon after breakfast Mr Labib Nasir telephoned to say that the head of the Social-Welfare Department of the Government, Mr Basri Alaudin, was asking for one hundred bundles of clothing for refugee families in Jerusalem. With all our workers either in Bethlehem or Ramallah and no one able to travel anyway, all I could do was to tell Mr Nasir that if he could get the place opened and a jeep for me, I would go down and do what I could. A jeep arrived at nine o'clock. In the next three hours I managed to make up seventy-eight bundles and was greatly relieved when Mr Alaudin sent jeeps to collect them and decided they would be enough. The snow is over, but it is so deep that only jeeps can travel in it.

[8 February] We had a request from UNRWA this morning for clothing for 1,555 families in camps who are in urgent need of clothing as a result of the snow. There is also another request for clothing for eight more Gaza refugees. The latter have sad stories to tell and these have been confirmed by Chris, of the Lutheran World Federation, our dear Danish friend, who has been in Gaza recently. He tells us that the people of Gaza feel trapped, isolated, and are in constant fear. He also confirms the thought that we have had increasingly, that Israel is getting encouragement from somewhere or she could not keep on defying the UN resolutions so openly.

We were in Cairo in the latter part of February as Willard had to attend committee meetings and consult with governments on bringing in relief. While there we had a good visit with Commander Elmo Hutchison, formerly of the Mixed-Armistice Commission stationed in Jerusalem, and now with American Friends of the Middle East. He gave us some interesting information on the treatment of the Jews in Cairo following the attack on Egypt. He feels that it was unique in history for tolerance. Foreigners had lived in Egypt for generations and been given all the advantages of foreign status. Jews had refused to stand up and let it be known where their loyalties lay, by failing to take out citizenship. However, they had been treated remarkably well in the circumstances. Three months had passed since the Suez attack and so far only a quarter of the Jewish Community had left the country; the rest had decided to await developments. Almost all Jewish firms were operating and there were no special laws against Jews as Jews; recent laws were directed against enemy aliens and foreign companies only. If Jews had British or French citizenship, these laws would affect them as they did others.

3 March found us again on our way to Beirut via Damascus. It was a beautiful trip in the spring. Jericho with its abundance of fruits and flowers, the whole Jordan Valley green and fertile after the rains, the fields around Irbid almost ready for a rich harvest, all were good for our souls. At the border of Syria customs officials were friendly, and as we sipped coffee with the official in charge of entry formalities, he told us of his studies in America and how friendly and wonderful Americans had been to him. He had seen more of the USA than we had, and as we were leaving he said rather wistfully: "If it wasn't for Israel, all would be well between the USA and the Middle East."

It took six UN resolutions and the threat of a measure being brought before that organization to impose sanctions on Israel to bring about a reluctant withdrawal. The feeling among Palestinians and members of the foreign community was that Israel was getting support from France and Britain in her refusal to obey UN resolutions. Eisenhower's reputation for statesmanship was still high and he was given credit for bringing pressure on Israel to follow the lead of Britain and France and withdraw from the occupied territories. For a brief period, America was the hope of the Arab World for justice in the Middle East. Pressures in the United Nations were certainly great, as the resolutions indicated, and on 6 March the good news came that Israel was leaving the Strip.

When this news reached the Arab Communities, especially on the West Bank, there was a tremendous sense of relief, as many had relatives in Gaza and reports that had reached them of life under occupation were grave indeed. I am inclined to think that they hoped that the whole effect of the Suez Crisis and its aftermath might make the international community wake up to the necessity of settling the Palestine Problem, particularly that of the refugees. That was apparently too much to hope for, as only expedient measures were to be taken.

One interesting development was the establishment of a United Nations Emergency Force to maintain peace on the Egypt-Israeli Armistice Line. When it was proposed, Israel refused to have it on her side of the line but Egypt accepted it and honoured it from the beginning. This force was drawn from ten member nations of the UN: Brazil, Canada, Columbia, Denmark, Finland, India, Indonesia, Yugoslavia, Norway and Sweden. The blue berets of this force were to become familiar sights in Jerusalem, for the men came on leave as often as they could and, like all foreigners, enjoyed the sights and sounds of this wonderful city. This force was to remain until the next major crisis ten years later, and it maintained a high standard of service.

I went to Gaza frequently and each time I went I found a busy population building new homes, opening up businesses, improving the city and, in general, carrying on wonderfully well even in their isolation, and always hopeful of the future. The flag of Palestine flew over the government buildings and Palestine was on its stamps. Under an able committee of the NECCCRW, an extensive programme for the refugees was carried on, notable for its diversity and excellence as well as for the way it was training hundreds of young people in useful occupations. My husband had to go almost every month to meet the committee to keep up with its needs, to let contributors know how their gifts were being used, and to encourage them to continue to assist in this great area of need. It was always a special treat for me when I could go with him, for we had Old Boys and Old Girls of our schools in Gaza and many friends from many lands, and a visit to the various programmes being carried on was heartwarming.

Our next crisis came in April and this time it was a domestic one and more critical than many of us realized at the time. It centred on a plot to assassinate the King, declare Jordan a republic, and free it from imperialist domination. Glubb Pasha and all the British officers of the Arab Legion had been sent out of the country a year before and there were those who wanted an Arab Federation, which they maintained could not be formed of republics and monarchies. For the moment, the future of Jordan and particularly of the West Bank was in jeopardy as Israeli troops began massing on the borders as soon as news of the attempted coup got abroad.

Strangely enough, most of us on the West Bank hardly realized how critical the situation was at first. There were rumours of frequent cabinet changes and disaffection in the army, but it was not until the crisis was almost over and an incident erupted in the Broadcasting Station that we woke up to some of the problems the King had faced and what dangers had been averted. We were to learn of them later.

In the Mandate days, the broadcasting studio was in Jerusalem but the tower was in Ramallah. It was told that when the government was trying to decide where to erect the tower, one official thought it would be romantic to have it in Bethel, where Jacob had his dream of a ladder going to heaven, or descending from heaven, but investigation proved that there was no good place for it in that village. Ramallah, close to Bethel, was next studied and science won where romance failed. When the British were about to leave Palestine, some of the studio equipment and furnishings were sent to Ramallah, and it was for years the station which served all of Jordan under the name of Jerusalem Broadcasting Station. In 1957 Amman had not yet a station as well equipped.

Thus it was that, when the crisis was resolved, King Hussein considered it his duty to report to his people all the facts and sent his message to Ramallah to be broadcast with the evening news. Incredibly, the staff shut down the station and refused to do the broadcast. The incident created quite a sensation and apprehension in our area, to say nothing of what effect it had in Amman. Several members of the staff were arrested, suspected of having communist sympathies, and later condemned to several years in prison.

The story which filtered through to some of us who could not keep up with the Arab Press was that a small faction in the army, headed by Abu Nawar, Commander-in-Chief of the army, a young man whom the King had trusted, and some of his officers, had planned the coup. They moved the troops about to suit themselves, and at one time Amman was almost surrounded. Fortunately for the King, there were many loyal soldiers and officers who were able to warn him of impending danger. At a most critical time, word went out that the King was dead. On hearing this, with a courage he had exhibited on more than one occasion, Hussein decided to have it out with the army and show that he was indeed very much alive. Taking Abu Nawar with him, he drove to Army headquarters in Zerka and boldly faced his troops. The reaction was electric; the men surrounded him with rejoicing and a great display of loyalty. Some leaders of the coup immediately fled across the border into Syria. Abu Nawar returned to the Palace with the King, who in a most unexpected gesture gave him permission to leave the country at once with his family.

There were some difficult days ahead as a new cabinet was formed, but eventually Hussein had a cabinet he could trust, the loyalty of the army was assured, and he had gained in stature both at home and abroad.

Before April ended, however, our sense of peace and order was again disrupted. A new factor was introduced into the life of the country, bringing on new demonstrations and all that went with them. And ironically it was called the Eisenhower Doctrine, but it was merely another extension of Suez. We remember that one aspect of the French, British, and Israeli collusion which had aroused the anger of President Eisenhower was the fact that France and Britain had violated the Tripartite Declaration of 1950. France and Britain had acted independently, secretly, and aided a violation of the Armistice Line between Egypt and Israel by plotting with Israel the overthrow of Nasser and opening the way for further Israeli aggression.

The Tripartite Declaration was now history; France and Britain had lost, for the time being, their place in the Middle East, and America, alone of the Western Powers, was still considered acceptable. But a new problem arose for the Western Powers and that was Russia. So far, she had been the one to gain from the Suez Crisis. And so it was that the Eisenhower Doctrine was proposed to meet the situation or to fill the vacuum left by France and Britain.

The Eisenhower Doctrine was primarily a ploy to keep Russia

out of the Middle East. To us, it was strange to think that was possible, for Russia was already in the Middle East. Perhaps Eisenhower hoped he could keep Russia from getting further into it. The proposal was that America would provide arms to Egypt for "reasonable defence of its borders in return for an agreement that it would never accept any Soviet offer." It was unfortunately couched in terms no sovereign state could accept and angered more than it appeased, for after its firm handling of the Suez Crisis America seemed to be backing down. Before Suez, America had refused to sell Egypt necessary arms "for reasonable defence of its borders," and after Suez had refused to sell wheat and medicines so much needed after the attack on Port Said and other points in Egypt. Furthermore, when Egypt asked America to release $27,000,000 of blocked currency, she was again refused. As she had done in the past, Egypt now turned to Russia for wheat and medicine and arms. Eisenhower's offer was late, too late, and was a bitter disappointment to Americans in the Middle East. The new doctrine savoured of bribery, if not of capitulation. Whatever her motives, Russia had been a friend in need to Egypt and America had lost the largest uncommitted area in the world. Russia won it by default; she was now in the Mediterranean and she was not to be easily dislodged. Almost any move from now on was to the Palestinians an attempt to make them accept Israel and make the refugees ready to give up their right of return. And so we were back again to curfews, demonstrations and martial law.

On 24 April Willard was in Beirut. There seemed to be a good deal of activity at the Iraqi Consulate in Jerusalem that day, otherwise there was a quietness that seemed to portend something new. It was not surprising then when I learned that a curfew would go on at five o'clock in the evening. It was not lifted until three o'clock in the afternoon of the next day, and then for only an hour. The radio reported that Ramallah, Nablus, Jerusalem, Irbid and Amman were especially tense and sources of disorder. The curfew was not lifted until eleven o'clock on Friday morning, and I hurried down to the post-office for the mail. It was rather comforting to see people going about in a business-like way, shops had opened and people paid little attention to the soldiers guarding the gates to the Old City and government buildings. Everyone was friendly and almost casual. When I got home, neighbours, knowing I was alone, came in with roses and pansies and we drank coffee together in the security of our home. However, I could not get over the feeling of being suspended between two worlds, one of peace and security, another one tottering on the brink.

Willard was able to get home on Friday afternoon and he immediately applied for a pass so that he would not be shut in as he
needed to be able to travel to Ramallah, Bethlehem, and Hebron
and to be in touch with friends in Jerusalem.

On Sunday morning we decided to drive down to Hebron to see
Ada and Ida Stoltzfus, the twins, who carried on our programme of
relief. They had remained at their post carrying on the work of our
committee as usual. We had been anxious about them, but they
assured us that Mr Hammouri, a member of an ancient Muslim
family and an associate in the work, had taken them into his own
home when feelings were running high. To say that they were
surprised to see us puts it mildly. We had a short Quaker Meeting
with them since regular church service was not possible, and we
all four felt that the hour together in their modest home had been
good. The drive to and from Hebron was lovely. At all the check
posts we were treated courteously. If guards were surprised to see
us, they did not show it; in fact, they expressed pleasure. The drive
between Bethlehem and Hebron was through a beautiful stretch of
terraced hills and fields and orchards well cared for. The grape-vines
were coming on, promising a good harvest of the famous grapes of
Hebron, famous before Abraham came to Palestine. The sky was
clear blue, a perfect day to be outdoors. Yet there were the soldiers,
the guns, and the ugly barbed wire indicating a partitioned country.
We wondered if we would ever be able to travel this road in a time
of peace as we had done so often in our early days in Palestine.

In the afternoon we drove out to Ramallah to call on friends
where the curfew was being strictly enforced. They were glad to
see people from outside, and to talk about happier days we had
shared. It helped get our minds off the present troubles for an hour.
It was always hard to know what was happening in Jordan or what
would bring about a crisis or how long it would last.

June came and with it the kind of thing that could happen only
in Jerusalem. We were invited to a party at the British Consulate
to celebrate Queen Elizabeth's birthday! It was a big gathering
which included some Palestinians. Disturbing as the April crisis had
been, Jordan was still with the West, and Palestinians may have
attended lest their absence indicate a lack of support for this decisive step of their government. One Arab friend said to me: "We
have taken our stand with the West again. It is up to the West to
justify it." I thought of Sharif Hussein in Mecca in 1916 throwing
his lot in with the Western Powers; I thought of the recent Suez
affair and hoped that this time there need be no reason for loss of
faith.

The year ended peacefully, though the Palestine Problem, ten years after the UN recommendation to partition the country, was not resolved. It had, in fact, grown in intensity and complexity with the scene shifting to Egypt increasingly, and the refugees becoming more and more a forgotten people. Each year we had prayed that the problem would be solved and the injustice done to the Palestinians would reach the conscience of the world community, but in the UN it stopped with relief, and that minimal.

The year 1958 started out quietly but it was to have its moments. Willard was in Egypt early in February when Egyptians were celebrating the formation, with Syria, of the United Arab Republic. We were under the impression at the time that Syria feared a Communist take-over and needed Egypt's help. The union seemed a good omen for the year.

Following the union of the two republics, there were rumours that the three kingdoms of Jordan, Iraq, and Saudi Arabia would form an Arab Federation. On 14 February, however, when a union was formed Saudi Arabia was not party to it. The young kings of Jordan and Iraq were cousins, great-grandsons of Hussein, the Sharif of Mecca, so that there was a strong blood-tie in the Federation. Under the terms of the union, both kings were to retain their thrones and capitals but would have a united army, foreign policy and educational system, and common trade agreements. Unfortunately for the rulers, a federation of republics such as that of the UAR appealed more to the people and the union did not get strong support in either country.

The relative quiet of our days was broken in April when we learned that Israel was making plans to celebrate ten years of statehood by having a big parade in Jerusalem. It happened that Jerusalem was not recognized as the capital of Israel by the United Nations nor by many governments, including Britain and the United States. Also, it was a border city and the decision of the Israeli Government to move guns and tanks into the area was a serious violation of the armistice agreement. Furthermore, the line of the parade was to be too close to the Armistice Line to be ignored. The people on the Arab side of this divided city learned of the plan with dismay and anger, and as the day approached tensions increased. The problem created for the United Nations Truce Observers by this defiant gesture was a difficult one, for they were responsible for peace on the Armistice Line. One rumour which did not allay fears was that some hot-heads on the Israeli side were boasting that they were going "to shoot their way to the Wailing Wall." When the Jordan Government learned of the parade, they informed UNTSO that they could not ignore such a blatant violation of the Armistice Agreements and would have no choice but to mobilize.

A few nights before the big day, 24 April, the Israelis began moving their tanks and guns up to Jerusalem, and we on the other side watched and heard. At the same time, the Jordanian army began to bring military equipment across the Jordan River up to Jerusalem. They took positions near the walls of the Old City from where they could observe the proposed route of the parade and at the same time be prepared in case of any further violation of the armistice. On the day of the parade, Jordanian civilians stood on the walls and buildings, quietly tense, but it was clear that Jordan would not violate the armistice and the army was there to prevent trouble on our side, too.

Our home looked out on the British Cemetery, the Hadassah Hospital, and the buildings of the Hebrew University on Mount Scopus. We could have walked to any of these places in less time than it took to walk down to the Old City. In a previous chapter I reported that a Jewish enclave was created in the summer of 1948, when the buildings were threatened by the Arab armies. The Israelis claimed that if fighting continued on Mount Scopus, and the buildings were destroyed, a valuable library and important scientific experiments would be lost. King Abdullah agreed to a temporary enclave as he, too, respected learning and often wore the distinctive garb of the scholar, and neither he nor anyone else expected the hostilities to last indefinitely. Under the agreement, the properties were to be under United Nations supervision, but a staff of Israeli scholars and caretakers would be allowed to occupy the buildings, the former to continue scientific research and the latter to maintain and protect the property. Since they would be cut off from the Israeli side, an arrangement was made for an exchange of scholars and maintenance crew every two weeks. A convoy system was set up for this fortnightly replacement of men, with provisions of every kind, including fuel. Since peace did not follow, the convoy was to be part of the Jerusalem scene for more than twenty years. The Arab Legion was pledged to meet the convoy at Mandelbaum Gate and secure its safety to Mount Scopus. I have seen that convoy a hundred times in the nine years we lived in Jerusalem, and never ceased to marvel at the dignity and order which accompanied it, for in time Mount Scopus became known as an Israeli fortress inside Jordan. Yet that convoy went through safely. The Arab Legion soldiers honoured the arrangement to the letter, but the

United Nations Observers were never allowed freedom of inspection of the buildings and on occasion were turned away at the point of a gun by the Israeli guards. At times of Jewish feasts, we often saw signals being flashed to the Israeli side and the entire enclave lighted. Arab mothers, whose homes looked out on Mount Scopus, as ours did, have told me that when they had to be up with their children in the night they would see signals being sent across; and it troubled them, for this enclave covered Arab Jerusalem to the south and the road from the north. I was alone at night much of the time while Willard was off to Beirut or Cairo, and I had an arrangement with a British neighbour nearby to call him at once should there be any signs of trouble from the "hill".

The night before the parade, I looked out on Scopus as usual before going to bed. The entire area was lighted and there was an occasional report of gunfire, and I wondered what the morrow would bring. Willard was in Beirut but was expected home next day. Our Clothing Centre was on the Arab side of Mandelbaum Gate, so would be close to the parade route, and our workers wondered if it would be safe to come to work, but we persuaded them that the rumour about "shooting our way to the Wailing Wall" was probably an idle one and that we could carry on as usual.

Surprisingly, the day passed without incident, and we thought that was probably due to activity at the UN in New York in touch with local UNTSO, who were doing all they could to prevent incidents. The Arab Legion was also there and they had given a good account of themselves when Jerusalem was under heavy assault for months in 1948. If a violation had not been prevented, violence had been; and we were grateful for the men in the blue berets, too. Another crisis was over.

Life was busy and relatively quiet until July, when we were shocked by the short but bloody coup in Iraq on the fourteenth of the month. The young King, the whole royal family, and the Prime Minister were all put to death. We had hardly recovered from the shock when the next blow fell. We learned that American marines had landed in Lebanon. We were preparing to attend a reception for Commander Elmo Hutchison, who had served in the Marines, and more recently was with the Mixed Armistice Commission in Jordan from 1951 to 1954. He was now with the American Friends of the Middle East in Cairo. Hutch, as we called him, left Jerusalem at once and the reception was called off. A few notes from my diary will help to show the effect of the Marine landing in Lebanon on us in Jordan.

[16 July] The situation grows in danger. The rumour is that the US Marines are in control in Lebanon; another, possibly a wild one, is that King Hussein is going to advance on Iraq. There is much speculation about British and American intervention in Jordan and Iraq. Most Americans and British subjects are leaving Lebanon. This action of the USA disturbs even friends of the West. Eric Bishop (British) and Harry Dorman (American) were here to lunch. The latter lives in Lebanon and he outlined for us what he thought the government would do in the next few days. It all sounded very comfortable, but where do the Arabs come in? Their rights seem to be the last consideration.

[16 July] We hear that British troops are coming into Jordan, perhaps fear for Hussein, perhaps to stop any advance toward Iraq if that was seriously considered. Shades of the Mandate and ten years ago! It is hard to know what is really happening, but it would seem that the Marines are solidly in Lebanon. But why?

[18 July] Willard had to go to Beirut today on business. Airports are trying to keep open. We wonder how long Russia and Egypt will stand quietly by. But life must go on. I attended the YWCA "graduation" programme this afternoon. Certificates were awarded to seventeen girls who had completed a dressmaking course. They asked me to present the certificates and a gift of cloth from the Refugee Committee. The girls do excellent work. We had a happy time together and I was glad it was possible to have this type of occasion in the midst of tension.

[19 July] Jordan is quiet but rumours abound and we watch and wait. It is possibly true that only British soldiers guard the palace in Amman. All cars and trucks are being checked. Willard arrived unexpectedly from Beirut. He says the town is dead. The Lebanese are feeling that the American troops are there more for Russia and Syria than for them and they are resentful of this occupation. The situation is increasingly involved and one wonders who is going to fight whom, and for what.

[20 July] Another day of watchful waiting. Black flags fly from all buses and cars and buildings. At noon today, all churches and mosques were having memorial services for the Hashemite and Jordanian victims of the Iraq coup. We attended the service in the cathedral.

A week of fairly normal life followed the events of the past days and we were able to carry on work for the refugees. The Clothing

Centre was a busy place and we had the usual spate of visitors and meetings. By Saturday, to our surprise, the American Consul was advising Americans to leave unless they had important work to do. We decided to remain, but had to go to Beirut on Sunday as Willard had meetings there on Monday morning. In Beirut there was much speculation about the future of Jordan and, although all seemed quiet on the surface, one was aware of anxiety and insecurity, and when we were with friends, the talk was usually concerned with how America was going to get out of this venture. A curfew, strictly enforced, did not allay fears. One subject on which all were agreed was the good image of the Marines. We returned to Jerusalem to find new developments. The British Council Library and one other building in Amman had been bombed and two young college students arrested, one a young woman. What would pent-up emotions and frustrations bring next! All was not well . . .

[8 August] The American Consul-General came to the house at half-past nine this morning. He fears that Americans may have to be evacuated at any moment and asked Willard to help in case of such an emergency. He outlined the steps to take, how to inform people, and his whole attitude indicated gloomy possibilities for Jordan. He was guarded in his remarks but we wondered if he thought his government feared that Israel would take the opportunity of the various crises to take over our side. We knew it would not take much to give her a reason to come over for her own protection. It is always easy to present the world with a *fait accompli* and get it accepted: it has succeeded often in the past and the West bows to it. People admit freely that the creation of the State of Israel in this area was a mistake, but back down when challenged to do something about it. What would the British soldiers do if Jordan is invaded while they are here: defend the Arabs against the invaders or stand by and see them lose more?

As I read my diary of the days following this warning of the possibility of evacuation, I am amazed to note how normally we seemed to carry on the usual activities and how freely and safely we moved about. Yet we never knew what the next hour would bring. Left alone, Jordan was getting along well, but living under daily threat of aggression was a trial.

In the middle of August, the Palestine Problem was discussed in the General Assembly and President Eisenhower again made an effort to be constructive with a Six-Point Plan for the Middle East. We knew that he was to bring forward a plan of some kind and hoped for something that would get to the basic problem, but the plan was disappointing. Money and social welfare were not the answer. The Palestine refugees had endured ten years of suffering and exile, and, what was more difficult, inability to get their cause presented and understood in the assemblies. They would endure more rather than give up their identity as a people and their right to their homeland. Only a courageous facing of the fundamental problem could bring peace; and so they were disappointed when Eisenhower had only this plan to present. The Arabs feared that he had sold out to politicians and buckled under Zionist pressures. There was one bit of good news: we learned that the Marines were leaving Lebanon and we hoped they had accomplished what they had been supposed to do. The fact that they were leaving was hopeful.

The tension of the summer months lessened by the end of August and it was with pleasure that I learned that Willard had meetings scheduled in the Gaza Strip in September and that I was invited to go to get notes for publicity. This meant flying first of all north to Beirut and then south to Gaza in the UN plane. I loved the flight down the coast over the tideless sea that had borne so much of the world's history on its waves through the long story of the human family. One thought of the Egyptians and the Cretans, the Greeks and the Romans, and of course the Phoenicians, the adventurous and clever merchants who travelled so far and to all of whom we owed so much. At such times Masefield's *Cargoes* would come to mind:

"Quinquireme of Nineveh from distant Ophir
Rowing home to haven in sunny Palestine,
With a cargo of ivory, and apes and peacocks,
Sandalwood, cedarwood, and sweet white wine."

Alas, from the days of the Crusades it was conquerors who came from the West bringing bayonets, battleships and bullets to sunny Palestine. We were never very high on this flight nor far from shore, and it always seemed so peaceful at that distance and that height. For me, this flight was always too short.

Gaza was getting back to normal, if a city set in a narrow strip along the coast with hostile neighbours on the north and east and miles of desert to the south, and host to 251,976 refugees, could be called normal. UNRWA was still at work doing a remarkable job with a limited budget, bringing to many sustenance and hope. The Baptist Hospital, the YMCA, and other voluntary agencies like ours were doing all they could to help lighten the burdens of the people, and where material aid was not always adequate their presence and care gave help beyond the material. The coming of the United Nations Emergency Force, with representatives from many nations, gave an international character to the city and the people some contact with the outside world, and promised a kind of peace.

I spent my time visiting refugee camps, refugee projects, of which there were many, and renewing acquaintance with former pupils of our schools in Ramallah. The boys used to bring back, after vacation, preserved dates stuffed with almonds, one of the most delectable preserves I have ever tasted, and it was good to know they were still preserving dates in Gaza. We found, also, that our old students were carrying responsibilities that were challenging in this crisis period.

Our committee in Gaza had developed many self-help projects that were becoming self-supporting. Sewing machines and knitting machines enabled women and younger girls to make thousands of garments for distribution in schools and in the camps. Classes for training large numbers of girls in dressmaking were spreading through the camps, and specially gifted ones were given further training to become teachers. Girls were also given secretarial training when possible, and scholarships were provided for them to get further education for school teaching. Young men were being trained in carpentry, cane-work, iron-work, auto-mechanics, cabinet-work and upholstery.

Two projects which were of special interest to me were the palm-branch project and the poultry project. The Egyptians have long known how to utilize almost every part of the date palm tree without cutting the tree down. At certain times the lower branches can be cut off. The stiff centre ribs are used to make porch and beach furniture and this was in great demand by the foreign personnel in the community in Gaza. The shredded leaves fluff up into upholstery material which never attracts insects or termites, making it excellent for mattresses also. The short spines make useful fruit baskets, and the in-between bits are good for brooms and scrubbing brushes. The twelve men employed in this project, when I was there, had made 10,000 fruit baskets for merchants to use in the date season.

Perhaps the most spectacular and, dare I say, the most romantic project was that of poultry raising at Deir el Balah, adjoining the Government Experimental Agricultural Station. It grew out of a great need after the Israeli occupation of the Gaza Strip during the Suez Crisis.

In order to supplement the limited rations of UNRWA, the

refugees had raised chicken and often could sell a few eggs or chicken to buy vegetables and fruit, so much a part of the normal diet of the Palestinians, but not provided in the UN rations. During the occupation their chicken were often taken from them or they had to eat them, so that no hatching was done, and the price of both eggs and chicken soared because they were so scarce. With the coming of the UNEF more than five-thousand strong and the return of the Egyptian Government officials and their families, something had to be done. Thanks to the initiative of the young Egyptian who headed our Gaza programme, and to the co-operation of government officials and grants from the Committee, a novel experiment was tried.

It was known to the Egyptians that in the village of Berma, in Lower Egypt, a special kind of incubation was practised which had come down from the days of the Pharaohs. The men of the village learned the method from their fathers and guarded it as a secret. Each year at the proper season they fanned out to surrounding villages to serve the people with their special skill. As the time of their coming approached, farmers began to collect eggs for hatching and had great quantities ready when the Bermawy arrived. Since modern incubators were out of the question, our Mr Henein wondered if it would be possible to get a man from Berma to come to Gaza to save the day for them. It was possible, and in October a man and his wife and daughter arrived to practise this ancient art, for it is an art.

Haj Mustapha immediately set to work to build a mud house with thick walls and domed roof. Eggs were brought in from Holland as a donation from the Heifers Incorporated, a Church of the Brethren project which encouraged farmers to share their stock and poultry with people in many lands, and from other sources, and soon all was ready. The inside of the house was divided into four compartments, each big enough to hold two thousand eggs. A small room for the incubator adjoins the hatching area, for the hatcher must live almost in isolation during the three-week incubation period, and his work is exacting and delicate. Ledges under the domed roof provide the heating area. Dried bean stems are used for fuel because they burn slowly without flame or smoke and hold the heat well. The eggs are carefully and swiftly tested with the aid of an oil lamp, eggs of abnormal shape or with the least crack are discarded, and the room is pre-heated without benefit of thermometer, the skilled artisan using his own body's sensitivity to guide him. The eggs are placed in a bed of clean sawdust.

Now the critical period begins: even heat must be maintained and each day the eggs must be turned. On the fourth or sixth day the hatcher tests the eggs by placing them against his eyeball, and in some magic way he knows if life is in them and if the temperature is right. Infertile eggs are discarded at this point. Great care must be taken at every step, as it would be disaster beyond words if so many eggs were lost. During the last few days, the eggs generate their own heat and the fire is allowed to die.

To my surprise and delight, Haj Mustapha allowed me to go into the incubator to watch him at work. The door to the house was so low that I had to stoop to get in, and I am not much more than five feet tall! Haj Mustapha was as kindly and gentle a man as one could ever meet, and as I watched him roll the eggs over with brown hands, slender and soft as the down of a mother-hen, I was lost in admiration. I watched him later, at the Experimental Station, pick up a fine big Rhode Island hen, gently stroke its gleaming feathers, and show us with pride what he had helped bring to Gaza. Five times during the season, November to late June in Gaza, the process was repeated, with more than ninety per cent success. As Mr Henein, our representative to Gaza, modestly said: "The project was a real success and fulfilled its purpose." The men of Berma count on from ninety to ninety-five per cent success with this method of incubation, and it surely worked out that way in Gaza.

Since our committee furnished the funds needed for this project, seventy per cent of the baby chicks were sold to refugees at cost or were distributed free to help refugees get a start on flocks again. The rest were kept for the committee to raise for present needs and future incubation, and soon the chicken-and-egg crisis in the Gaza Strip was over. Not only was there a supply of chicken and eggs, but the price of both came down. Eggs that were sixty piastres a dozen were now thirty-eight.

But one never got away from the fact of the refugees and their isolation from their friends. They were still living in the memory of the Israeli occupation and of the anguish so many of them suffered at the time. It is estimated that eight hundred were put to death for, or on suspicion of, being involved in *fedayeen* activities. We were grateful for all that was being done to lighten their burdens, and were helped ourselves to see how the human family can be "beaten to earth and rise again." One could not leave Gaza for a more free area without a deep sense of sorrow for the people, but one admired their optimism. They welcomed us warmly and gave us such hospitality as they could under difficult conditions. I suppose isolation and exile from kinsmen and homes and country is deep down one of the hardest burdens to bear; and for the Gaza people the additional fact that they were so near their homes must have added to their frustration. We visited Gaza in 1965 and found great progress in housing and in beautifying the city, and the flag of Palestine still flying over the government building. Seventeen years after partition, their stamps still bore the much-loved name.

Surprisingly, the end of the year brought large numbers of tourists to Jordan. Many of them were dedicated churchmen and laymen wanting to know more about the situation in regard to the refugees and the political problem that appeared to defy solution. We were called on increasingly to meet various groups and to enable them to meet Palestinians who could at least present their side of the story. Sometimes we were ashamed when questions were couched more in words of criticism or attack than as sincere seeking after truth. Repeatedly the Arabs were told that they could not turn the clock back and how much they needed Israel. We could only hope that they might tell the Zionists, on the other side, that they could not turn the clock back either. Our people had the advantage of still having the keys to their homes in their pockets and, in many, many instances, could have walked home easily. As I sat through many such sessions, I was impressed by the patience and courtesy of the Palestinians. After one such session, I asked a prominent Muslim whom we had invited to be on a panel if we were asking too much of him and others by exposing them to the tactlessness, ignorance, and, at times, arrogance of the visitors. He simply smiled and said he thought they did not mind as it was good to know what people were thinking. Incidentally, he was a graduate of Oxford and a member of an old and distinguished Jerusalem family. I am happy to say, however, that most of the American visitors were genuinely sincere, polite, and sympathetic even when they might not agree, and we were glad for them to meet Christian and Muslim Arabs.

Willard was due to retire in 1959, but the NECCCRW Committee persuaded him to continue for another three-year term in the hope that the big programme of relief would not be needed after that. The hope of a settlement was never given up. So they sent us to the USA for two months, presumably for rest and recreation. December and January are not the best months to be in the States if one wants to get about to see friends and family, but it was good to be able to spend Christmas with our son and daughter once again.

When we arrived in New York, a dear friend took us to her apartment for a few days to "orient" us to American life, which was changing too fast for us. She told us with some amusement that a Jewish reporter had written a "terrible tirade" against us, that tourists should be warned about us and not even be allowed to see us. Most amusing to us was the charge that Willard was responsible for certain UN resolutions against Israel. The writer also denied any injustice to the Palestinians and the fact of Jewish terrorism. We never saw the article, nor do we know who was the writer, but it was an interesting bit of news and an unusual welcome home. We could only hope that it was dismissed for its very extravagance, and it surely did not dampen our precious days with our home folks. As a matter of fact, Willard had conscientiously taken no part in political matters at any time, and had taken pains not to be involved in politics lest it prejudice the work he had been called on to do for the refugees and his freedom of movement in all the Arab countries. On one occasion, the NECCCRW directed Willard to send a letter to the UN on behalf of the Bedouin, but how much good it did we never knew. When Americans, or people of other lands, asked to meet Palestinians, he was willing to arrange panels, but he always let the Palestinians speak for themselves. I was frequently asked to give the background of the problem and tell of the work of the committee, but neither of us had anything whatever to do with the UN decisions. A host of people were available and officially appointed to do that. As for the Zionist terrorism, the writer should have checked at the UN or Whitehall, London.

Christmas in Cincinnati was wonderful. As we looked over the city from a high place in the evening, it looked so beautiful and peaceful, aglow with lights, secure and celebrating joyously, and we wished that we could share the abundance and security with our friends in Jerusalem and Bethlehem and wherever they were to be found in the Middle East. Later we listened to the bells ringing out from the Church of the Nativity in Bethlehem and we were seeing the refugee camp within walking distance of the church. We could only ask how such things could be. Peace was far off that night in Bethlehem, but we could still hope that perhaps in the coming days before we would be leaving there for good, we could rejoice in the Peace of Jerusalem.

Our Bedouin Friends

We arrived in Jerusalem on 10 February 1959, after our brief furlough in the United States, and were immediately caught up into the work of the committee. It was a sad homecoming for us, as Mr Hanna Atalla, Chairman of the International Christian Committee, the area committee of the NECCCRW, was seriously ill. We went almost at once to his home only to learn that there was no hope for his recovery. He died in the night and it was our sad duty to attend his funeral that same day. He had guided us well through the period of crisis in 1956 and for the following years had given of himself generously to the committee. His warm sympathy for the refugees, of whom he was one, having lost his home on the other side of Jerusalem, his legal training, excellent judgments, and his long acquaintance with people from the Western countries, were all most important at this time, so we knew we would miss him greatly. He was buried in the grounds of the Garden of Gethsemane, a very special tribute and a deserved one as he had been an active layman all his life. Greek, Russian, and Arab priests joined in the service in the Russian Church in the Garden and a large number of Arabs and friends from the international community attended.

We had hardly stepped off the plane when another matter was called to Willard's attention. This was a request from the British Consul-General to get in touch with him as soon as possible. We were told that this was an urgent matter, so Willard responded at once. To his surprise, he was asked to administer relief to Bedouin of the Azazma tribe who had been driven out of Israel and were in East Jordan, and in great need. The government of Jordan, already burdened with a reduced economy and a population one-third refugees, was taxed beyond its ability to care for thousands of new refugees, yet could not return these Bedouin to their homes in Israel. Their tents had been burned and their flocks were gone. The Consul-General explained that this had been brought up in Parliament in London and his government had voted to send £50,000 (approximately $140,000) for relief to them. However, as confidence in the British Government had not been fully restored since

Suez, this relief could not be carried on through their representatives. During the discussion in Parliament on how best to get relief to a people needing it at once, Willard's name had been brought forward with the thought that he could administer it in connection with the programme of the NECCCRW. He was now being asked if that would be possible.

Willard's first response was that he could not complicate or prejudice the work of the NECCCRW by accepting funds from, or being responsible to, a government, however worthy the cause. It was true that the Committee distributed large quantities of surplus foods from America, but these had come through Church World Service and responsibility for distribution was to that organization. He assured the Consul-General that he was sympathetic to the desire of the British Government to give aid to this group beyond the capacity of a voluntary agency, and he was also deeply concerned over the fate of these proud and hitherto free people, now destitute and homeless. He was also sympathetic with the problem faced by the Jordan Government. Unfortunately, these Bedouin were not eligible for relief from UNRWA as they were displaced after the relief rolls were closed. Surely a way must be found to meet this great human problem, this further tragic link in the chain of events following the partition of Palestine, and he thought there was one possible solution.

It happened that the British Council of Churches, next to Church World Service in the USA, was the largest contributor to the ecumenical programme under which the NECCCRW operated; in fact, proportionally, their giving was remarkably large. Willard's suggestion was that if the British Government was willing to turn the £50,000 over to the BCC and if they in turn would entrust the NECCCRW to administer it for relief for the Azazma Bedouin, he felt that his committee would approve and accept full responsibility for this added relief project. An exchange of telegrams between Jerusalem and London followed and, within hours, the matter was concluded as Willard suggested. An interesting sidelight came to us in the next few days when the formal request came from the British Council of Churches. A member of Parliament had gone to it for advice about the use of the money the government wanted to give, and it was the BCC which had suggested Willard's name in the first place. Without knowing this, Willard had done what they hoped he would do, and they fully approved the conditions he had laid down and his policy of keeping the work of the NECCCRW, the service arm of the Christian Community, free from government control or direction.

The programme of relief was carried out by our regular workers and a few others, as it was not easy to get to the southern part of East Jordan where the Azazma were located and our regular programme could not be sacrificed either. Transportation was difficult and expensive, but by pooling our resources of staff from both sides of the Jordan, a tremendously big programme was possible. A survey revealed that there were 12,432 families comprising 73,476 persons to be cared for. We kept overheads to the lowest level possible, and statistics show that, in a period of almost eleven weeks, flour, vegetable oil, sugar, tea, dates and rice were distributed to that large number, and including all other costs such as transport, wages, rents, porterage and additional office expenses, the total expenditure per person was $1.90. Dates might seem like a luxury item to people of the West, but to the Bedouin they are a staple food and I have been told a Bedouin can subsist on a very few each day.

One of the happiest factors in the situation was the donations that came from other sources as the relief story spread. The British Council of Churches, Church World Service, and the Oxford Committee for Famine Relief sent money to purchase fat-tailed sheep and goats to help families start new herds and flocks, provide blankets and clothing and meet emergencies. One English woman sent, at her own expense, one thousand new blankets. The desert countries get very cold at night and winters in the south of Jordan can be severe, so that blankets were a great blessing.

A still further development grew out of the attempt to start flocks of sheep, and that was the need for water. Our Committee, in co-operation with government, began projects such as cleaning and restoring old Roman cisterns, making water channels and reservoirs, searching for hidden springs, and even terracing waste lands which could be used when water became available for growing fruits and vegetables.

Our Jerusalem Committee made school outfits for the children, and school-bags, which I think they loved even more than the clothing. When we visited the schools it was wonderful to see how happy the children were and how earnest they were in their studies. These children had an ability to concentrate that was amazing and they could memorize poems and passages from the Quran with apparent ease. Providing for the Bedouin captured the imagination and sympathy of large numbers of people, and there was an enthusiasm that was contagious. So after the £50,000 was spent, the work continued and increasingly the lot of the Azazma improved.

Perhaps a word should be said about the Bedouin of Palestine, for there is so much misunderstanding about them. Of course, in the first place, people in America were given the impression that all Arabs, including the Arab people of Palestine, were nomads, and that settling them somewhere else was a simple matter: they had no roots. As a matter of fact, only about one-tenth of the Palestinians were Bedouin, and they were only semi-nomadic. They lived in the south in the Negeb area, where they raised crops in the rainy season and in the dry season took their flocks to places where there was water. They came from the desert near Egypt, travelled across to Transjordan or into the northern part of Palestine, setting up their tents near springs, then returned to their traditional home bases in time for the winter rains. They used to come into our area after the harvest season was over and pitch their tents in the fields, and, as far as I know, they never encountered or created difficulties. I asked one of our farmer neighbours once if their coming was a problem, and he smilingly assured me that, on the contrary, they were a help. The flocks enriched the soil and the Bedouin never left the fields worse for their having been there.

From time immemorial and, more recently as the history of that ancient land goes, in four hundred years of Turkish rule and during the British Mandate days, the grazing and water rights and seasonal migration of the Bedouin were accepted and respected. The Bedouin did not roam aimlessly; they were in search of food and water, and their adaptation to desert conditions was as sound as that of all people settled in their special geographical regions. Their law, their hospitality, their tribal warfare, their treatment of law-breakers might be studied valuably by our modern governments, for surely we in the West do not have a blameless record in regard to war, social relations, and international relations.

In the old days, by which I mean before partition, many of the Bedouin were rich in herds of camels, sheep, and goats, had pure-blooded Arab horses, and lived well in their "houses of hair". Goat's hair was woven into cloth for the *abayeh*, the outer garment so familiar to us in pictures, and for the tents they lived in. Goat's hair cloth is strong and waterproof and flexible enough to be rolled up when the migrating season begins. The pride of a Bedouin was a camel's hair *abayeh*, a luxury garment, soft and silky, which draped gracefully over the shoulders. But a Bedouin did not talk of his house, he talked of his "house of hair".

Bedouin women did their part in the life of the community by weaving the cloth and the rugs which were so necessary, and they had an eye for beauty of colour and design. A sheikh's tent might be carpeted with beautiful oriental rugs or lined with what we called Egyptian tent-work decorations in appliqué similar to those found in Egyptian tombs. One such tent was at Friends' Boys' School, and was brought out on special outdoor occasions. Bedouin women, like their sisters in other lands, took pride in their homes. In turn, they could dress well and sometimes one found them well adorned with silver and gold bracelets and necklaces.

Each tribe had its sheikh, who was expected to provide, plan for, and protect the whole group. He also settled quarrels and granted rewards. If there was poverty, it was shared by all. His role in the tribe was honoured, and he resembled more a patriarch of old than the kind so often portrayed by the moguls of Hollywood.

They were not prepared for the intrusion of Israel with its aggressive policy of expansion and its need for land if it was to bring millions into this small country. It was reported in the United Nations in 1953 that seven thousand Bedouin had been expelled, approximately half of them from the Azazma tribe, and this policy of expulsion was followed through the years. If there was resistance, can anyone be surprised?

The full story of the relief programme which started early in 1959 is long, too long to be recounted now, but a footnote may be inserted. Although Willard was not responsible to governments, he consulted both Jordanian and British officials who knew the problems and customs of the Bedouin well, for relief funds were too precious for experimentation and the need for expert advice was imperative. It was therefore most reassuring and gratifying when one day he received a letter from Major Bromage, of the British Embassy in Amman and an expert on the Middle East, after the initial programme was over. Major Bromage confessed that when the NECCCRW was asked to expend the £50,000, he had grave doubts about the ability of a voluntary agency to undertake such a large and sensitive programme. However, he had followed the programme closely and wanted to congratulate Willard and his splendid staff warmly for the manner in which the whole operation was carried out, for the imagination and careful detail that had gone into it, and for the careful accounting and economy of resources that had been exercised, doing more than could have been expected with the money.

It was our good fortune to visit some of the Azazma in East Jordan in June 1962, two weeks before we retired, and it is one of the wonderful memories of that last month in the Middle East.

We left Jerusalem one morning at half-past six with Victoria Nasir and Abdullah, two of our colleagues who had rendered able assistance in the early days of the relief programme, doing more than we could ever repay them for. It was a beautiful morning as we descended the winding road to Jericho into the Jordan Valley, still green from the later rains and the broad-leafed banana trees still bearing their precious fruit. We crossed the valley before the heat of the day, the Dead Sea on the right and the oasis of Jericho on our left. What a world of history this valley holds! We were soon climbing the hills of Moab on the east and skirting Amman, the capital of Jordan, seventy-five miles from Jerusalem, as we drove on to Kerak with its great Crusader Castle dominating the scene. We were to travel farther south to the Azazma tents, but Willard had to stop at the Italian hospital in Kerak to say good-bye to the Sisters, who had always offered kind hospitality when he had to be in the area on refugee business. The hospital combined the offices of a hospice for travellers with care of the sick. We took time to visit the Crusader Castle, which I had not seen since 1924: I wanted to refresh my memory. It is a most impressive ruin, which must have been a magnificent example of mediaeval architecture in its day. It is still of great interest to scholars and builders; to me it was part of the story of the crusades and the crusaders who left so many strongholds, names, and, unhappily, a history of bloodshed and cruelty. The blood of the crusaders still runs in the veins of the people of Palestine and Lebanon in certain towns and villages, combining with the Semitic strain to produce interesting physical characteristics. The crusaders' castles, still remarkable in decay, are ironical monuments to followers of the Prince of Peace.

We sped on from there to our appointment in the Arid el-Hausa area, where our hosts were awaiting us. Our goal today was not for romancing over a bygone day but a rendezvous with a people whose way of life had its romance, too. We arrived in time for dinner, more than a dinner, a feast! The tent of the sheikh, somewhat tattered but clean and comfortable, was all ready for the big event. If the setting was not like the tent of a better day, there was no apology and all the rules of hospitality were observed: "Welcome. You honour us. What we have is yours." Greetings expressed in more beautiful language than our English translation. The District Governor and other local dignitaries were also there to greet us and we settled down to enjoy the afternoon.

With due regard for the feelings of our hosts and for the present state of their fortunes, Mahmud, our faithful representative in East Jordan who had worked closely with the Azazma programme of relief, had arranged for the meal so tactfully that the sheikh could preside over it without embarrassment and could perform the courtesies of a host. We sat on low pillows on the ground, and after a proper exchange of the polite expressions of hospitality, large trays of rice and lamb were placed before us. A salad of cucumbers, tomatoes and finely chopped onions with dressing accompanied the meat and rice dish. Before eating began, a servant came around with ewer and towel for us to wash our hands, and we could then form small balls of rice with our clean fingers and as delicately as possible toss them into our mouths without touching our fingers to our lips. Flat loaves of bread could be broken into small pieces, which we could form into spoons to dip into the salad bowl. A kindly Azazma seated beside me handed me from time to time succulent pieces of lamb which I ate with relish. Fruit brought from Amman was passed after we were sated with the main course, and by that time we were ready for the ritual of coffee, a remarkably satisfying end to the meal.

We could smell the coffee beans roasting as we were eating, the fragrance filling the tent for our delight and happy anticipation. Presently, a young son of the tribe brought in the mortar filled with the hot crisp beans and began to pound them into the finest of powder with a practised hand, rhythmically creating a kind of music for our entertainment. The coffee was then boiled in the artistically shaped coffee-pot of the Bedouin. It was served in small cups from which we sipped slowly with smiles of appreciation to the coffee-maker and to our host, and our cups were refilled until, having shown proper appreciation, we turned the cups in our hands indicating that we were satisfied and friendship was sealed. We were quite hungry when the feast was spread, for we had not eaten since six o'clock that morning, and I think I have never enjoyed a meal more.

Because we were leaving our work, there were speeches in beautiful Arabic, and I enjoyed hearing my husband being referred to as *Abouna*—Father. There were also gifts: mine was a short jacket made by the women after their own kind, but without the embroidery. This coat can be worn either side outward, being made with two pieces of cloth sewn together so perfectly that all the seams are hidden. It is the ideal car-coat and I still wear it with pleasure and comfort.

Willard's gift was a beautiful camel-hair *abayeh*, now a treasured possession. It must have come from Saudi Arabia, for it has the silken quality of the finest camel-hair, and when worn hangs in soft folds and has all the warmth and comfort of this special garment, a garment made famous in the great days of the Arab Empire when Arab scholars in Europe wore it and it became the mark of the scholar. Our modern academic robes can trace their ancestry to the Arab *abayeh*, or *aba*, as it is more familiarly called in the West.

More than thirty school children later came to share in the general festivities, wearing the school uniforms we had made at our sewing centre in Jerusalem, carrying their school bags, for they were very proud of them. Fortunately, we had brought sweets for them, and attractive china dishes filled with Jordan almonds and chocolates for the women of the tribe who had prepared the food. Our gifts were indeed modest compared with the hospitality and the gifts they had given us at considerable sacrifice.

As we sat with our Azazma friends, I was reminded of another Bedouin feast we had attended on the West Bank. This one was by special request for a party of Americans from California. Our wonderful Victoria planned this one, and it was well arranged. This tribe of Bedouin had been a wealthy one, but in spite of their poverty they had lost none of their dignity, nor their manners. One woman of the American party had not wanted this particular experience and was sure she should take her own food with her. I happened to sit beside her at the meal, which I noted she ate, and as we rose to leave she turned to me and said, feelingly: "These kindly people."

The twentieth century had been catching up with the Bedouin of Palestine, with the coming of automobiles, radio, and aircraft, with their children in schools and all aspects of modern life so close, but they were not prepared for the sudden ruthless dispossession of their lands and the disruption of their way of life. An alien people had come in with foreign laws, had burned their crops and tents and forced them from their homes into a way of life for which they had no desire. The Bedouin, too, had a culture and a code of laws, and centuries of desert life had given them an inner freedom. Many were illiterate, but they could read the signs in the sands and the heavens, and understood natural elements, and Allah was constantly in their language.

A small cement house could not replace their *beit shar*, "house of hair," the freedom of the desert, nor the traditions of their ancestors. Our lives were enriched by our brief relations with them, and we were deeply moved as we realized how they had built up a culture under the challenge of the winds and the sands of the desert, and we left them hoping that the future would be kind and that the best of their culture would not be lost.

AL-QUDS KHATERKUM
Goodbye to Jerusalem

Looking back, one recalls particular days, and 1 January 1954 is one of special memory, for it was the day we moved from Friends' Boys' School to Jerusalem, where Willard could now devote full time to his new assignment, which had begun in September 1953. It was a beautiful day, a good omen, we hoped, for this new phase of service in Palestine.

Since the Near East Christian Council Committee for Refugee Work, NECCCRW, had a special committee in each host country, and since numbers and needs varied, my husband's duty was to keep the needs of the separate committees before the contributing agencies, and, under the guidance of an executive committee, to distribute funds and material aids as wisely and as impartially as possible. This involved much travel, but we were both granted courtesy visas to all the host countries and the privilege of travel on the UN plane.

Willard's appointment was originally for two years: it was thought that by the end of that period the problem of the refugees would be settled, that even the task of helping their return to their homes would be completed. In our innocence we believed that the UN, which had arbitrarily partitioned the country without regard to the wishes or the needs of the majority of its people, would not let the tragic aftermath of the decision continue. Yet, though the right of return was restated, but not implemented, every November at the UN, the refugees themselves were becoming mere numbers on relief rolls, and were continuing to endure hardships and to pray for a settlement. Theirs was a good land, and they loved it. We could understand, for we were caught in its spell, too.

With the best areas of Jerusalem occupied by Israel, with Arabs excluded from their homes, their places of business, and many amenities, Arab Jerusalem had little to offer in 1954. I am indebted to Ruhi Bey el-Khatib, Arab Mayor of Jerusalem, for the following account of the conditions in East Jerusalem when fighting ceased in April 1949.

"Arab Jerusalem was confined to the part inside the city walls and to a few residential centres falling east, north, and south of the city; an area not exceeding two and a half square miles out of twelve and a half square miles that was the total area of Jerusalem, and it comprised remnants of inhabitants not exceeding 33,000 out of a total of 90,000 Arabs who were living in Jerusalem before 1948. Our heritage from the Mandate Government in this part of Jerusalem was a distressed city of shaky buildings, a paralysed commerce and industry, devoid of any financial resources and without a government, water, or electricity. The city was suffering from poverty and bad destiny . . . and sustaining the calamities of war. The catastrophe left us only the sacred shrines and the legacy of our ancestors, their remembrances and their landmarks, and with these it retained for us the spirit of co-operation, faith in God, in humanity, and in the homeland."

The story of how the mayor and his council set to work to rebuild Jerusalem, to maintain stability and public security, to restore electricity and a water supply, to get industry going, to create a city the refugees could return to, to encourage the tourism which was its greatest source of foreign money, to rebuild houses and to reconstruct is an inspiring record of success achieved with difficulty and at great sacrifice. When we moved from Ramallah, there were few houses in the ten miles between that town and the city. Before we left Jerusalem, a whole new community had arisen at Shafat, and houses, many like the lovely ones the Arabs had lost in 1948, now occupied by Jewish immigrants from many lands, began to rise all along the way, until Jerusalem, Ramallah, and Bireh merged into an extended community. Having lost their airport at Lydda, the Arabs built a new one half-way between Ramallah and Jerusalem, and thousands of tourists began to pour into the country all through the year. During the Easter and Christmas seasons, hotel accommodation was at a premium. The area to the north and west of Herod's Gate, *Bab ez-Zahri*, previously a quiet residential suburb, became the commercial centre of Jerusalem, with shops, tourist offices, government buildings and hotels. A new YMCA building arose on the Nablus Road nearby, a beautiful building which incorporated the art as well as the crafts of the Palestine so recently war-scarred.

I travelled the Nablus Road several times each week, and as I watched the new construction I wondered if the owners were merely foolish, or had more courage than we had the right to expect of any people. What was true for Jerusalem was true for the rest of the country then left to the Palestinians, and it would take a volume or two to tell the whole story of that period. And, though much of that story is dark, it is good to be able to record that light did shine in. As we watched the city grow, I often thought that if a single stone of the new buildings was dislodged, I could not bear it. We had come to Palestine when it was in rebirth after one great war; now we were seeing another, and this time we could understand its meaning better, for we had seen its travail.

George Antonius, author of *The Arab Awakening*, writing almost forty years ago said: "The most formidable obstacle to an understanding, and therefore to a solution, of the Palestine Problem lies not so much in its inherent complexity as in the solid jungle of legend and propaganda which has grown up around it. To the ordinary task of a student dealing with the facts is thus added an obligation to deal with the pseudo-facts and dethrone them from their illegitimate eminence. It is as much his duty to expose the fallacies as to assert the truth, and the duty is all the more imperative as he is dealing with tragedy in enactment in which innocent lives are being sacrificed every day and human beings kept in anguish and suffering."

People in the United States and Britain have come to believe that because the Palestinians resisted partition they are the aggressors. Nor has public opinion in the West counted the cost of maintaining the Armistic Line. It has cost the UN millions of dollars, and it has probably taken more of its time, filled more of its filing space, employed more secretarial staff, than any other single matter, while Israel has defied decisions and ignored directives more than any other member nation.

To list the committees, commissions, and other bodies of the UN —UNRWA, UNTSO, UNSCOP, MAC, UNEF, UNPCC—indicates not only the enormous amount of money and numbers of men but also the complexity of the problems.

A few nights before my husband and I retired, I stood on the roof of the YMCA on the Arab side of Jerusalem with an English friend who had spent his life in the diplomatic service of his country in the Middle East. He was now retired, but had come back to serve voluntarily in the work of relief. As we looked across the lines to Occupied Jerusalem, he turned to me and said: "Not only the greatest injustice but also the greatest political blunder of the twentieth century." Two terrible wars had been fought within the previous forty years to prevent just such injustices, yet we were more than ever involved all over the world in attempting to achieve peace by force.

As we looked first to one side and then to the other, Arab Jerusalem seemed so vulnerable; a small area between the "fortress" on the hill to the north and the armed forces so near on the south, waiting for the moment to strike. We had hoped that the Palestine Problem would have been solved before we had to retire, but it was not to be. We had to say goodbye to everything that had meant so much to us through the years: friends, places, and rich experiences, but now with the dread thought that this little country might still have to face years of insecurity and pain.

Our friend, Musa Bey Nasir, Foreign Minister of Jordan, in a speech before the General Assembly of the United Nations sadly reminded that body in 1960 that: "unless there is a change of attitude, unless a wrong is called a wrong, and unless there is open recognition of the aggression and the injustice, and unless there is undoubted willingness to remove the injustice inflicted on the Palestinian Arabs, there can be no hope of solving the Palestine Problem or of establishing real peace in the Middle East."

I have made no attempt to present a solution. I hope merely that I may have offered some insights into the problems the peace-maker must face. I hope I have paid a tribute to the people of Palestine, those we knew best, whose suffering we witnessed, who are the real heart of the problem.

The Arab is accused of not being "realistic". The loss of home and country and national identity are painfully real to him, and the suffering he has endured through recent years lacks nothing in realism. He is aware of the whole story. If attempts at peacemaking have failed, it may be because the peace-makers have not been realistic. Our friend the Reverend Eric Bishop, long resident in Jerusalem during the Mandate and now retired in England, wrote to us recently: "They (Western leaders) don't understand that moral wrongs weigh much more in the Orient than in the Occident; people's resentments at injustice count far, far more than material advantage." Too often the peace-makers begin with the situation which has developed rather than with the underlying causes of the conflict. They would like the Arabs, especially the Palestinians, to forget all the sufferings of the twenty and more years since Partition, and to accept what outsiders think is best for them. And how much does the peace-maker know of the history of the Middle East during the past century? And does he remember that the Arab people were the inhabitants of Palestine when Moses first entered that land?

Historically, Palestine has been the victim of its geographical situation, but Allah has compensated for it in many ways. One needs to experience the cycle of the year in the country to appreciate its charm and to understand the love which its children have for it. There were times when I have wished that one could gather up this small country in one's arms and move it to a quiet spot on the globe for a little space of time, to give it a rest from the ceaseless movements of the armies of the world.

No, I shall not propose a solution, but I hope I may have helped a little towards the understanding which is needed more than anything else at the moment, and which alone can bring about a solution and a lasting peace.

When we moved to Jerusalem, a friend wrote wistfully: "It is a privilege to live in Jerusalem." For us, it was, as it was for so many others. But with privilege there is responsibility. There may also be heartache.

As we were leaving Palestine, we were shown more kindness than any two people deserved, and we were given mementos we shall always cherish. In closing this chapter of our life there, we may perhaps be forgiven if we share with the reader two of them which we hold dear.

On 27 May 1962, our fortieth wedding-anniversary, we broke ground at the YMCA Centre in the Shepherds' Fields for a youth-centre or camp to bear our name.

And at our departure we received this poem, written by one who had been our pupil at Friends' School in Ramallah, and who later taught there, as her mother and her grandmother had done before her.

> You have lived with us long, known our hates,
> Our sorrows, the reasons for our loves:
> You have seen the children of the land
> Cry out with hunger, both of mind and heart,
> Their eyes staring at their cruel fates.
> In love, you sought to help, to bind the wounds
> That men, in war, had wrought.
> You followed in the footsteps of Him who sought
> To comfort and to heal. In spirit and in truth,
> You did your part.
> Now, you must go.
> Our thoughts will be warm, for having known you.
> For you are, now, the people of the Holy Land.
>
> Affectionately,
> May Mansoor

Printed by Clarke, Doble & Brendon Ltd, Plymouth

LIBRARY OF DA'